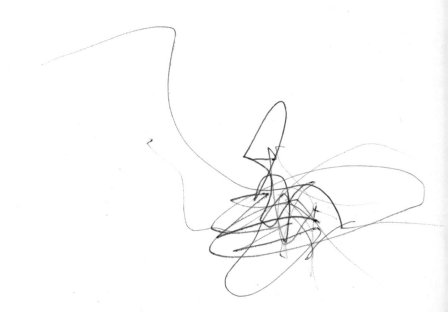

THE LIFE OF JAMES MADISON

JAMES MADISON, AGE 76

Bust by John H. J. Browere

Made in 1827. In possession of the Virginia Historical Society at Richmond,
and now published for the first time.

THE LIFE OF

JAMES MADISON

BY

GAILLARD HUNT

EDITOR OF
THE WRITINGS OF JAMES MADISON

NEW YORK

Russell & Russell

FIRST PUBLISHED IN 1902
REISSUED, 1968, BY RUSSELL & RUSSELL
A DIVISION OF ATHENEUM HOUSE, INC.
L.C. CATALOG CARD NO: 66-27105
PRINTED IN THE UNITED STATES OF AMERICA

To

HARRY A. GARFIELD, Esq.

NEARLY a generation has passed since you and I as boys used to settle the affairs of state, which your father with the assistance of mine was trying to solve. The friendship we formed then time has deepened. On my part it is based not only upon our youthful association, but upon an understanding of your character and of the purpose you have set before yourself of striving to mitigate some of the evils in government which have developed since the Constitution left the hands of Madison and his coadjutors. And so I dedicate this book to you as a token of my friendship and as a tribute to your work.

CONTENTS

vii

THE LIFE OF JAMES MADISON

THE
LIFE OF JAMES MADISON

CHAPTER I

THE AMENDMENT TO THE BILL OF RIGHTS

THE HOUSE OF BURGESSES of Virginia held its last session May 6, 1776, when forty-five members, assembling at Williamsburg, declared that the ancient constitution of the colony had been subverted by the King and Parliament of Great Britain. Accordingly, they disbanded, and the last official evidence of the subjection of Virginia to Great Britain disappeared. Another body met on the same day to inaugurate the new era of independence. Public opinion had unwillingly reached the point of desiring separation. It was dominated by the wealthy and educated men, and was in consequence conservative, and clung to the hope of an amicable settlement of differences; but events forced the people into a position of irrevocable rebellion. The final circumstances were: September 1, 1775, Lord Dunmore, the royal governor, seized the printing-press of John Holt because of his seditious articles; October 26, George Nicholas fired the first shot of the Revolution at one of Dunmore's tenders sent to destroy the town of Hampton; November 7, Dunmore issued his infamous proclamation, urging "all indented servants, negroes or others," to secure their freedom by joining in the forcible reduction of the colony; December 8, Leslie's attack on Woodford near Norfolk was repulsed; January 1, 1776, Norfolk, the largest city in Virginia, was bombarded and burned.

Added to the grievances which had gone before, these made reconciliation an impossibility, and the Virginians who still adhered to the crown were an unimportant minority.

There was no doubt, therefore, that the convention of May, 1776, which was held, at the invitation of the Continental Congress, to institute a new government, would do so. The elections of the delegates were spirited,* but the rivalry between the candidates was rather personal than political, and there was no party in the field opposed to independence. The result of the elections was an assemblage, not of young or untried men, but of the ablest, most experienced, and most trusted men in the colony. In organizing, Edmund Pendleton, who had been president of the Convention of the year before, after Peyton Randolph's death, was chosen to preside over the new Convention. He was fifty-two years old, and had held offices of trust for more than twenty years, being at different times justice of the peace for Caroline County, a member of the House of Burgesses, president of the Caroline Court, county lieutenant, member of the Continental Congress of 1775, and president of the Committee of Safety. These distinctions he had attained, as he says in a brief autobiography,† "without classical education, without patrimony, without what is called the influence of family connection, and without solicitation." His remarkable charm of manner and easy and graceful eloquence made him a model presiding officer. Before the convention met he was a Whig, and was suspected of British proclivities, but in reality his attitude was merely that of the most conservative wing of the patriot party. "When the dispute with Great Britain arose," he says, "a redress of grievances and not a revolution of government was my wish. In this I was firm but temperate; and whilst I was endeavoring to raise

* Kate Mason Roland's "Life, Correspondence and Speeches of George Mason," I, 222.

† MS. in the possession of Erasmus Taylor, Esq., of Orange County, Virginia.

the spirits of the timid to a general united opposition, by stating to the uninformed the real merits of the dispute, I opposed and endeavoured to moderate the violent and fiery who were for plunging us into rash measures, and had the happiness to find a majority of the public bodies confirmed my sentiments, which, I believe, was the corner-stone of our success."

The master spirit of the Convention was George Mason, of Gunston Hall, also a man past the meridian of life, and also untouched by radicalism. Unlike Pendleton, he avoided public office whenever he could, and had performed his first official service in 1775, when he took Washington's place in the Colonial Convention, upon Washington's appointment to the command of the Continental Army. He was a sound scholar, especially in the legislative and political history of England, and until the Revolution his sympathies were those of an Englishman, and liberty meant to him English liberty. He was free from personal ambition, strong and immovable in his convictions, forceful and uncompromising in debate. His personal influence with men of consequence was probably as great as that of any man in Virginia, and the chief work of the Convention fell to his hands. Patrick Henry resigned his military command in disgust just in time to be elected a member, but the Convention was a body with constructive work before it, and Henry's genius lay not in that direction. The power he exerted in the proceedings of the Convention was not as great as that which had swept people along with him before, or which he exercised afterwards upon successive legislatures of the State. According to Edmund Randolph, who was one of the few young members, those of the Convention who were most in the public eye, beside Mason, Pendleton and Henry, were James Mercer, Robert Carter Nicholas, Richard Bland, Thomas Ludwell Lee, Richard Henry Lee, George Wythe, John Blair, and, younger than any of them, and one of the youngest of all the members, James Madison, Jr., of Orange County. "Until the meet-

ing of this Convention,"* says Randolph, "he was un-
known at the metropolis. He was educated at Princeton
College in New Jersey, and had been laborious in his
studies which ranged beyond strict academic limits, but
were of that elementary cast, subservient in their general
principles to any science which he might choose to cultivate in detail. As a classical scholar he was mature, as
a student of belles lettres, his fancy animated his
judgment ; and his judgment, without damping his fancy,
excluded by the soundness of criticism, every propensity
to tinsel and glitter. . . . His diffidence went
hand in hand with his morals, which repelled vice,
howsoever fashionable. In Convention debate, his
lips were never unsealed except to some member,
who happened to sit near him; and he who had
once partaken of the rich banquet of his remarks, did not
fail to wish daily to sit within the reach of his conversation. It could not be otherwise; for although his age
and the deference which in fewer circles had been paid
to him, were apt to tincture him with pedantry he delivered himself without affectation upon Grecian, Roman
and English history, from a well digested fund, a sure
presage of eminence. A very sensible foreigner observed
of him, that he never uttered anything which was not
appropriate, and not connected with some general principle of importance. Even when he commented upon
the dignity with which Pendleton filled the chair, it was
in that philosophic spirit, which looks for personal dignity in officers of a republic as well as of a monarchy.
While he thrilled with the ecstasies of Henry's eloquence,
and extolled his skill in commanding the audience, he
detected what might be faulty in his reasoning. Madison was enviable in being among the few young men
who were not inflated by early flattery and could content themselves with throwing out in social discourse
jewels which the artifice of a barren mind would have
treasured up for gaudy occasions."

* MS. History of Virginia, in Virginia Historical Society at Richmond.

When Madison was elected to the Convention he was twenty-five years of age, and he looked younger than he really was. He was five feet six and a quarter inches tall,* and his body was thin and delicate. His pale face was lighted up by a pair of hazel eyes which were ready to reflect a quiet humour, but his features were irregular and not handsome, and his countenance bespoke the suffering of bad health. His hair was light, combed back and gathered in a small queue behind, tied with a plain ribbon. He was clothed so soberly that he looked more like a dissenting divine than the heir of a planter of large estate, and before his election his neighbours declared he was more of a minister than a statesman. This was the first large assemblage of men in which he had ever taken part, and he shrank timidly from observation, and rose only once to offer a motion, which, however, he did not support with a speech. Randolph's statement that he was one of the delegates most in the public eye is doubtless an exaggeration. He was known as the son of James Madison, lieutenant of Orange County, and probably the most influential man in it, but his own reputation was merely that of a precocious young scholar who had shown zeal for the Revolutionary cause. He met the great men of the Convention for the first time, and did not pretend to rank with them.

The great question before the Convention was announced by the president, when he said that the time had come when it was necessary to decide whether the present condition of public affairs could be continued. On May 15 the answer came in a clarion note, and the Convention instructed the delegates of Virginia in the Continental Congress, "to propose to that respectable body to declare the united colonies free and independent states, absolved from all allegiance to or dependence upon the crown or Parliament of Great Britain, and that they give the assent of this colony to such Declaration, and to whatever measures may be thought proper and

* Randall's "Jefferson," III, 262.

necessary by the Congress for forming alliances, and a confederation of the colonies." It was also resolved that a committee be appointed to prepare a Declaration of Rights and Plan of Government for the colony. Who drew up the instructions is not known. It was an impression of Madison's, expressed many years afterwards, that they originated in a letter from Thomas Jefferson, then in Philadelphia, to George Wythe; but Edmund Randolph declared they were drafted by Pendleton and proposed by Nelson. The point is not important, as the people had resolved on independence, and resolutions to that effect would have been offered by one delegate or another. Charles Patterson and John Càbell, the delegates from Buckingham County, had these orders from their constituents: "We instruct you to cause a total and final separation from Great Britain to take place as soon as possible; and a constitution to be established, with a full representation and free and frequent elections." The inhabitants of Augusta and Transylvania and on the rivers Watauga and Holstein sent similar messages,* and those parts of the colony which made no specific expressions fully expected the action that was taken. On the same day with the passage of the resolutions thirty-two members were appointed a committee to prepare a Declaration of Rights and Plan of Government. In the first list Madison's name did not appear, for he did not take his seat till the 16th, but on that day, upon special motion, he was added. Two days later, May 18, George Mason arrived, and he too was added to the committee, and became virtually its head, and wrote the Declaration of Rights which preceded the Constitution and was an enunciation of the principles upon which it was based. These principles were English,—those of Magna Charta, the Petition of Rights, the Acts of the Long Parliament, and the doctrines of the Revolution of 1688 as expounded by

* Bancroft's "History of the United States," VIII, 376.

Locke.* But the constitution of society in Virginia was also English, and some of the members of the committee had an abiding fear of the common people and a deep-rooted belief in the superior rights of an upper class. The first clause of the Declaration of Rights, proclaiming the equal rights of all men to freedom and independence, met with strenuous opposition, and called forth numerous amendments from aristocratic members, Robert Carter Nicholas, especially, expressing the fear that it might prove the forerunner of civil convulsions. A number of the suggestions offered to other points in the Declaration were absorbed by Mason, and their best features were embodied in his final draft. On Monday, May 27, Archibald Cary, chairman of the committee, reported the Declaration to the Convention; it was discussed in committee of the whole, several amendments were accepted, and June 12 it was adopted by a unanimous vote. It declared that all men were born equally free, and with inherent rights of which they could not divest their posterity—life, liberty, the means of acquiring property and pursuing happiness; that all power was vested in and derived from the people; that government was instituted for the benefit of the people, and when it failed to fulfil this purpose the people had a right to change it; that no offices should be hereditary; that the legislative and executive powers should be distinct from the judicative, and for the two former there should be frequent elections; that elections ought to be free; that there should be no arbitrary power of suspending laws, nor excessive bail; that no man should be deprived of his liberty except by law, and trial by jury should be preserved; that there should be freedom of the press; that standing armies should be avoided, and the military subordinated to the civil power· and that there should be free exercise of religion. Such was the Declaration

* See Rives' "Life and Times of James Madison," I, 119 et seq.; also Henry's "Life, Correspondence and Speeches of Patrick Henry," I, 405, et seq.

which preceded the Declaration of Independence by nearly a month, and which contained within it all the general principles of the Declaration of Independence. It has stood at the head of the five Constitutions that Virginia has had, and either in form or in substance was embodied in the first Constitutions of New York, Pennsylvania, New Hampshire, Massachusetts, Maryland, Delaware and North Carolina, of the original States, while it has since been incorporated into the Constitution of every State of the Union.

The Declaration of Rights having been agreed to, the Convention proceeded to construct the Constitution itself, and on June 29 it was finally agreed upon. The preamble was taken from a plan of government which Jefferson sent Pendleton by Wythe, who was returning from Philadelphia, and a few of the other features of Jefferson's plan were included. The chief draftsman of the Constitution was, however, Mason; Madison had no hand in it, nor did he approve of all its provisions, or of the method of its adoption.

The last section of the Bill of Rights, relating to religious liberty, read as follows:

"Sec. 16. That religion, or the duty which we owe to our Creator, and the manner of discharging it, can be directed only by reason and conviction, and therefore all men are equally entitled to the free exercise of religion, according to the dictates of conscience; and that it is the mutual duty of all to practise Christian forbearance, and charity towards each other."

This was the result of a compromise, and differed materially from the clause as first introduced by Mason. It then read: "That Religion, or the duty which we owe to our Creator, and the manner of discharging it, can be directed only by reason and conviction, not by force or violence; and therefore, that all men should enjoy the fullest toleration in the exercise of religion, according to the dictates of conscience, unpunished, and unrestrained by the magistrates, unless under colour of religion any man disturb the peace, the happiness, or safety of society. And that it is the mutual duty of all to practise Christian forbearance, love and charity towards each other."

The single occasion when Madison's voice was heard in the Convention was when he offered this amendment: "That Religion, or the duty we owe to our Creator, and the manner of discharging it, being under the direction of reason and conviction only, not of violence or compulsion, all men are equally entitled to the full and free exercise of it, according to the dictates of conscience; and therefore that no man or class of men, ought, on account of religion, to be invested with peculiar emoluments or privileges, nor subjected to any penalties or disabilities, unless under colour of religion, the preservation of equal liberty and the existence of the state be manifestly endangered."

This was the day of an established church, and in Virginia dissenters were suffered to exist only by favour, and were often persecuted. The section of the Declaration of Rights, as it was adopted, declared the persecutions unjust, but took no ground inconsistent with the existence of a state church. It was preferable to the original draft, which used the word *toleration*, thus leaving room for the implication of *permission* of free exercise of religion, instead of proclaiming it as a *right*. Madison's amendment, as he offered it, not only proclaimed this right, but made a state church or any state interference with religious matters an impossibility. The bill for assessments for support of teachers of the Christian religion, which was afterwards introduced in the Assembly, and which he and his friends defeated in 1786, would have been in direct conflict with the proposed declaration that "no man or class of men, ought, on account of religion, to be invested with peculiar emoluments or privileges," and if Madison's amendment had been adopted the long struggle over this and kindred measures would not have occurred. Nor would there have been occasion for the famous bill for religious freedom which Jefferson wrote, and which Madison finally carried through the Assembly ten years afte his amendment to the Declaration of Rights had been shorn of its far-reaching power. The pith of Jefferson's bill was: "That no man should be compelled to f equent or support any religious worship, place or ministry, nor shall be enforced, restrained, molested, or burdened in his body or goods, nor shall otherwise suffer on account of his religious opinion or belief," and this was hardly more than Madison had said.

The proposed amendment was an expression of what was at the time he offered it the strongest sentiment James Madison possessed, and it came from a man who was deeply religious. After finishing his course at Princeton he returned to the plantat on in Virginia much enfeebled by overstudy and not expecting a long life. His mind was charged with religious inquiry and his mental life was solitary. The consequent introspection in which he indulged was tinctured by the Presbyterianism under which he had lived at Princeton. Writing, November 9, 1772, to his college friend, William Bradford, afterwards Attorney-General of the United States, concerning expectations of happiness and prosperity in life, which he said were natural to all men, he remarked that they were harmless provided they were not allowed "to intercept our views toward a future state." We must, he added, always keep a watch on ourselves, lest while building ideal monuments of renown and bliss on earth, "we neglect to have our names enrolled in the annals of Heaven." He would have Bradford season his other studies with "a little divinity now and then, which, like the philosopher's stone in the hands of a good man, will turn them and every lawful acquirement into the nature of itself, and make them more precious than fine gold."

All of his family surroundings were strongly religious. His father was vestryman of St. Thomas' parish and a lay delegate to the Episcopal Convention of 1776; his mother was a pious communicant; his second cousin and friend of the same name, James Madison, who became president of William and Mary College in 1777 and afterwards Bishop of Virginia, had recently returned from England, a consecrated Episcopal clergyman. His tutor before he went to Princeton was an Episcopal clergyman, Rev. Thomas Martin, who lived in his father's house, and for whom Madison had a high regard. But at Princeton he breathed another atmosphere, and he saw in New Jersey and Pennsylvania a greater degree of religious freedom than existed in Virginia. Especially in the section of the State where he lived he saw greater persecution of dissenters than existed in other portions of the State. Nevertheless, the dissenters were rapidly increasing in numbers about him, daily growing stronger as the established church grew weaker. That such should be the result was only natural, for the Episcopal Church in Virginia was steeped in scandal. Quarrels, contests of authority, expulsions and general demoralization existed. The livings were so poor that only the lower order of ministers came from England or Scotland to fill them. Without instancing the scores of individual cases in proof of the bad condition, it will be sufficient to quote the sweeping condemnation of Bishop Meade: "At no time from its first establishment was the moral and religious condition of the church in Virginia even tolerably good."* Madison's contempt for the church as a state institution knew no bounds. Writing to Bradford, January 24, 1774, he said: "If the Church of England had been the established and general religion in all the northern colonies as it has been among us here, and uninterrupted tranquillity had prevailed throughout the continent, it is clear to me that slavery and subjection might and could have been gradually insinuated among us. Union of religious sentiment begets a surprising confidence, and ecclesiastical establishments

*"Old Churches and Families of Virginia," by Bishop Meade, II, 351

tend to great ignorance and corruption; all of which facilitates the execution of mischievous projects."

Active persecution of the Baptists was in progress when he wrote, and he had about this time the experience of standing by the jail in Orange and hearing several Baptist ministers, who had been imprisoned because of their opinions, preach through the prison bars. And thus it was that while he was studying theology and writing erudite notes upon the gospels, and was himself an attendant at the Episcopal church, he believed that human liberty was impossible of attainment, unless legislative interference in concerns of conscience disappeared from the face of the earth.

In constructing his amendment, Madison acted alone, and made no effort to save it from being moulded into the milder paragraph finally adopted. He must have realized that he was in advance of his colleagues, for a majority of them did then favour state control of religion. There was one Virginian of influence, however, who would have sided with Madison ; but Thomas Jefferson was busy in the larger field at Philadelphia. In October, 1776, six months after the Convention adjourned, he came to Williamsburg to take his seat in the new Assembly, of which Madison also was a member, and he and Madison met for the first time. They lived in adjoining counties, but Jefferson was eight years older than Madison, and as a successful lawyer and busy man of affairs, his pathway had not crossed that of the modest bookworm. In the Assembly their service threw them together, for both were members of the Committee on Privileges and Elections. There then began that extraordinary friendship which lasted without interruption for fifty years, when Jefferson died. Their strong personal affection went hand in hand with a mutual admiration and general co-operation in public life which have no parallel in our history. This co-operation, however, did not attain its full proportions until parties formed after the Constitution of the United States was adopted.

CHAPTER II

PRINCETON

ONE REASON why the ruling class in Virginia acted with such unanimity in the Convention of 1776 and other crises of the Revolution was that a large proportion of them had received the same kind of education. This usually came first from clergymen of the established church, who added to the scanty subsistence of their livings by teaching. Happily, these were the better class of parsons, the others not having the industry or stability necessary for the task. From this schooling the regular course was to go to "Their Majesties' Royal College of William and Mary," which was one of the four chief colleges of the colonies, the other three being Harvard, Yale and Princeton. To call the names of notable Virginians in the Revolution is almost to call a roll of graduates of William and Mary. Peyton Randolph, Richard Bland, Benjamin Harrison, Archibald Cary, Paul Carrington, William Cabell, George Wythe, Thomes Jefferson, Edmund Randolph, James Monroe, James McClurg, were all William and Mary men. Seven of the eleven members of the Committee of Correspondence appointed March 12, 1773; six out of eleven of the Committee of Safety appointed by the Virginia Convention of 1775; eleven out of thirty-two of the committee that drew up the Declaration of Rights, and four of the seven Virginia members who signed the Declaration of Independence were from that college. The small proportion of well-to-do Virginia boys who went elsewhere were educated in England or by private tutors, and still fewer went to the Pennsylvania colleges or to the College of New Jersey.*

*"William and Mary Quarterly," VII, 1 et seq.

Among the last-named was James Madison, and his rudimentary schooling came from a Scotchman who was not a divine. Donald Robertson kept a school in King and Queen County, and there the boy was sent at the age of twelve. He studied the usua classica course, and was taught Spanish and French besides. These, as he explained in after life, he learned as dead languages; and when he was at Princeton, being called upon to act as interpreter between a visiting Frenchman and Dr. Witherspoon, he discovered that, while he was able by hard attention to pick out a few words that the Frenchman spoke, the latter was unable to understand a single word of Madison's French. He improved his accent afterwards, but never succeeded in ridding himself of the "Scotch French," as he called it, that Robertson had taught him.* From Robertson's school Madison came under the tuition of the Rev. Thomas Martin, of New Jersey a graduate of Princeton of the class of 1762, who was made rector of St. Thomas' parish in 1767, and who lived with the Madisons.

When the time came for him to go to college, there were several reasons why William and Mary was not chosen. The boy's health had always been delicate, and Williamsburg was regarded as an unhealthful spot.† Also, there was unseemly strife at the college between the board of visitors and the faculty, and the president, Rev. William Horrocks, was unpopular. It may be, too, that the general infidelity which was actually rife at this institution, officially so orthodox, weighed against it. Princeton was the nearest of the other great colleges, and the tutor naturally urged his scholar to go there. He was seventeen years old when he entered the sophomore class, and he took the degree of Bachelor of Arts in 1771. He had the advantage of broader surroundings than would have been possible if he had completed

---

* This, it is stated upon contemporaneous authority, was one of Madison's favourite after-dinner stories. Randall's "Jefferson," II, 192, *n.*

† "William and Mary Quarterly," VII, 66.

his education elsewhere in America; for William and Mary was a local college, and so were Harvard and Yale, with few students coming from any other colony than the one in which each was situated. At the College of New Jersey, on the other hand, every colony was represented among the students; and while New Jersey had a few more than any other one colony, she had not a fourth part of all the students, the actual figures being, when Madison entered, only nineteen Jerseymen out of eighty-four students. Of the twelve students who graduated with Madison, only one, Charles McKnight, afterwards distinguished in the medical department of the army of the Revolution, came from New Jersey. Chief among Madison's companions in his own class were Gunning Bedford of Delaware, Hugh Henry Brackenridge of Pennsylvania, and Philip Freneau of New York. In the class below him was Aaron Burr, and here he met for the first time Henry Lee, a sophomore when he was a senior. His intimate associates were serious students—Caleb Wallace, who was ordained a Presbyterian clergyman and afterwards became a lawyer and judge of the Supreme Court of Kentucky; Samuel Stanhope Smith, also a Presbyterian divine, the first president of Hampden Sidney College in Virginia and Witherspoon's successor as president of Princeton; his brother, John Blair Smith, also a Presbyterian clergyman, who succeeded to the presidency of Hampden Sidney; and William Bradford, who studied divinity but preferred a lawyer's career.

The most important act of Madison's undergraduate life was the founding of the American Whig Society in 1769, for the purpose of cultivating literature, friendship and morality among the members, his associate founders being Samuel Stanhope Smith, Bradford, John Beatty, John Henry of Maryland, Nathaniel Irwin, Wallace, Bedford, Brackenridge, Freneau, and McKnight. It was a patriot organization and had for its object the reading of essays and holding of debates, and here, behind locked doors and among his friends, Madison had his first practice in discussing questions of government which occupied his chief attention during the rest of his life.

His favourite studies at college were the history of the free states of antiquity, and all subjects relating to government. He was the deepest student in college, and for several months he spared only three hours out of the twenty-four for sleep.* Finding his constitution unable to endure the strain, he relaxed, but allowed himself only such an amount of sleep as was absolutely necessary to his health. He became famous for his conversation, and formed the centre of a circle which the other students deemed it a privilege to enter. Dr. Witherspoon remarked to Thomas Jefferson, many years afterwards, that during Madison's whole college course "he had never known him to say or do an indiscreet thing." He was too diffident to face a public audience, and those college honours which were given for oratorical achievements were not for him. The contemporaneous account of the commencement exercises when he graduated contains this note: "Mr. James Madison was excused from taking any part in the exercises." The reason probably was that he was ill at the time.

Having graduated, he remained a year longer to pursue advanced studies under Witherspoon. The course was essentially an ecclesiastical one, embracing chiefly Hebrew and ethics, and was pursued by students who intended to embrace the ministry as a career. Such an intention Madison doubtless had, but it was not definitely formed, and probably did not extend beyond a desire to sound his own mental and moral suitableness for a clergyman's life. At any rate, after leaving Princeton he never recorded any desire nor took any visible steps towards consummating the logical result of his post-graduate studies.†

* "Eulogium," by James Barbour, who states that Madison informed him of this personally.

† See "Memoir of James Madison, Founder of the American Whig Society," by Professor Henry Clay Cameron, in "The Centennial Celebration of the American Whig Society," Princeton, 1871.

He left Princeton in 1772 and returned to Virginia. His nature had expanded in the varied social life of college and the congenial atmosphere of learning, and he chafed miserably at home. Probably, if he had been a free agent, he would have fled from the region of the established church and domestic slavery to Pennsylvania or New Jersey, where conditions were then more to his liking. Domestic exigencies, however, kept him at home. Thomas Martin, his old tutor, died in 1770, and Madison took his place as tutor to his younger brothers and sisters. Then came the transition period of the young man's life, when he was solitary and purposeless. His religious studies and enfeebled health darkened his thoughts, and he turned from poetry and romance, of which he had once been fond, to laborious reasonings on freedom of the will and elaborate studies of the Scriptures. The surrounding robust country life was not for him. The young Virginians of the time were, as a class, merry, easy livers, loving sports, horse-racing, cock-fighting, cudgelling and wrestling matches, fond of big gatherings and heavy feasts with many toasts, visiting freely through the country-side, making love to their neighbours' daughters, quarrelling and fighting not a little, fond of dancing and of the fiddle, which many of them played; but at the age when Patrick Henry and Thomas Jefferson were mastering the intricacies of that instrument Madison's soul was wrapped in deep books and sombre reflections. He was a youth in years without a youth's tastes or mind, and he found few associates. What was there for him to do in the world? Life must have something .more in it than the mere reading of books, roaming through the woods of Orange County, and imparting knowledge to a few boys and girls. There was ready for him a planter's life, or he might become a lawyer; but before the decision was made came the great crisis in American affairs, and an unforeseen occupation opened for him. He wrote the reply of the Orange Committee, May 9, 1775, to "Captain Patrick Henry and the Gentlemen Independents of Hanover," and desired to enter the army. For this, however, he was entirely unfitted by reason of his physical deficiencies, and he occupied himself in recruiting others. Largely through his father's influence, he was elected a member of the Virginia Convention of 1776.

CHAPTER III

FAMILY INFLUENCES

IN EMBRACING, as he did at the beginning, the patriot cause, Madison was unhampered by any regrets that might have come from a living family connection with England. His second cousin James went to England a few years before the Revolution to be ordained as a priest, the voyage being necessary, because Virginia was under the spiritual jurisdiction of the Bishop of London and had no bishop of her own. He did not remain long, and formed no strong English ties. He was the only member of the family who received any part of his education outside of the colonies. England was not, therefore, home to the Madisons as it was to so many other American families. They were purely a colonial family, almost coeval with the Anglo-Saxon settlement of the New World, and the record did not extend beyond that.

"Captain Isaac Maddyson," an artisan, one of the colonists of 1623, and mentioned in John Smith's history as a good Indian-fighter, was the first Madison to reach the New World.* A hundred years later, November 15, 1723, his descendant, Ambrose Madison,† in conjunction

---

* Mr. Gay in his "Life of Madison," denies that Isaac Madison was an ancestor of the Virginia Madisons, but Mr. Rives, whose source of information was the family tradition, asserts that he was.

† John Madison, ship carpenter, patented lands in 1653 in Gloucester County; his son John was sheriff of King and Queen County in 1704; his son was Ambrose, who married Frances Taylor, August 24, 1721, Zachary Taylor, President of the United States, being her collateral descendant. Ambrose Madison's third child, Frances, great-aunt of James Madison, Jr., married Jacob Hite, who was killed by the Indians, July, 1776. James Madison and Eleanor Conway had the following issue: James, born March 16, 1751, died June 28, 1836; Frances, born June 18, 1753; Ambrose, born January 27, 1755, died October—, 1793, Catlett, born February 10, 1758, died March 8, 1758; Nelly Conway, born February 4, 1760, married Isaac Hite, January 2, 1783; William, born May 5, 1762, married Fanny Throckmorton, died July 20, 1843; Sarah, born August 27, 1764, married Thomas Macon; Elizabeth, born February 9, 1768, died May 17, 1775; Reuben, born September 9, 1771, died June —, 1775; Frances Taylor, born October 4, 1774, married Robert Rose, died October —, 1823. "William and Mary Quarterly," IX, 39. Family Bible record of Major Isaac Hite and of the Willis family of Orange.

with Thomas Chew, patented 4,675 acres of land in that part of Spottsylvania County which became in 1732 the county of Orange. Ambrose Madison dying in 1732, his eldest son James, the father of the subject of this book, inherited the interest in the land, and by purchases at different times acquired the whole of it.* This was the estate which came subsequently to be known as Montpelier, and upon which James Madison, the son, spent his whole life. As it happened, however, he was not born there.

He was the eldest child of a young husband and wife who had ten children in all, seven of whom lived to maturity, four being sons and three daughters. His father, James Madison, married Eleanor Rose Conway, September 15, 1749, at Port Conway on the Rappahannock River in King George County. She was seventeen years old, and he twenty-seven. Her father, Francis Conway, was the grandson of Edwin Conway of Worcester County, England, who came to Virginia about 1640; her mother was Rebecca Catlett, also of English descent.† Immediately after the wedding the young couple went to Orange, and to the wooden house which the bridegroom's father had built a few years before. It stood on a gentle slope about half a mile west of the spot where the Montpelier house now standing was erected.

About sixteen months after their marriage they journeyed back to Port Conway in order that the young wife might be with her mother during her first confinement. The route lay first to Fredericksburg by a road following nearly but not precisely the track of the present road, and at Fredericksburg they were ferried over the river and followed the highway which was then the main stem of travel between North and South. It was a journey of between fifty and sixty miles and probably took nearly three days, as progress on wheels was necessarily slow, the roads being bad. About a mile from

---

* MS. records of Orange County, Virginia.
† Hayden's "Virginia Genealogies," 255.

the river and a short distance back from the road stood Francis Conway's house, and here at midnight, March 16, 1751, Nelly Conway Madison gave birth to a son.* The house was many years ago razed to the ground, and nothing now remains to mark the spot but a few bricks of the cellar.† Twenty-one days after his birth the baby was christened and given his father's name. The parish clergyman, Rev. William Davis, officiated, and the sponsors were John Moore, Jonathan Gibson, Mrs. Rebecca Moore, and the Misses Judith and Elizabeth Catlett, all neighbours and relatives of the young mother. Soon after the christening the journey was made back to Orange, so the child had no associations with the spot where he was born. Between 1756 and 1760, after the family circle had been enlarged by the birth of two more children and invaded by its first sorrow in the death of one of them, a new brick house was completed, probably the first one built of that material in that part of the world. It was a plain rectangular structure, with a hall running through the centre and two rooms on either side. It still stands, but its identity has been so moulded into the grander house which was subsequently added to it, that its orig nal proportions are hardly discoverable. Thus, for upwards of seventy-five years, Madison lived under the same roof, and on the same estate all his life. His grandfather had settled upon it, driving the Indians before him, and it went from father to son, remaining with the three generations for one hundred and thirteen years.

The influence of the father and mother continued with their first-born during his maturity. The father died in 1801, when he was seventy-seven years old, after his son had become Secretary of State; and the son had run his course and retired to private life when his mother

* Hayden's "Virginia Genealogies," 261.
† R. H. L. Chichester, judge of King George and Stafford counties, through the clerk of the court of King George County, E. L. Hunter, Esq., furnishes this information. It has been confirmed by the personal knowledge of Professor H. C. Cameron of Princeton University.

died in 1829, in the ninety-eighth year of her age, and only seven years before his own death. During all these years they shared the same house. Eleanor, or as she was commonly called, Nelly Madison was not a beautiful woman, but her face was strongly marked, and her son in the latter years of his life bore a striking resemblance to her in her old age. Although not robust in youth, her health became good in the latter half of her life. She lived a simple, unostentatious life, surrounded by her family and relations, by whom she was held in great reverence. She was noted for her piety and was a communicant in the Episcopal Church from the time of her girlhood, although she was not confirmed till she was eighty years old; this, as it happened, being her first opportunity. The Episcopal Church in Virginia almost disappeared from the face of the earth for a quarter of a century succeeding the Revolution, and St. Thomas' parish had no regular rector. Rev. James Waddel, the famous blind Presbyterian minister, whose eloquence has been enshrined in one of William Wirt's most picturesque passages, preached regularly at Belle Grove church, near Gordonsville, about eight miles from Montpelier, and at intervals in the Episcopal church nearer Montpelier, and Mrs. Madison took great delight in his preaching and attended his ministry whenever possible. She was thus not a strict sectarian, but for many years there were hardly any strict Episcopalians in her part of the State.

Madison's father was a careful planter and patriotic citizen, accepting his public duties without aspiring to fame in them. He acted on the revolutionary committee of his county, served as vestryman of his parish and was county lieutenant. As he was probably the largest landholder in Orange, and as landholding was the chief test of consideration, his influence was as great as that of any other man of his section. He was not a man of high education, but, it would appear, possessed as much learning as the average planter of his time, and in his letters which have been preserved he expresses himself plainly and directly. When his son was born Orange was a frontier county in Virginia, and did not have a society as important or wealthy as that of the lower and river counties. In the State as a whole, therefore, the Madisons and their numerous connections did not occupy a position as high as that of many other families, especially those few that had relatives of consequence in England; but from a local point of view their place was at the top, and as the region became more settled their importance increased.

Primogeniture in Virginia was not abolished by law until 1785, and the principle of family importance, and its maintenance through the recognition of the superior position of the eldest son, did not die with it. The young James Madison was, accordingly, treated by his parents as the chief heir to the estate, and immediately after his return from college became the head of the family, next to his father, sharing the responsibilities and consideration. He was well fitted for the position, for his nature was already mature and stable, and he sowed no wild oats.

CHAPTER IV

THE TASTE of public life which Madison had in 1776 was pleasant to him and, the Assembly having adjourned, he offered himself for re-election to the House of Delegates. He was young and he had not yet secured a firm hold upon his constituents. He attempted, nevertheless, to secure their votes, while at the same time he combatted one of the election customs to which they were firmly attached. This was the custom of treating the voters liberally with rum and punch, a form of corruption which was always practised in colonial elections, and which George Washington himself had observed when he was elected to the House of Burgesses in 1758. But Madison conceived that a new and better order of things had now begun, and he determined to endeavor to put a stop to a practice demoralizing to candidates and voters alike, and to secure his election without making his supporters tipsy. His motives were commendable, but his opponents represented them as springing from a parsimonious spirit and an indifference to the wishes of the people. He was a rich man's son, and it was proclaimed that he was not the poor man's friend, and a successful appeal was made to class prejudice. His opponent, Charles Porter, treated lavishly and was elected. A number of Madison's supporters presented a petition to the House of Delegates, May 16, 1777, saying Porter had used bribery and corruption and praying that his seat be declared vacant. It went to a committee, but was allowed to drop.*

The victim of Porter's punch had no occasion to press

* Journal of the House of Delegates.

the petition, for he soon received official recognition from the General Assembly itself, being elected, November 13, 1777, a member of the Privy Council or Council of State, and taking his seat January 14, 1778. This body consisted of eight members, chosen by the Assembly from its own members or from the people at large, and was intended by the Constitution to be an advisory cabinet for the Governor. It elected its own president, who acted as Lieutenant-Governor of the State when the Lieutenant-Governor was away, and two members were removed by joint ballot of the Assembly every two years, and were ineligible for re-election for the next three years, their places being filled by election by the Assembly. It was considered a body of exceptional dignity, and when Madison entered it was recruited from the most influential class. His colleagues were John Page, afterwards Governor, John Blair, who went to the Federal Convention with Madison in 1787, David Jameson, of the Revolutionary army, Thomas Walker, the pioneer and soldier who was Jefferson's guardian and Washington's friend; B. Dandridge, Nathaniel Harrison and Dudley Digges,—all members of important families. Madison was much the youngest member, and his selection was proof that he had made an unusual impression during his service in the Convention and the Assembly. The Council, however, was not a field in which an ambitious man had much opportunity to extend his reputation. In writing to Jefferson in 1784 (March 16) Madison described it as a grave for talent and "objectionable in point of expense."* Of the eight members seldom more than five or six were present at the meetings. Madison was more assiduous in attendance than any other member, but he had one prolonged absence from July 13 to November 7, 1778. The chief business of the body was the issuing of warrants for war purposes, arranging the drafts on the counties, authorizing appointments, and raising troops and supplies. Jefferson is authority for the statement

* "Writings of Madison" (Hunt) II, 40.

that in the meetings of this small body Madison's diffidence disappeared and he became accustomed to speaking. He acted as interpreter when foreigners communicated with the Council until Belini became secretary and interpreter in June, 1778,* and as he prepared most of the papers for the Governor's signature, he was termed the "Secretary of State."

The most important question with which the Council had to deal, and the one which furnished the most valuable training to Madison was that of raising money, and the Virginia system may be taken as an illustration of the methods which prevailed in the other States to a greater or less extent. The problem presented was, how to recruit and equip armies and pay the expenses of government, including a proportion of those of the continental establishment, and yet increase taxes as little as possible, for, naturally, the people were distressed in their circumstances and would not bear heavy levies. When such a condition of affairs exists, States issue paper money, or borrow, or do both, and try to meet the crisis of the present without undue solicitude for the future.

In 1776 the Virginia Assembly provided for the office of Treasurer, to receive all taxes, and laid special taxes on carriages, land, licenses, and legal documents, beside providing for a poll tax.† The payment was to begin in 1784, and in the meantime, "to suit the distressed circumstances of the inhabitants" and as "the only expedient" the Treasurer was ordered to borrow upon the credit of the taxes at an interest of four per cent. per annum as much money as he could procure, and if he could not borrow to issue treasury notes up to £500,000. The notes were to be legal tender for all debts and taxes, and heavy penalties were laid upon those who should refuse them, or exchange gold and silver at a premium.

---

* Journal of the Governor's Council MSS., Virginia State Library.
† Hening's Statutes at Large for the dates given in the text contain the laws cited.

All the notes were to be redeemable January 1, 1790, and if the taxes should prove to be insufficient for this purpose the "whole estates, real and personal, of the inhabitants" of the colony were pledged to make good the deficiency. This marked the beginning of the Virginia emissions of paper money after the Revolution began. In May, 1777, the Treasurer was ordered to call in the outstanding paper, and issue in its place $1,000,000 in notes. Of course, the law forbidding the holding of coin at a premium had no effect, but it was repeated this year with heavier penalties, against "the pernicious artifices of the enemies of American liberty to impair the credit of the said bills, by raising the nominal value of gold and silver."

At the October session, 1777, the Assembly recognized the depreciation of the paper money and the necessity for a more promising provision for its redemption, and passed an elaborate and comprehensive tax measure. The proceeds of the tax were to be applied first to Virginia's quota of the principal and interest of money borrowed on treasury notes by the Continental Congress, and then to the redemption of the State emissions. To tide over the period till the taxes should begin to be paid, $1,700,000 of treasury notes could be issued. Profiting by the example set by the Legislature, individuals began to issue bills of credit or notes payable to the bearer, and a law was passed to prohibit the practice. In May, 1778, a new emission of $600,000, was authorized, and in October, $1,700,000 more. These acts necessarily caused unevenness in the assessment of taxes, some assessors valuing the lands at their selling price in gold or silver, others at what they would bring in paper. At the May, 1779, session they were ordered to assess on the paper valuation. At the same session £100,000 more of paper money was authorized and the people were encouraged to pay taxes in wheat, corn, rye, barley, oats, hemp or tobacco. The act forbidding any person from asking more in coin than in paper for any article was repealed, as causing "many inconveniences and much injustice." The fact was frankly recognized that matters could not go on much longer at the present rate of paper emissions—that there must be found some basis for them. An additional tax was accordingly laid in October, 1779, and at the same session an act to provide a fund upon which to borrow money was established. It laid a tax of thirty pounds of inspected tobacco in transfer notes upon every tithable person, except free whites between the ages of sixteen and twenty-one years. Five-eighths of the proceeds were to constitute a fund upon which the Treasurer was empowered to borrow not to exceed £5,000,000 current money, paying annual interest. One hundred pounds of inspected tobacco was to be taken as equal to thirty pounds current money, and every lender was to receive indented certificates. The payment of the tax was, however, suspended until December 1, 1780. Another act increased the general taxation one-half per cent. So far as the general condition in both Nation and State was concerned the Assembly understood it and stated it frankly in the act passed at the spring session, 1780: "Whereas, the just and necessary war into which the United States have been driven, obliged Congress to emit bills of credit before the several States were sufficiently organized to enforce the collection of taxes or funds could be established to support the credit of such bills, by which means the bills so emitted soon exceeded the sum necessary for a circulating medium, and consequently depreciated so as to create an alarming redundance of money, whereby it is become necessary to reduce the quantity of such bills; to call in and destroy the excessive mass of money now in circulation, and to utter other bills, on funds which shall ensure the redemption thereof. And, whereas the certain consequences of not calling in and redeeming the money now in circulation in the depreciated value at which it hath been generally received would be to encrease the national debt thirty-nine times greater than it really is, and consequently subject the good people of this commonwealth to many years of grievous and unnecessary taxation"—therefore, a fund was created and new taxes laid to call in the State's quota of the $200,000,000 of continental money issued by Congress and to destroy the State money in circulation. On the faith of the United States and on the funds of the State new bills to the amount of $1,666,666 2-3 bearing interest at five per cent. per annum were authorized, to be redeemable in coin by December 31, 1786. The rate of exchange of the old bills for the new was fixed at forty to one. The efforts to make money out of paper were not the result of any general delusion or desire to pay for something with nothing, but were simply the result of necessity. Another way was tried but without success.

There lived at Collé, a plantation a short distance from Monticello, a Tuscan scientist named Philip Mazzei, who, with a small colony of other Italians, came to Virginia to cultivate grapes for wine.* He became an ardent American and threw himself heart and soul into the Revolution, and being prolific of schemes he hit upon one for borrowing money in Italy. He described his scheme and the situation in the State in a confidential letter to Richard Henry Lee, one of his friends, dated March 25, 1777.† "The redundance of the paper money; the unavoidable necessity of new emissions; the successful malice of so many villains in depreciating it everywhere; the repugnance of the people to the service, artfully increased, and even suggested by many wandering ministers of the Gospel; the daily growing discontent on account of the great scarcity and exorbitant prices of several necessaries of life, especially salt, which is not now to be had on any terms; the reigning mercantile spirit, by which it appears, that the making great fortunes at the expense of public calamities, is now the

* Randall's "Jefferson," I, 235.
† Lee MSS., University of Virginia.

only cherished object, and the possibility, that the British ministry, either by the strange acquisition of some degree of prudence, or by fear or compulsion, may be induced to offer such terms, as might disunite us, give me the greatest apprehension. I can't help thinking, that I could probably contribute not a little to remedy these evils, or lessen their effects, was I sent to Europe in company with some clevar fellow, such as Mr. Maddison, Mr. Man Page, Dr. McClurg, Dr. Jones, &c."

No "clevar fellow" was sent with him, but soon after the date of this letter he was commissioned by the Governor and Council to proceed to the Italian States and solicit a loan for Virginia. The Grand Duke of Tuscany or the Genoese would, he thought, lend money, if it was expended for supplies, etc., in the country of the lender, his people thereby deriving the benefit of it.* This plan appears to have commended itself to Madison and the Governor, and it was arranged that Madison should be Mazzei's chief correspondent. On June 13, 1779, when on the eve of embarking, Mazzei wrote enclosing the cypher they were to use, and saying he had put his papers in a bag with a four-pound ball to throw overboard in case of capture by the enemy. He set sail and was captured, and the shot carried his commission and instructions to the bottom of the sea. After a season of imprisonment he was released, and went to France to consult Franklin on the subject of his mission, but Franklin disapproved strongly of the efforts of individual States to borrow money, because his own exertions for national loans were thereby interfered with. So he told Mazzei he had no authority to borrow and Mazzei wrote back to Virginia for a new commission, but it was never sent. He went to Florence where he was soon reduced to extremity, was without money, and chafed at his neglect. He ceased asking for pay and begged only for money to come back to America. He did not like Italy, and said he wanted to spend his evenings once more with

* Department of State MSS.

Blair, and Lomax, and President Madison, of William and Mary, and their families, and declared there was more virtue among the ladies of Virginia than among a whole cargo of European women.* By some means other than official he succeeded in getting back to his beloved Virginia, and became a man with a grievance, and as Franklin had thrown cold water on his mission he pursued him malignantly. The State had, in truth, treated him but shabbily, but affairs at home were too pressing to admit of much consideration for a man who wanted money in Italy. In fact there was none to send him, and Lemaire and Schweighausen, two other agents, who actually bought military supplies in Europe under Arthur Lee's direction, were no better off for payment than was Mazzei.†

* Department of State MSS.
† Arthur Lee to Richard Henry Lee. Lee MSS. University of Virginia.

CHAPTER V

FEDERAL FINANCES

AFTER having served two years as a Councillor of State, Madison was elected a delegate to the Continental Congress by the General Assembly and took his seat March 20, 1780. He described the situation as it then existed in a letter to his father: "Our army threatened with an immediate alternative of disbanding or living at free quarters; the public treasury empty; public credit exhausted, nay the private credit of purchasing agents employed, I am told, as far as it can bear; Congress complaining of the extortion of the people; the people of the improvidence of Congress; and the army of both; our affairs requiring the most mature and systematic measures, and the urgency of the occasion admitting only of temporary expedients, and these expedients generating new difficulties; Congress recommending plans to the several States for execution, and the States separately rejudging the expediency of such plans, whereby the same distrust of concurrent exertions that has dampened the ardour of patriotic individuals must produce the same effect among the States themselves; an old system of finance discarded as incompetent to our necessities, an untried and precarious one substituted and a total stagnation in prospect between the end of the former and the operation of the latter. These are the outlines of the picture of our public situation."

Robert Morris said the authority of Congress was almost "reduced to a metaphysical idea."* The payments of the several States into the Federal treasury

* Sumner's "The Financier and the Finances of the American Revolution," I, 286.

under the requisitions of Congress were hardly tangible.
The army was kept from starving and total prostra-
tion of the Government was prevented by drafts upon
the States for their unpaid requisitions, and the States
met the drafts by fresh outputs of paper money and not
by increased taxation. The State currency was more
worthless than the continental currency. At the close of
the year 1781 Ambler, the Treasurer of Virginia, said the
paper of the State could be reduced to specie at the rate
of 1,000 for 1. The people shuddered at paper and were
wild to get specie, but the few who got it hoarded it and
thus furnished fresh excuse for more paper emissions.*
August 13, 1781, Madison said the exchange between
the old continental currency and specie was about 135 to
1. Yet there was a good deal of specie in the country in
1780 and 1781. It came from the French army, from
Havana, in exchange for supplies for the Spanish forces
there, and from illicit trade carried on, in spite of legal
prohibition, between Americans and the British. Hardly
any of this specie was in circulation in Virginia, however,
where imported articles cost 100 per cent. more than
they did in Philadelphia.† When the French troops
departed for Virginia in October, 1781, there was joyful
anticipation of an influx of specie in that State, but their
expenditures really brought little relief, for commerce
had almost stopped, and the hard money remained in
the hands of a few fortunate people. Little specie ever
got into the Federal treasury, for Morris wrote to Franklin, November 27, 1781, that since June, when he entered
upon the duties of his office, he had not received over
$100,000 in coin. May 11, 1782,‡ Ambler wrote Madi-
son that since he had been Treasurer of Virginia there
had not been ten pounds of specie in the State treasury.§
In a report made by Morris to Congress, August 28, 1781,

* Edmund Randolph to R. H. Lee, Richmond, September 24, 1785.
Lee MSS. University of Virginia.
† Sumner's "Financier of the American Revolution," I, 99.
‡ Id., I, 97.
§ Department of State MSS.

he gave the amount of requisitions upon the States, March 1, 1780, as $5,000,000, worth only $401,450 in specie.* The lamentable condition of affairs was not due to inability of the people to support the Government, for the testimony is ample that they could have done so. As Wilson explained in a speech in Congress, January 27, 1783,† they were unwilling to submit to taxation, which they had regarded as odious under the old Government, and which they were now loath to accept when it was laid in a direct manner instead of indirectly, so that the payments would not be noticed. There was general complaint that taxes were too high, and Richard Henry Lee wrote Madison, November 20, 1784, that it was one cause of the large emigration then in progress from Virginia to the more Southern States. He suggested, as a remedy, that the State debt be funded and taxes lessened; but the collection of the taxes laid the year before had been postponed and there was nothing with which to meet the obligations of the State.‡ John Francis Mercer, a colleague of Madison's in Congress and generally opposed to him on financial questions, was disposed to abandon what seemed to be a hopeless struggle against bankruptcy. In November, 1784, he had a conversation with Robert Morris, who told him that no money came into the treasury, that several of the States had taken no notice whatsoever of the Congressional requisitions, and others declared they could not understand them. Morris said Virginia was about the only State that kept the wheels of Government moving, so Mercer could see no object in continuing to pay, and thereby merely postponing the inevitable stoppage of the wheels.§

When Madison entered Congress the continental bills of credit amounted to $200,000,000. Forty dollars

* Sumner's "Financier of the American Revolution," I, 299.
† "Writings of Madison" (Hunt) I, 328.
‡ Department of State MSS.
§ Id.

paper to one dollar specie was the ratio of exchange fixed by resolution of March 18, 1780, but it fluctuated and was really much higher. This resolution also substituted for these issues not more than $10,000,000 of new bills payable in specie six years after their date, in the meantime drawing interest at five per cent. per annum. This was virtually an act of bankruptcy, and before it went into effect the old continental bills depreciated to 400 to 1. It was at this stage that Congress urged the States to pay their quotas in produce instead of more worthless paper. Some produce was thus furnished, but paper was piled on paper and the finances of the country were in an appalling condition.

The hopes of Congress centred in Europe where Franklin, Adams and Jay were soliciting loans, but when Franklin informed Morris that France had granted an additional 6,000,000 livres it was found that the whole had been anticipated by bills of exchange, purchase of supplies for the army, Beaumarchais' debt of 2,500,000 livres due in 1782, interest, &c. When the Secretary of War told Congress in May, 1782, that the Department of Finance was unable to furnish the means for supporting the army, Madison said Congress was shocked but not surprised. Such desperate straits had the country reached that Morris called upon Congress to appoint a committee to devise with him measures of temporary relief. Madison, Osgood and Rutledge were appointed January 10, 1783, and after consultation decided to draw upon the *applications* for loans in Europe !* These drafts upon the bank of hope, as Jay called them, were absolutely necessary to prevent a complete wreck. Peace negotiations with Great Britain were in progress at the time and there was deep mortification at the confessed poverty of the Government of a country about to be independent. April 8, 1783, the grand committee composed of one member from each State, reported the foreign debt as $7,885,085, the

* " Writings of Madison " (Hunt), I, 306, 307.

domestic debt as $26,615,290, the total, $36,500,375.* As a means of ameliorating the conditions, Madison proposed to Congress to address a formal recommendation to the States to discontinue their paper emissions, but the proposition met with a cool reception and he abandoned it. He believed Congress should have power to coerce recalcitrant States into contributing their quotas to the expenses of the general government, and followed Washington's opinion that Congress, "after hearing the interests and views of the several States fairly discussed and explained by their representatives must dictate and not merely recommend and leave it to the States to do afterwards as they pleased; which, as I have observed before, is in many cases to do nothing at all." This view came to be generally held in Congress, but there was a difference of opinion as to whether the necessary power existed under the Articles of Confederation, and Madison favoured an amendment granting jurisdiction over the trade and property of contumacious States. The subject never went beyond the stage of discussion, for its unpopularity among the objects of it was foreseen.

The Articles of Confederation provided that Federal taxes should be apportioned among the States according to the valuation of lands, but Madison, Hamilton and a majority of the members of Congress believed the rule to be an impracticable one and impossible of execution without friction, expense and delay. During the war, at any rate, it was manifestly impossible to put it into effect, as the country was overrun by the enemy. Another plan was proposed which Madison advocated with all his might as a basis of relief. This was the levying by Congress of an import tax on foreign merchandise. A request to the States for the necessary power was made by Congress, February 3, 1781, and Virginia acquiesced in June; but later, hearing that all the other States had not taken similar action, she quali-

* " Writings of Madison " (Hunt) I, 443.

fied her assent, by instructing the Governor not to make
it operative until the other States should also agree.
Massachusetts at first remonstrated against the proposition, Rhode Island absolutely rejected it, and Georgia
failed to take any action. Madison, Fitzsimmons and
Hamilton were appointed a committee to draw up a
reply to the refusal of Rhode Island. Hamilton wrote
it and it met with Madison's full concurrence. It con-
tradicted the contention of Rhode Island that an import duty would bear hardest on commercial States,
and pointed out that every duty on imports is incorporated in the price of the commodity, and ultimately
paid by the consumer, with a profit on the duty itself,
as a compensation to the merchant for the advance of
his money. As the merchant was himself a consumer
he too paid his share of the tax. A deputation was appointed to proceed to Rhode Island, lay the reply before
the officers of the State, plead the desperate urgency
of the situation, and ask a reconsideration of the State's
action by the Legislature.

The envoys set out December 22, 1782, and had proceeded half a day's journey when a rumour reached them
that Virginia had wholly repealed the act of assent. If
this were true, as it was, it would be a crushing calamity
and would make an appeal to Rhode Island a waste of
breath. The deputation, therefore, returned to Philadelphia to learn the truth, and learning it, abandoned
their journey. The Virginia Assembly had several
reasons for its action.* Personal enmity played a part,
for the Lee family was hostile to Robert Morris and
opposed the proposed tax because Morris desired it.
The ill-feeling began in 1776, when Morris by defending
Silas Deane aroused the enmity of Arthur Lee. There
was also a jealous feeling that the State had already contributed more than the other States to the Federal expenses and should refuse further aids of which she would
probably have to bear an unequal share. Another

* "Writings of Madison" (Hunt), I, 295 n.

reason was set forth in the preamble to the act of repeal:
"Whereas the permitting any power other than the
General Assembly of this Commonwealth, to levy duties
or taxes upon the citizens of this State within the same,
is injurious to its sovereignty, may prove destructive
of the rights and liberties of the people, and so far as
Congress might exercise the same, is contravening the
spirit of the Confederation in the eighth article thereof,"
etc. If this ground were adhered to there could be no
Federal tax for general revenue.

The functions of a member of the Continental Congress were diplomatic and executive. Elected by the
Legislature of his State he was supposed to carry out its
orders implicitly and to apply for instructions, when he
doubted what his orders were. The State Legislature
was the seat of power, and in Virginia, as Edmund
Pendleton said, it was given to "cutting out large,"* and
had a due sense of its own importance. To disobey its
orders, to advocate a measure which it specifically condemned, was an act of insubordination hitherto unheard of; but Madison, without hesitation, and apparently
without fear of the consequences, deliberately put the
resolutions of the Virginia Assembly aside. These
resolutions were formally laid before Congress by Bland,
January 27, 1783, and on January 28, Madison introduced a new modelled resolution in favour of providing
general funds. It was: "That it is the opinion of
Congress that the establishment of permanent and adequate funds, to operate generally throughout the United
States, is indispensably necessary for doing complete
justice to the creditors of the United States, for restor-
ing public credit, and for providing for the future exigencies of the war." The issue was between those who
favoured increasing Federal power and those who feared
the increase would subvert State power. Alexander
Hamilton made a speech on the day Madison's resolution was brought in, declaring all collectors of Federal

* To R. H. Lee, May 17, 1777. Lee MSS. University of Virginia.

taxes should be both appointed and paid by Congress, because they would then be interested in supporting the power of the Federal Government. Bland and Lee and other State rights members smiled when they heard this, and observed among themselves that he had let out the secret of the purpose of the proposed measures for Federal funds. Madison himself afterwards said that Hamilton's remark was injurious to the cause it was intended to serve: In Madison's speech in favour of his resolution he said it was needless to go into proofs of the necessity of paying the debts, as the idea of erecting our independence upon the ruins of public faith and national honour was an abhorrent one. His resolution, therefore, must be agreed to, unless some one could show another plan that would accomplish the same purpose. It was admittedly impossible to pay any part of the principal of the debts; the question involved was how to pay the interest. Periodical requisitions on the States had proved a failure. If the States themselves established separate funds they must be founded upon a final adjustment of accounts between the States and the United States, and the difficulties, complications, and delays would be interminable. If the funds were first in the hands of the several States they might be diverted from their proper use at any time upon any excuse. There would also be a perpetual jealousy between the States as to amounts levied and contributed. A general fund under the control of Congress obviated all of these difficulties. It was apparent that unless a general provision were made Pennsylvania would pay her own troops as she was then threatening to do.* Her example would be followed by other States, and what then would become of the authority of Congress and the Union? Grave dangers confronted the Government and it must not be

* The Pennsylvania Legislature, in a memorial presented to Congress November 20, 1782, expressed a desire to pay the creditors of the United States in the State from the revenues alloted by the State for Federal uses. Madison, Hamilton and Rutledge were appointed a committee to meet and dissuade the committee of the Legislature.

forgotten that it was the clamours of the army for their
pay and pensions that had brought about the present
crisis. It would not be safe to drive an army to des-
peration. It had been objected that the scheme was
subversive of the sovereignty and liberty of the
States [Virginia had said it], but Congress already had
authority over the purse and a requisition for money
was now a law to the States, although it was a law that
was not enforced. The proposed scheme would simply
make it an effective law. He admitted that the States
showed no fondness for the scheme, but insisted it was
gaining in popularity all the time. As for Virginia's
opposition he was always anxious to follow the behests
of his constituents, but the present considerations prevailed over it. A member owed something to the col-
lective interests of the whole people. He thought there
were occasions when personal consequences should not
deter a legislator from acting according to the clear
dictates of conscience for the good of the whole; he
thought Virginia would not have repealed the law if she
had had full knowledge and would even yet change her
action.*

A reason why Madison wished to obtain a general fund
for the disposal of Congress was that such a fund was
necessary in order to pay the National debt, and to pay
the debt was necessary to preserve the Union. If the
Union broke up there were many people who would
favour a return to English allegiance. He thought, too,
that military uprisings were inevitable, unless there was
a settled way of paying the troops. A general fund
would prevent disputes among the States, which were
now dangerously jealous of each other, the Eastern
States thinking they were creditors of the Southern
States. It the confederacy broke up the Eastern States
would be strong at sea; the Southern States would be
opulent and weak. Mutual reprisals would follow and
the weaker side would call in foreign aid, and finally both

* " Writings of Madison " (Hunt), I, 333, *et seq.*

sides would be subservient to the wars and politics of
Europe. In a speech on February 21, 1783, he said he
would concur in every arrangement necessary for an
honourable and just fulfilment of public engagements,
but in no measure unnecessarily increasing the power
of Congress, and he had, therefore, no desire to per-
petuate the public debt.*

The attitude of the several States toward the project
of providing general funds and strengthening the confederacy was thus summed up by Madison: New Hampshire was in favour, because she wished to be free from
taxation by the States through which her trade passed;
Massachusetts because she was a creditor state and
wished the public debt to be provided for. Rhode Island
should have been in favour, because she was so weak
that the Union was necessary to her protection, but she
was loath to give up the opportunity of taxing her
neighbours which her geographical position afforded her.
Connecticut was interested in anything to enable her
to escape taxation of her commerce by New York and
Rhode Island. In New York many influential citizens
were concerned for provision for the public debt. New
Jersey needed protection against taxation by Pennsylvania and New York. In Pennsylvania were many
citizens who had subscribed for the domestic debt of the
United States. Deleware was too weak to stand without
the confederacy to help her. Maryland occupied a
unique position. She had never been the seat of war,
and not many of her citizens were creditors of the United
States. She had, however, a general wish for National
tranquillity. To Virginia the confederacy was necessary
to protect her large commerce against the maritime
supremacy of the Eastern States; but she disliked giving up the privilege of taxing North Carolina. North
Carolina, like Virginia, needed protection against the
maritime power of New England, and also against the
taxing power of Virginia and South Carolina. South

* " Writings of Madison " (Hunt), I, 382.

Carolina was weak and exposed. She suffered severely during the war and was a creditor of the United States. Georgia was weak and rich, and as a frontier State required protection.*

Following the resolution of Madison the committee on revenue made a report on March 7, reviving the recommendation of 1781, that the States yield to Congress power to levy, for the use of the United States, a duty of five per cent. ad valorem at the port of importation upon all foreign merchandise with a few exceptions; and asking for a like duty on all prizes condemned in the court of admiralty, and a tax on salt, wines, liquors, sugars and teas imported. The taxes were to run for twenty-five years, and the collectors were to be appointed by the States, and to serve under the orders of Congress. None of the taxes were to take effect until all had been agreed to by every State. March 19, Morris reported to Congress that the credit of the United States was at an end, and that no further aids were to be expected from Europe.†

Among the most earnest supporters of Madison's resolution was Alexander Hamilton, but on the report of the revenue committee he and Madison parted company, Hamilton insisting upon direct taxes as the proper way to secure revenue and the direct appointment of collectors of taxes by Congress. His scheme would have been the best, but the States never would have adopted it, if it had passed through Congress. The plan of the revenue committee, with some amendments not affecting its general provisions was adopted by Congress, April 18, 1783, all the States voting for it but New York, which was divided by Hamilton's vote in the negative, and Rhode Island, which opposed it.‡

It was computed that the amount of the tax would not exceed $6,000,000 a year, which was not sufficient, and

* " Writings of Madison " (Hunt), I, 389, n.
† Id., 397, 410.
‡ Id., I, 453.

left a million and a half of interest on the debt to be provided for. It was decided to apportion this sum among the States and leave them to collect it by such taxes as they chose to impose. The apportionment was to be based upon population, counting all the whites and free persons and three-fifths of the slaves. This computation emanated from Madison. The Southern members contended that as a slave was not nearly as productive as a white man, it was obviously unjust to compute him as the same in any scheme of taxation, and after many tentative ratios were suggested, Madison's was accepted as the least objectionable.

April 26, 1783, Madison submitted the address to the States urging the acceptance of the import duty and it passed unanimously. It set forth the necessities of the occasion and declared taxes on consumption were least burdensome, because they were least felt, and that taxes on consumption of articles of foreign commerce were "most compatible with the genius of free States." The whole problem was stated lucidly and simply and an earnest plea was made for paying the debt (1) to our ally, (2) to those foreigners who had stood our friend and trusted us, (3) to the soldiers who had fought for us, and (4) to our own citizens who had loaned us their funds.*

Two months later Madison's Congressional service terminated for the time being and he went home. The impost was finally agreed to by each of the States, at scattering dates, but it was not until the eve of the Constitutional Convention at Philadelphia that all had taken favourable action.

* " Writings of Madison," II, 454, *n.*

CHAPTER VI

THE SURRENDER OF THE "BACK LANDS"

DURING nearly the whole period of the Revolution, until March 1, 1781, the American Union existed by common consent and the general Government performed its functions without a charter. The Articles of Confederation were agreed to by Congress, November 15, 1777, but they were not operative until ratified by all the States, and after the other States had acted favourably Maryland continued to withhold her consent and blocked the way. Her objections were based upon the ground that the proposed articles confirmed the existing sovereignty of the States; and before this could properly be done those States which had, or claimed to have, unoccupied Western territory, or "back lands," as they were commonly called, should yield them up to the sovereignty of the United States. Maryland individually had no such lands, and she was jealous of the overweening power of her richest and largest neighbour, Virginia.* On September 6, 1780, Congress appealed to the States to make liberal surrender of the lands, and to Maryland to authorize her delegates in Congress to ratify the Articles of Confederation. The response of Virginia was a liberal one. In making it she was actuated by a desire to consummate the Union as a legal fact, and to secure a definite Western boundary of general recognition chosen by herself. There were also vexatious questions and obligations connected with holding the enormous territory she claimed which she could profitably shift upon the general Government, thereby relieving herself of the burden of administration.

* Rives, I, 210, *et seq.*

44

The plan of cession originated with George Mason, and as actually adopted by the Assembly of the State was substantially the same as that outlined by him in a letter to Joseph Jones, July 27, 1780. It proposed to surrender the territory west of Pennsylvania and north of 39° 45′ 18″ parallel, between eighty and ninety miles long, and in breadth from east to west the whole distance between the western boundary of Pennsylvania and the Mississippi, between three and four hundred miles; also the country between the Ohio and Mississippi, lying north of parallel 39° 45′ 18″. The whole area was about 50,000,000 acres in extent, and comprised all of Virginia's holdings, possessed and claimed, north-west of the Ohio, and extending thence to the Mississippi and the Great Lakes. From it the States of Ohio, Indiana and Wisconsin were afterwards formed. Title to the lands was asserted by the Virginia Assembly in the spring of 1779, in an act declaring that all deeds or cessions previously made by the Indians to the crown should vest in the State, and all deeds made by the Indians for the separate use of any individuals should be considered void.* The State also claimed title by conquest.

Early in 1777 George Rogers Clark's scheme of conquering the Illinois country was approved by the Governor and Council of Virginia, and he was authorized by the Assembly to raise troops, and promised a liberal quantity of land for himself and his soldiers if he succeeded in his proposed undertaking. About one hundred and eighty men went with him, and after great hardship and heroic daring, he reduced a large section of the country and the important posts of Kaskaskia and Vincennes.

The act of the Virginia Assembly (January 2, 1781), offering the back lands to Congress, accordingly exacted, as a condition of the gift, that Clark and his men should have a quantity of land laid aside for their use. It also

* Rowland's "Life of George Mason," I, 360, *et seq.*

stipulated that the State should be reimbursed for the expense incurred in conquering and defending the country; that the friendly inhabitants should be protected in their rights and property; that the promises of bounty land for Virginia troops in the Continental army should be met; that the territory should in due season be laid off in "Republican States"; that the unappropriated lands should constitute "a common fund for the use and benefit" of all the States, and consequently that all deeds from Indians to private persons or companies should be disregarded. Congress was also to guarantee to Virginia all her remaining territory after the cession.*

There were three classes in Congress who opposed these conditions:—first, those who wished to force a larger cession and thereby restrict the boundaries of the State, thus crippling its preponderating influence; second, those who thought all territory formerly known as crown lands now belonged of right to all the States equally and not to any one within whose boundaries it happened to be; third, those who had an interest, pecuniary or otherwise, in the land companies.

These companies were the Indiana, Vandalia and Illinois. In contravention of Virginia law they had obtained from the Indians for mere trifles titles to more than 40,000,000 acres of land within the chartered limits of Virginia. When the question of the cession came before Congress they threw their influence might and main against its acceptance, and it was rumoured and generally believed at the time that some of their stock was held by members of Congress.

Two States besides Virginia also offered lands, Connecticut and New York, the former giving up all claim to the soil west of New York and as far as the Mississippi, but reserving political jurisdiction; the latter giving all lands, without reservation, west of a certain boundary "drawn on the occasion."† Both cessions covered

* Hening's Statutes at Large, X, 564.
† "Writings of Madison" (Hunt), I, 172.

some of the lands claimed by Virginia. New York's title rested upon treaties with the Six Nations tribe of Indians, surrendering all the territory claimed by that tribe and tributary tribes, making a domain of incalculable extent.

In the autumn of 1781 all the acts of cession and the memorials which the land companies submitted in support of their claims were referred by Congress to a special committee for a report. By combining their forces the interests opposed to Virginia were in the ascendency, and the committee appointed reflected the views of the majority, being made up of members from New Hampshire, New Jersey, Maryland and Pennsylvania, all but Pennsylvania small States which hoped to accomplish a restriction of Virginia's western boundary. The committee called at once for proof of title to the lands, but this demand the Virginia delegates resented, holding that the State had already declared itself on this point, and that the resolution of Congress calling for the surrender of the lands professed to bury such discussions.* They also felt the uselessness of arguing the case before prejudiced men. An endeavour to obtain action from Congress prohibiting the committee from entering into the question of titles met with no success, but the agents of the land companies appeared and made their arguments. November 3, 1781, the committee reported in favour of rejecting the offers of both Virginia and Connecticut, and declared that "all the lands ceded, or pretended to be ceded," by Virginia were a part of the original territory of the Six Nations and tributary tribes and were now under the government of New York. Accordingly, they recommended the acceptance of that State's offer. As it embraced the lands southeast of the Ohio, the western boundary of Virginia would thus be the Alleghany mountains. The report also favoured the absolute confirmation of the Indiana Company's claims, and treated those of the Vandalia and Illinois

* "Writings of Madison" (Hunt), I, 160, 161.

Companies as having an equitable basis. Nothing could have been more obnoxious to the Virginia delegates than this report; yet to permit its consideration by Congress would at this time have resulted in its adoption. Resort was accordingly had to dilatory tactics, and by adroit parliamentary manœuvring Madison succeeded in preventing its consideration. As it was plain to him that no favourable action was to be expected from Congress as matters stood, he turned his attention to the State government, and wrote to Jefferson, urging him to carefully trace Virginia's title and be prepared to defend it.* In May, 1782, he suggested that the Legislature reconsider its act of cession and either repeal it or set a limit of time for its acceptance. By thus presenting a bold front he had no doubt Congress would change its attitude.

In the meantime one of the chief objects of the Act of Surrender had been accomplished, for Maryland had given her adhesion to the Articles of Confederation, and on Thursday, March 1st, 1781, they were announced to the world.

Madison's suggestion that Virginia reconsider or modify her act of cession, so as to force the hand of Congress, was not pursued, and in the summer of 1782, before further action was taken by the State, the Grand Committee of Congress, composed of a member from each State, called the attention of Congress to the fact that if the back lands were at its disposal, they would furnish an excellent means of raising some of the revenue so pressingly needed. The debates showed, however, that at this time Congress was hopelessly split on the subject, enough States favouring one plan or another to make it impossible to find a majority for any.† There was danger, therefore, of such delay that the individual States, having lands, or claiming to have them, would open land offices and sell land patents without reference to Federal action, and an already complicated situation

---

* " Writings of Madison " (Hunt), I, 170, *et seq.*
† Id., I, 225.

would thus become still more confused, while the general Government would be deprived of any benefit from the lands. In this aspect of affairs Madison became convinced that the occasion was one for a compromise, or both the Federal Government and Virginia would suffer. It was desirable for the additional reason that the lands in question were being settled, and the time was not distant when the inhabitants would be making demands of their own. Virginia would then lose the territory and the United States would not gain it. "A separate government," wrote Madison, "cannot be far distant, and will be an insuperable barrier to subsequent profits. If, therefore, the decision of the State on the claims of companies can be saved, I hope her other conditions will be relaxed."*

In the autumn of 1782 the New York cession was brought up by itself with a proposition to accept it without prejudice to the Virginia and Connecticut propositions; but the Virginians opposed it, because it would merely substitute the United States for New York in the boundary questions then pending.† Six months later (April, 1783,) Congress received a memorial from Moses Hazen, Colonel of the 2nd Canadian regiment, "Congress' own," as it was called, praying that a tract of land on Lake Erie be allotted for the use of the Canadian soldiers, who had fought for the American cause. Wilson, of Pennsylvania, improved the opportunity afforded by the reading of the memorial to propose that a committee be named to report proper measures to be taken with respect to the Western lands, as emigration thither was rapidly increasing. Madison opposed the motion as inopportune. Efforts were then in full progress to secure consent of the States to a scheme for raising general revenue and Wilson's motion, if agreed to, would arouse jealousy among the States with consequent op-

* "Writings of Madison" (Hunt), I, 232, 233.
† Id., I, 251, n.

position to Federal measures. Until Congress should acquire the lands through their cession by the States no steps to dispose of them could properly be taken, he said. Pending such acquisitions it was the duty of the States to suppress irregular settlements. Wilson replied that there was no need of waiting for action by the States, as all the territory over which the States had not actually exercised jurisdiction belonged of right to the United States. Madison called his attention to the fact that Pennsylvania had on a former occasion, in a territorial dispute, contended that exercise of jurisdiction was not a proper test of the territorial rights of the States; but if it were, Virginia had exercised jurisdiction over the Illinois territory and other places northwest of the River Ohio. As a matter of fact, he declared, the treaty of peace with Great Britain did not comprehend any territory not already claimed by some one of the States. He was of opinion that subsequent action by the States might render any action at the present time unnecessary.* Alexander Hamilton shared Wilson's view, that the right to the lands lay with the United States, but he thought the private claims deserved consideration and moved an amendment in their favour, June 10, 1783. As the consideration of the question proceeded, however, these claims were "tacitly excluded," and the land companies in consequence opposed the inpending settlement. Yet, it would appear that their interests lay upon the side of a settlement, for non-action upon their claims would enable them to ask Congress to consider them later when they would have only Congress to deal with. At present they might be sure that Virginia would not recognize their right to an acre of land, and it was equally certain that Congress would not extend authority over the Western territory by use of force against Virginia.

On June 30, 1783, the first step was taken positively

* "Writings of Madison" (Hunt), I, 444, *et seq.*

pointing to an acceptance of the Virginia cession upon
a compromise. The committee having the matter in
charge reported in favour of that part of the Virginia
conditions providing for the State's re-imbursement
for reducing the British posts at Kaskaskia and Vincennes.* At once New Jersey sent a vigorous remonstrance to Congress, calling attention to the claim of
the State made as early as 1778 to a share in the Western
territory, which was the common property of all the
States, and belonged no more to Virginia than it did to
New Jersey. The Virginia conditions of cession were
characterized as "partial, unjust and illiberal."† The
coalition against Virginia at this time comprised, beside New Jersey, Pennsylvania, Maryland, Rhode Island
and Delaware. Maryland proposed an ingenious substitute for the Virginia offer. With considerable minute-
ness it described the territory France had ceded Great
Britain in 1763, and the portion of it ceded to the United
States by Great Britain in the treaty of ⌐eace. It was
the United States "as one undivided and independent
nation, with all and every power exercised by the King
of Great Britain" that succeeded to the British title.
Congress was reminded that as early as 1779 Maryland
had instructed her delegates in Congress to maintain
"that a country unsettled at the commencement of
this war, claimed by the British crown, and ceded to it
by the Treaty of Paris, if wrested from the common
enemy, by the blood and treasure of the 13 States,
should be considered as common property, subject to
be parcelled out by Congress into free, convenient and
independent governments, in such manner and at such
times, as the wisdom of that Assembly shall hereafter
direct." Accordingly, Congress was now requested to
appoint a committee to report what territory lay without
the actual boundaries of the individual States, and

---

* " Writings of Madison " (Hunt), I, 474, *et seq.*
† Journals of Congress (Ed. 1800), VIII, 204-205.

within those of the United States, and what parcels were most eligible for one or more independent States, and to provide for the opening of a land office forthwith. New Jersey alone voted with Maryland for this proposition.*

The Virginia proposal was now in the hands of a friendly committee composed of Rutledge of South Carolina, Ellsworth of Connecticut, Bedford of Delaware, Gorham of Massachusetts, and Madison. The report which they submitted reflected the compromise which had been arranged under Madison's advice. The condition that the claims of the land companies be specifically declared void was rejected. The promise that the ceded territory would be a common fund to be used for the benefit of all the States was deemed sufficient to satisfy this point. The condition that all of Virginia's remaining territory be confirmed to her was also rejected, because it would be obviously unfair for the United States to thus take the side of one State against any other State with which she might have a boundary dispute. If there was no such dispute the Articles of Confederation presented sufficient security in the clause which confirmed each State in its sovereignty; if there was a dispute, the Articles themselves provided all the legal machinery for settling it. All the States voted in favour of accepting the committee's report, except New Jersey and Maryland, New Hampshire being divided.† The action of Congress being referred back to the State, the Virginia Assembly acted favourably, after a hot fight by a vote of fifty-three to forty-one. Many members were accused of deriving personal profit from the new arrangement and some of them were defeated for re-election the following autumn.‡ On March 1, 1784, the delegates in Congress, Thomas Jefferson, S. Hardy and Arthur Lee, signed the deed of cession.

* Journals of Congress (Ed. 1800) VIII, 254.
† Id., VIII, 258.
‡ Benjamin Hawkins to Madison, Sweet Springs, September 4, 1784, Department of State MSS.

The final consummation thus occurred, as it happened, after Madison left Congress, but the guiding hand throughout the proceedings had been his, and it was his patience and tactical skill that prevented defeat, and his advice that secured a timely compromise and practical success for Virginia's conditions.

CHAPTER VII

INTIMATELY connected with the subject of the back lands and of more vital consequence to the future of America was the question of the boundary between the United States and Spanish territory and the right of navigating the Mississippi River.

By her chartered limits and Clark's conquests, Virginia claimed the territory to the banks of the river, and the General Assembly by resolution of November 5, 1779, ordered the delegates in Congress to favour the free navigation of the river to the sea. The question was, of course, an international one, and involved negotiations with Spain by a Power not yet independent.

In June, 1779, Spain and England were virtually at war, and the opportunity seemed to be ripe for securing Spain as an ally of the United States. In 1756 she had lost the Floridas to Great Britain, and by resolution of September 15, 1779, Congress held out to her the prospect of regaining them with America's help, provided "the United States should enjoy the free navigation of the River Mississippi into and from the sea." John Jay, our minister at Madrid, reported that the desired alliance was impossible at this price, but Congress agreed unanimously to adhere to the condition, and October 4, 1780, appointed Madison, Sullivan, of New Hampshire, and Duane, of New York, a committee to draw up an instruction to Jay on the subject, a copy of the instruction to be sent to Franklin at Paris. The paper was prepared by Madison, and October 17 he presented the completed draft, which Congress accepted without change. It was the first important State paper to come from his pen in Congress, and it put him at once in the front rank of the members, for it is probable that no other member could have prepared an argument so faultless and adequate from the American point of view.

It laid down the principle that, as the question of boundary between Spanish and British territory in America had been settled by the treaty of 1763 between Spain and Great Britain, the United States succeeded to all the benefits Great Britain had derived from the treaty. The King of England had exercised sovereignty over his American colonies not because he was recognized as King by the people of England, but by the people of America. The territory held in his name was held for them, and became theirs when they threw off his yoke and assumed sovereignty themselves. Certain portions of the territory in question were in the possession of Spain when her relations with England were broken off, but these were only a few unimportant places and it could not be successfully contended that they controlled the surrounding territory. If the right to the country depended on conquest the United States had a more extensive claim than Spain, having conquered all the important posts on the Illinois and Wabash and established civil government over the inhabitants. It was true Great Britain held parts of the territory, but these parts were not subject to conquest by any power other than the United States. To admit otherwise would be to admit that any part of the United States captured or to be captured by Great Britain was subject to such conquest, and New York, Long Island, and other places in the enemy's hands might be permanently severed from the American Union. The most natural boundary between the United States and Spanish possessions was the Mississippi, and it was less likely than any other to become a subject of dispute. As the sovereignty of the soil was a descendible right, so was the free navigation of the river, and the fact that Spain was in possession of both banks at the mouth was neither a natural nor an equitable bar to prevent the use of the river. The usages of nations under such circumstances gave no further right than the imposition of a moderate toll on commerce. Vattel was quoted to show that an innocent passage was due all nations at peace even for troops through a friendly State, and this applied equally to water passage. In this case, however, it involved also a free port at the mouth of the river, as to navigate the river vessels must be so constructed that they could not go to sea. Stress was laid upon the material advantages to be derived by Spain if she agreed to America's wishes. The Western country would soon be overspread with people, and in the nature of things they would for years to come be engaged wholly in agricultural pursuits. Their consumption of foreign manufactures would necessarily be large, and the most natural channel for exchange of products would be the Mississippi. If this channel were closed, commerce would perforce go northward up the rivers having their sources near the lakes, thence by short portages to the lakes or rivers flowing into them, thence through the lakes, down the St. Lawrence to England, instead of down the Mississippi to the benefit of Spain and France.*

The bold argument advanced in this instruction was negatived by the fears of America herself. In less than a year after it was written British military successes in the South were such that it seemed probable the whole of South Carolina and Georgia, and even possibly Virginia and North Carolina, would fall into the hands of the enemy. The armed neutrality of Europe under Catharine II of Russia began to make itself felt, and serious fears were entertained that the allied neutrals would force a peace between the United States and Great Britain upon the basis of each belligerent keeping such territory as each actually held—the *uti possediis.* As this would mean a disastrous dismemberment of the United States a cry arose outside of Congress and within

* " Writings of Madison " (Hunt), I, 82.

it to abandon the Mississippi for the sake of an alliance with Spain. A little more than a month after the instruction to Jay had left, Georgia and South Carolina moved its reconsideration, and Theodoric Bland, Madison's only colleague at the time, changed front completely, and wrote to Jefferson, then Governor of Virginia, November 22, 1780,* saying he thought the distant prospect of free navigation of the river ought to be abandoned for the immediate benefit of an alliance and probable independence. He showed the letter to Madison who refused to sign it, but Jefferson transmitted it to the Assembly, December 5. Madison and Bland sent a joint letter dated December 13, asking for instructions, which was laid before the Assembly.† The instructions were passed January 2 and were: "Every further or other demand of the said navigation to be ceded, if insisting on the same is deemed an impediment to a treaty with Spain." Fortunately, Jay himself was then opposed to the abandonment of the American position, and when the instruction of Congress rescinding that which Madison had drafted reached him, he stated to the Spanish Government that the American offer must be availed of at once, as there was no obligation to renew it in the future. Spain did not accept, no alliance was formed, and the Mississippi remained an open question when Madison's first service in Congress ended.

When Madison took his seat, the law of Virginia did not permit a delegate to serve more than three years in any term of six years. Madison's service would, therefore, have terminated in the autumn of 1782, but in May of that year the law of eligibility was repealed, and he was chosen for a fourth consecutive year, at the end of which there remained four months when he would be eligible to serve under the Articles of Confederation, which established a triennial rotation, but did not go into effect till the ratification, March 1, 1781. It was

* Department of State MSS.
† " Writings of Madison " (Hunt), I, 102, *n.*

proposed to re-elect him for this brief period, but he declined to allow it. He was not, however, popular with all the members of the House of Delegates, a considerable opposition having developed from those who were habitually jealous of Congressional power and his advocacy of it.

The treaty of peace with Great Britain terminated the desirability of a treaty of alliance with Spain, but in place of it came a demand from the Eastern States for a treaty of commerce. Unfortunately, diplomatic negotiations with Spain were rendered difficult by the terms of the treaty of peace, a secret article of which provided that, if England should at some future· day gain West Florida from Spain, the Southern boundary of the United States should extend beyond the line actually named in the treaty. This secret article became known at Madrid almost as soon as it was agreed upon, and the Spanish Government informed Congress, June 25, 1784, that Spain would not admit that the boundary between the United States, Louisiana and the Floridas had been truly described in the treaty, and that until a correct description should be given Spain would maintain her right to the exclusive navigation of the Mississippi and would not permit American boats to use the river.

Don Diego Gardoqui presented his credentials as Minister from Spain July 2, 1785, and John Jay, who had succeeded Livingston as Secretary of Foreign Affairs, was instructed to negotiate a commercial treaty with him. Gardoqui soon let it be known that he was commissioned to sign a liberal treaty, provided it did not touch Spain's right of exclusive use of the Mississippi. August 25, 1785, Jay was instructed to adhere to the position originally taken by the United States on this point, as set forth in the Madison instruction of October, 1780. It was, of course, apparent to Jay that an insistance upon this position meant the failure of the negotiations, and he asked for a committee from

Congress with which he could secretly consult. Such a committee he hoped would have a majority of its members from those States which cared more for commerce with Spain than for the use of the Mississippi, and his move was successful, for Monroe was the only member of the committee who regarded the Mississippi question as paramount to the commercial question. The negotiations with Gardoqui, therefore, proceeded upon a basis of closing the river for twenty-five or thirty years; and August 3, 1786, Jay laid his plan before Congress. Everything pointed to the probability of its success.

Madison was not then in Congress, but his efforts for the right of free navigation of the river were as active in Virginia as they had been in Philadelphia. Except the problem of how to strengthen the Federal Government there was no subject which interested him so much. He never doubted that he was right and that the salvation of the country required that his views should prevail. Any agreement to close the river, even for a time, would, he believed, precipitate strife. "An impolitic and perverse attempt" of Spain to exclude American boats would, he wrote to Jefferson, August 20, 1784, merely *delay* the development of the Western country; and, he added: Spain "can no more finally stop the current of trade down the river than she can that of the river itself." He declared that Spain would not persist in her present attitude if America stood firm, for right was on the American side. Above New Orleans, there would soon be a population of millions, and it was too much to suppose that their interests could be sacrificed to those of a paltry Spanish town. Moreover, every argument now used by America for the freedom of the river Spain had herself employed in 1609 when she contended for the freedom of the river Scheldt. Furthermore, American trade down the river would make New Orleans one of the most flourishing ports in the world and a loyal Spanish city, instead of

remaining, as it was, a half-French town which hated
Spain for her oppression.   It was worth while for Spain
to consider that the friendship of the United States would
be better than the planting of seeds of permanent dis-
sension and probable conflict.   Spain also must be influenced by public opinion in Europe, which was opposed
to the notion that ownership of the mouth carried with
it the control of the whole length of a river.*   "The
use of the Mississippi," he wrote to Monroe in Congress,†
"is given by nature to our Western country, and no
power on Earth can take it from them." He impressed
his views upon everyone who could influence a favourable settlement of the subject.   During the intimacy
of a journey from Baltimore with Lafayette in September, 1784, he unfolded his arguments and told
him that such was the clash of interests between the
United States and Spain that an actual rupture was
imminent, unless France mediated between the two.
If she did not she would, as an ally of Spain, share the
odium of Spain.   Lafayette said Spain was such a fool
that allowances should be made for her, and he promised
to write to Vergennes on the subject.   He did so; but
after leaving Madison he fell into the hands of the commercial party, and when he sailed for France was under
the impression that many people were willing to yield
up the navigation of the Mississippi in return for commercial advantages.   Madison wrote him a long letter,
March 20, 1785, showing the impossibility of the maintenance of the Spanish position, and Lafayette lent his
influence in Paris on the side advocated by Madison.

That side, however, was not only losing ground in
Congress, but outside of Congress, and even in Virginia.
Henry Lee, who at this time usually followed Madison's
lead on public questions, failed to do so on this occasion,
voted with the Jay party in Congress, and lost his re-election to that body in consequence.   Washington, also,

* " Works of Madison " (Cong. Ed.), I, 93, *et seq.*
† January 8, 1785, Id., I, 121,

thought the navigation of the river not absolutely necessary, and that it could be postponed until such time as the
bordering country was more thickly populated. Madison's information, however, showed that Lee and Washington were wrong. He had a number of relations
and friends who had emigrated to the Western country
and kept him informed of the trend of Western public
opinion, and he knew that there was grave danger if
the river was surrendered that the pioneers would abandon the Federal Union as useless to them and seek the
protection of a foreign power. George Muter wrote to
him from Kentucky, February 20, 1787: "Our people
are greatly alarmed at the prospect of the navigation
of the Mississippi being given up, and I have not met
with one man who would be willing to give the navigation up, for ever so short a time, on any terms whatsoever." From Pittsburgh, February 21, 1787, John
Campbell wrote: "The minds of all the Western people
are agitated on account of the proposed cession of the
Mississippi navigation to Spain. Every person talks
of it with indignation and reprobates it as a measure
of the greatest Injustice and Despotism, declaring that
if it takes place they will look upon themselves released
from all Federal Obligations and fully at Liberty to
seek alliances & connections wherever they can find
them and that the British officers at Detroit have already
been tampering with them. I am apprehensive that
these matters will hasten the Separation of the District
of Kentucky prematurely from the other part of the
State, the Inhabitants of North Carolina to the Westward of Cumberland mountain being desirous to join
the People of Kentucky in forming one State."*

When the success of the Jay party appeared to be
most probable Madison was in the Virginia Assembly
and the news caused him serious embarrassment. As
the champion of extension of Federal power, he had
been telling his colleagues that Congress was attentive

*Department of State MSS.

to the wants of all parts of the country equally, and that the interests of the West would be served better if Congress were granted more authority. The news from Philadelphia seemed to be a denial of these promises. The jealousy of the influence of the Northern States in National affairs increased. There were thirty members of the Assembly from Kentucky, and their opposition to a Government apparently about to barter away their interests was to be expected. Many Virginians who had been Federalists heretofore became lukewarm, and worst of all, Patrick Henry, whose aid for Federal measures Madison had been hoping to secure, became cold. The opposition of the Western members to the project of closing the Mississippi was, however, the very feeling upon which Madison now worked to prevent them from leaving his party. He pointed out, truly enough, that if the right of navigation of the river should be abandoned by Congress it would be because the Federal Government was too weak to assert it, and feared a war for which it was powerless to prepare. The remedy, therefore, was to do away with the powerlessness and give real authority to the general Government. Caught by this reasoning the Kentucky members supported Madison's resolutions for the Philadelphia convention, and it was passed November 9, 1786. In return he wrote a vigorous protest against the contemplated treaty, which was adopted by a unanimous vote November 29th.*

Soon afterwards Madison sought and secured an election to the Continental Congress, his chief object being to continue there his efforts to defeat the projected treaty. In the meantime occurred those circumstances which usually happen to hasten a political crisis and which no statesmanship can foresee. An adventurer named Thomas Amis, living in the Western country, loaded a boat with merchandise and attempted to go down the Mississippi. On June 6, 1786, he was

* Rives, II, 109, *et seq.*

seized and his cargo confiscated by the Spanish authorities at Natchez. He was himself released and left to make his way homeward overland, and as he journeyed he told his story and it aroused the settlers. When the inhabitants of the American post at Vincennes heard it they were so wrought up that they looted the store of a Spanish merchant in the place by way of reprisal. Vincennes then being in Virginia territory, the State took measures to protect Spanish interests, and the affair was reported to Congress in the spring of 1787. At the same time a memorial was presented from North Carolina setting forth the seizure of Amis's boat. These incidents were a practical argument against the possibility of stopping emigration to the West, and showed that if trade down the river were stopped trouble would follow. They furnished a reason for a call upon the Secretary of Foreign Affairs for a report upon the condition of the negotiations with Spain.

The position of that officer was always a peculiarly difficult one. He was obliged to report to the full Congress whenever called upon and Congress had no stable policy, but changed his instructions whenever it saw fit. He could not even be certain of being permitted to manage the affairs intrusted to him without interference, for the members of Congress did not hesitate to communicate directly and without his knowledge with foreign ministers. Such communication Madison accidentally had with Gardoqui in March, 1787. The Spaniard attempted to support the position of his Government by using the Tagus River as an illustration. It flowed from Spain through Portugal, but Spain had never claimed a right to navigate it, deeming the possession by Portugal of both banks of the river at its mouth an undisputed barrier. He was then asked whether he contended for the same right of Spain to the Mississippi, where Spain had only five acres of territory at the mouth of the river. He replied that Spain had more territory than this, but when pressed to specify what it was, he could make no definite reply. He hinted, however, that the consequences would be dangerous if Virginia's views prevailed. In order to placate him his attention was called to the recent action of the Virginia Assembly denouncing the seizure of Spanish property at Vincennes; and with a view to alarming him he was told that the feeling in the West against Spain was becoming bitter and that the inhabitants were even threatening to go over to Great Britain.

The report made by Jay to Congress, April 11, 1787, was a frank disclosure of the state of his negotiations with Gardoqui. Repeated conversations with the minister had, he said, produced nothing, for the minister would not yield on the Mississippi question. He would not even agree to an article clearly implying the right of the United States to navigate the river, and "expressly forebearing the use during the term of the treaty"; but Jay thought he might agree to an article accomplishing this object by stipulating merely that the river would not be used by the United States during the term of the treaty, and observing silence on the question of right. The abandonment of the navigation while the treaty should run was an alternative for war, and Congress must decide upon one or the other. It was developed also that Jay considered himself empowered by the votes of seven States to proceed with the negotiations upon the basis outlined in his letter.

The division on the subject had generally been that of the North, which voted for the treaty, against the South, which voted with Virginia; but New Jersey and Pennsylvania had never been permanently on the Northern side. The Assembly of the former State now sent positive instructions to the delegates in Congress to oppose the treaty and the personnel of the Pennsylvania delegation changed, a majority going with Virginia. This was a natural development, as part of the State lay in the Mississippi valley. Rhode Island also changed her vote, but from unworthy motives. Judging other States by herself she supposed that the Eastern States desired to close the river, so as to throw out of competition in the market for public lands the extensive Western country. The real reason, however, was simply that the Eastern States desired commerce with Spain; and they did, undoubtedly, prefer that the Missisippi should be closed, since if it became a highway of commerce it would take much of the trade which otherwise would be forced to the Eastward. This reason was frankly avowed by Gorham of Massachusetts, in the course of the debate.

Jay's report being made, Madison moved its reference to a committee, and the vote on the subject disclosed the fact that the party in favour of the treaty was probably in the minority. On April 18, he moved that the negotiations be transferred to Madrid. If this could be done they would be taken from the hands of Jay to those of Jefferson, who would be sent as minister. This motion was a revival of one made by Pinckney of South Carolina when Madison was not in Congress. Of course, Jay reported against it with considerable feeling. Madison also called upon Congress to declare that the vote of seven States ought not to be regarded as sufficient authority upon which to negotiate the treaty. King, of Massachusetts, showed. that there had been twelve States present when Jay received authority to negotiate upon the basis of the non-use of the river. This was true, but it was equally true that the Articles of Confederation required nine States to assent to a treaty before it could become effective, and that only seven States had since been shaping the negotiations. What would they avail, if it was obvious that their result would be rejected? The object of Madison's motion was, however, dilatory, and to kill the treaty by debate. In the midst of the debate an adjournment was had and the treaty disappeared from view for eighteen months. When Madison left New York to go to

Philadelphia to attend the Federal Convention he was able to announce that the project of shutting the Mississippi *"was at an end."* And so it was for the time being, thanks chiefly to Madison. But Jay and his party had strong arguments on their side. A commercial treaty with Spain would have benefited many. Their mistake was in supposing it would have lessened the friction between the two Powers, whereas it would really have increased it, for the Western adventurers would have broken the treaty.

CHAPTER VIII

ONE REASON why Madison held a commanding position in the Continental Congress was that he was more assiduous in attendance than most of his associates, who came and went having regard chiefly to the affairs of their respective States and their own personal convenience, and holding the concerns of the Union as of secondary importance. As he was always on the spot his influence was naturally greater than theirs. While his public duties were thus laborious, his private circumstances were trying and his pressing pecuniary embarrassment caused him incessant worry.

The provision made by Virginia for her delegates in Congress would have been a liberal one if it had been paid. At first they were allowed food for their horses and servants, house rent and fuel, and twenty dollars for each day of attendance on Congress, and two dollars for every mile of travel going and coming. To encourage economy they were required to submit their household accounts to the State auditors.* At the May session of the Assembly, 1782, this provision was repealed, and they were allowed eight dollars a day specie standard, while in actual attendance. As a bachelor of unostentatious habits Madison's expenses were not heavy. He kept but one servant and two horses, and he had no separate house. But the treasury of the State could seldom pay him or his colleagues, and they were compelled to make common cause in their poverty; when one received a draft he shared it with the others. In March, 1783, the State auditors adjusted

* Rives, I, 518, *et seq.*

Madison's accounts and found £865 8s. 3d. due him,* the whole of which he never received, at any rate while in Philadelphia. His father sent him money from time to time, but not enough, and October 8, 1782, he wrote Edmund Randolph that he then owed about $350. In his distress he had recourse to two Jew brokers, Cohen and Haym Salomon. The latter was a native of Poland, a friend and fellow countryman of Pulaski. He refused to receive interest for loans to members of the Congress and when he died in 1784 his family received nothing from his estate.†

In the same boarding house with Madison were the other Virginia delegates, the French minister, Barbé de Marbois (also a client of Salomon's),‡ General James Floyd, a signer of the Declaration of Independence and a delegate in Congress from New York, and his daughter Catherine, a beautiful, vivacious girl, just sixteen years of age. There were several older ladies in the house one of whom acted, as it would appear, as the friend and adviser of Miss Floyd.

In those days a girl was accounted to be a woman at an early age and usually entered society at sixteen, and Catherine Floyd took her place among the other boarders as a young lady. Madison thus saw her every day and one of his few absences from the sittings of Congress was when he accompanied her and her father from Philadelphia as far as Brunswick, New Jersey, on their way to New York early in the spring of 1783. The chief romance of his life was then taking place, for he and Catherine were engaged to be married. He was double her age, and youth lay far behind him, and he was too old and sedate for a young girl in the first flush of womanhood. He was her father's friend and contemporary rather than hers. What did she care that a great career was predicted for him? She wanted pleasure, ardour,

* Department of State MSS.
† New York Public Library (Lenox) MSS.
‡ Id.

the young life; not politics, prosy discussion and repose. Yet the young statesman laid at her feet a treasure which a tamer, maturer nature would have prized. He was the soul of honour, reared in surroundings healthful to moral and mental development, looking at life through the eyes of a gentleman, chivalrous, highminded and pure, and after the habit of men of his class he held women in perfect respect and reverence. The poetic temperament which he had suppressed after he left Princeton must have revived under the influence of his passion, and the pleasing prospect was before him of a riper domestic life than he had thus far known, which should keep pace with his expanding public usefulness. Unfortunately the prospect was not pleasing to Catherine Floyd. She was docile enough for a time, and appeared to yield to Madison's suit, which her father also urged; but there was a young clergyman in Philadelphia, who, report says, "hung round her at the harpsichord," and made love to her while Madison and her father were discussing paper money; and when the affairs of a continent were being shaped with Madison as a chief actor in the Continental Congress, the affairs of his heart and Catherine Floyd's were being discussed and settled with the aid of the older woman who belonged to the young parson's party, in the little boarding house world where she and Madison lived. She decided in favour of the younger man, and jilted the Statesman, sending him his dismissal in a letter sealed with a piece of rye dough.* It is tradition also that she returned him, at the same time, his miniature, painted on ivory by C. W. Peale, in the back of which was set a knot of his hair and hers.

He was not a man to burden his friends with his private griefs, and of the mortification and distress which this affair must have caused him he left no record behind. Jefferson, as a privileged friend, ventured a few words

* The author cannot find any reason for the use of rye dough. A good account of the jilting of Madison may be found in Gay's "Madison," 43, *et seq.*

of philosophical condolence, but the affair was not one
to call for expressions of sympathy. He took up the
burden of his work in which his interest was so great
and found there the substitute for higher hopes, and the
episode passed, leaving no permanent trace of bitterness in the victim.

From the worry of debt and the cheerlessness of the
Philadelphia boarding house Madison escaped early in
December, when he returned to the congenial atmosphere of his home in Orange County. He had been in
public office for nine years, first in the county, then at
Williamsburg, then at Philadelphia, and his experience
was greater than that of any other Southern public man
of the same age.

The winter of 1783–84 was a severe one and unfavourable to open air employment, and in the solitude of the
long hours Madison applied himself assiduously to the
study of law. It was then his intention and desire to
practise it as a profession, in order to avoid a planter's
life, and gain a subsistence depending, as he said, "As
little as possible upon the labour of slaves."* His dislike of slavery was never concealed. From Philadelphia
he wrote his father, September 8, 1783, that his negro
boy Billy, who had run away and been recovered, should
not be sent back to Virginia as he was not a safe companion for the other slaves. Accordingly he sold him
in Philadelphia for seven years, the limit permitted by
Pennsylvania law. He was unwilling, he said, to trans-
port him and punish him for simply "coveting that
liberty for which we have paid the price of so much
blood and have proclaimed so often to be the right, and
worthy the pursuit of every human being."† During
the progress of the war, he proposed to Joseph Jones
(November 28, 1780,) to complete the Virginia quota
of troops by liberating and making soldiers of the blacks.
This would be "consonant to the principles of liberty,

---

* " Writings of Madison " (Hunt), II, 154.
† Id., II, 15.

which ought never to be lost sight of in a contest for liberty; and with white officers and a majority of white soldiers, no imaginable danger could be feared from themselves, as there certainly could be none from the effect of the example on those who should remain in bondage, experience having shown that a freedman immediately loses all attachment and sympathy with his former fellow slaves."*

Whatever the merits of the scheme as a measure of emancipation it was a weak one from a military point of view, and is one of the few instances where he ventured to give military advice. In reply, Jones pointed out with perfect truth that the plan, if put into effect, would probably tend to increase the army of the enemy, who would also be sure to arm the blacks. He added: "The freedom of these people is a great and desirable object. To have a clear view of it would be happy for Virginia; but whenever it is attempted, it must be, I conceive, by some gradual course, allowing time as they go off for labourers to take their places, or we shall suffer exceedingly under the sudden revolution which perhaps arming them would produce."†

The leading minds in Virginia were in favour of emancipation. When Jefferson introduced his digest of laws for the State in 1779 he intended to add an amendment providing for the freedom of all blacks after a certain date and their deportation after a certain age, and his proposed Constitution for the State, written in 1783, had an emancipation article. Of his amendment he wrote in his old age: "But it was found that the public mind would not yet bear the proposition, nor will it bear it even at this day." He regarded the ultimate freedom of the blacks as certain, and their deportation as a necessary consequence, as the two races could not live both free under the same Government.‡

* "Writings of Madison" (Hunt), I, 106.
† "Letters of Joseph Jones" (Ford), 63, 64.
‡ Randall's "Life of Jefferson," I, 227.

How George Mason felt on the subject may be gathered from his speech in the Philadelphia Constitutional Convention in 1787.

"Slavery discourages arts and manufactures," he said. "The poor despise labour when performed by slaves. They prevent the emigration of whites, who really enrich and strengthen a country. They produce the most pernicious effect on manners. Every master of slaves is born a petty tyrant. They bring the judgment of heaven on a country. As nations cannot be rewarded or punished in the next world, they must be in this. By an inevitable chain of causes and effects, Providence punishes national sins by national calamities. He lamented that some of our Eastern brethren had, from a lust of gain, embarked in this nefarious traffic."*

Edmund Randolph wrote to Madison in 1789 that he desired to go to Philadelphia to practise law. "For if I found that I could live there I could emancipate my slaves, and thus end my days without undergoing any anxiety about the injustice of holding them."†

Patrick Henry, who did not think in unusual channels, is supposed to have introduced, as he certainly approved, the liberal law permitting the emancipation of slaves passed at the May session, 1782, of the State Legislature. It recited that application had been made by people disposed to manumit their slaves for permission to do so, and it should, therefore, be lawful for any person by will or other written instrument under his hand and seal, attested and proved in county court by two witnesses, to free any or all of his slaves. The friends of this law hoped it would be followed by a still more liberal provision.‡

In November, 1785, a petition was presented to the House of Delegates in favour of a general manumission.

* Madison Papers (Gilpin), III, 1390.
† Conway's "Life of Edmund Randolph, 125."
‡ Henry's "Life of Patrick Henry." II, 174.

It produced no action, of course, but many members expressed their entire approval of the principle it expressed. So general became the feeling against slave-holding that a rumour gained currency that the chief planters intended to rid themselves of their negroes. Jacob Read, of South Carolina, wrote to Madison, August 29, 1785, from Congress, where, he said, Madison was sorely needed: "An opinion prevails in South Carolina that the principal holders of slaves in your State wish to divest themselves of that kind of property and that tolerable good purchases might be made on good Security being given for payments by instalments with a regular discharge of the interest.

"Under the impression of this opinion the Honourable Mr. J. Rutledge of South Carolina has addressed a letter to me wishing to become engaged in any purchase I may be able to make, to make a joint concern."*

The Quakers in Virginia formed "The Humane or Abolition Society," and after the adoption of the Federal Constitution, Robert Pleasants, the president, wrote to Madison (June 6, 1791)—"believing thou art a friend to general liberty"—to ask him to introduce in the House of Representatives a memorial which had been prepared against the slave trade. He said he had a strong desire to see some plan of general emancipation introduced in the State and added: "Knowing the sentiments of divers slave holders, who are favourable to the design, I wish to have thy judgment on the propriety of a Petition to our assembly for a law declaring the children of slaves to be born after the passing such act, to be free at the usual ages of eighteen and twenty-one years." A little later he sent the petition to Madison, but it was inopportune.† "The public mind would not yet bear the proposition."

Kentucky was settled chiefly by Virginians, among whom were many of Madison's friends and several of

---

* Department of State MSS.
† Id.

his relations. They frequently wrote to him for advice in the period of their State making, and H. Taylor, his cousin on his father's side, described the emancipation sentiment in the Constitutional Convention of 1792 in a letter from Danville, April 16. "The manumission of slaves," he said, "was a matter much debated in the house, some was for its taking place immediately others for a gradual mode, but Col° Nicholas w^d not give up the plan adopted in the Resolve for that purpose, a considerable number, as well as myself w^d have been very glad to have seen a stop put to the ingress of slaves after a certain period and an immediate prohibition of any for sale—instead of leaving the matter so much to the legislature."* The clause which George Nicholas insisted upon inhibited the Legislature from emancipating slaves without the consent of the owners, or without paying the owners, and from preventing immigrants from bringing their slaves with them, but laws might be passed permitting owners to emancipate their slaves and preventing slaves from being brought into the State as merchandise. That Nicholas should have resisted the emancipation sentiment in the convention is explicable on the theory that he did not believe the people of the State would ratify the Constitution if it contained an emancipation clause.

An extract from a letter from Francis Corbin, a typical Virginia planter, with many acres, many children and many slaves, may be quoted here. He was an ardent patriot and a devoted friend and admirer of Madison, to whom he wrote from his place, "The Reeds," June 15, 1797:

"The dislike I have had all, my life, to slavery increases as I advance in years. Indeed now I have become a *married* man, and am obliged to be more conversant with it than I ever was before, I find it to be intolerable. Reluctant as I shall be to leave the *Old Dominion*, yet my aversion to slavery will conquer all

* Department of State MSS.

my native predelictions and cause me to emigrate East-ward."* He did not go, but died as he had lived, an owner of slaves.

Among the Madison papers is a half-finished essay he wrote on "The Influence of Domestic Slavery on Government," which shows how clearly he understood the incompatibility of slavery with democracy: "In proportion as slavery prevails in a State, the Government, however democratic in name, must be aristocratic in fact. The power lies in a part instead of the whole; in the hands of property, not of numbers. All the ancient popular governments were for this reason aristocracies. The majority were slaves, of the residue a part were in the country and did not attend the Assemblies, a part were poor and tho in the city, could not spare the time to attend. The power was exercised for the most part by the rich and easy. 'Aristotle (de rep. lib. 3. cap. 184) defines a citizen or member of the sovereignty to be one who is sufficiently free from all private cares, to devote himself exclusively to the service of his country. See also Anacharsis, vol. 5, p. 28. The Southern States of America, are, on the same principle, aristocracies. In Virginia the aristocratic character is increased by the rule of suffrage requiring a freehold in land, which excludes nearly half the free inhabitants, and must exclude a greater proportion as the population increases. At present the slaves and non-freeholders amount to nearly 3-4 of the State. The power is therefore in about 1-4. Were the slaves freed and the right of suffrage extended to all, the operation of the Government might be very different. The slavery of the Southern States throws the power much more into the hands of property, than in the Northern States. Hence the people of property in the former are much more contented with their established Government than the people of property in the latter."†

* Department of State MSS.
† Id.

There is something pathetic in the spectacle of these fine individuals,—men like Corbin, Jones, Mason, Jefferson, Randolph and Madison,—and the thousands of others of their type, helpless in the folds of this monster which was crushed seventy years later in the blood of their descendants. They saw the idleness, shiftlessness and brutality that slavery engendered among their own race. They felt keenly what a glaring contradiction to their expressions of love of liberty it presented. They knew its injustice to the blacks,—that it was, as Mason said, a fundamental sin which carried sure retribution. And those who knew all this most thoroughly were the very ones whose higher qualities slavery did much to develop. It habituated them to the exercise of authority, and accustomed them to responsibility for the welfare and happiness of many human beings. Their dependents were so wholly dependent that they felt called upon to constantly exert their utmost endeavours to faithfully discharge their duties of dominion. And in the domestic economy the duties that fell to the women were such as expanded their better natures to an extraordinary degree, for to them fell the care of the sick and bereaved and the spiritual welfare of the poor souls whose condition never permitted the compassion of the mistress to sleep.

Madison, like his associates, found himself the child of circumstances and yielded to them almost unconsciously. In August, 1784, his father formally deeded to him a farm of 560 acres, a part of the Montpelier tract,* but Madison never lived upon it and came into virtual possession, during his father's life, of Montpelier itself, and gradually fitted into his father's place as a planter, accepting the industrial career thus provided for him with its interests and cares, and unavoidable accompaniment of slave-holding.

* MS. Orange County records.

CHAPTER IX

THE Virginia State Assembly elected Madison a member of the Governor's Council, because he had made his mark in the State Convention and in the Assembly of 1776, and the Assembly sent him to Congress and kept him there because it had confidence in him; but the people of his county had given no sign that they held him in especial regard, for his election in 1776 had been accomplished chiefly by the prestige of his father. When he tried for a re-election, he was beaten by an insignificant opponent, who bribed the voters with whiskey. Therefore, when his law studies were interrupted by his election, with slight opposition, as a member of the House of Delegates in April, 1784, it was the first time since he had risen to prominence that he had fairly stood before his people and received a pronounced endorsement from them. He went to Richmond, where the State Capitol had been moved from Williamsburg in 1782, early in May, 1784, having as the chief purpose of his service to concert measures by which the general Government might be strengthened.

The two rival figures in the Legislature were Patrick Henry and Richard Henry Lee, and they were pitted against each other in spectacular forensic displays for which the Virginians had a peculiar weakness.* The ascendancy over the Legislature was with Henry. At the session of 1783 the two leaders measured forces in the contest for the speakership, when John Tyler was put forward by Henry in opposition to Lee and was elected by a vote of 61 to 20. At the session of 1784, Lee him-

*Rives, I, 537.

77

self put Tyler in nomination and thus gracefully avoided another defeat.* There was less difference, politically, between Lee and Henry than appeared on the surface. While Lee was receiving his education in England and moving on terms of equality with the highest fashion of London, Henry was idling in backwoods country stores; but the polished aristocrat and the half-educated man of the people both had in common a craving for popularity and applause, which often dominated their actions as public men. When Madison approached Henry on the subject of augmenting the power of the Federal Government, Henry expressed himself as being strenuously in favour of it, but he had no plan. Lee, Madison reported, could not be depended upon.*

As a matter of fact, both would have been willing to add to the powers of Congress if, at the same time, nothing of the powers of the State should be lost, but it was obvious that whoever threw his influence on the side of Congress necessarily threw it against the power of the State, and his popularity in the State would be sure to diminish in consequence. Madison's energetic efforts on the side of Congressional power had raised up a party opposed to him in the State Assembly and among his constituents his position was never impregnable until after the adoption of the Constitution, when, conditions being reversed, he found himself opposing an increase of national authority. It was not, however, the question of extension of Federal Power that first engrossed Madison's attention when he entered the Legislature, but the subject of religious freedom which from his early manhood had aroused in him the fire of passion as nearly as any subject ever did.

After the separation from Great Britain the Episcopal Church in Virginia was under a cloud. Its disestablishment meant the withdrawal from the clergy of their means of subsistence, and many of them sympathized

* Journal of the House of Delegates.
*"Writings of Madison" (Hunt) II, 51–52.

with the mother country, prompted so to do by their own interests. The non-Episcopal clergy, on the other hand, were of the patriot party and were men of better character generally than the Episcopalians, and while the Episcopal churches closed their doors or were unattended the Baptist and Presbyterian congregations increased.* But religious observances were not as strictly kept as they had been in the old days, and war, with its consequent disordered conditions of society, brought an increase of crime and dishonesty. The two facts were put together—a decline in church attendance and an increase of immorality—and it was conceived that Legislative interference to help the churches would operate to improve the moral tone of the people. This view was held by Washington, Richard Henry Lee, Patrick Henry, Henry Tazewell, John Marshall, Joseph Jones, and a large number of representative men, not all of them strong churchmen, but all of them men who believed that the State should compel the people to support the churches.† It was not without a struggle that the older and more conservative planters gave up all idea of the State maintaining the Episcopal Church, for it had been, from their infancy, a part of themselves, and a social as well as a political and religious institution. When some non-Episcopalians came to Richmond to urge the Legislature to repeal all acts giving the Episcopal Church peculiar privileges, they approached one of these old-school cavaliers who said "he was clear for giving all a fair chance, that there were many roads to heaven, and he was in favour of letting every man take his own way; but he was sure of one thing, that no *gentleman* would choose any but the Episcopal."‡

Petitions against favouring the Episcopal way were

* Edmund Randolph's MS. "History of Virginia."   Virginia Historical Society.
† Rives, I, 602.
‡ Meade's "Old Churches and Families of Virginia," I, 50.   The anecdote was told by Madison himself.

presented soon after Madison took his seat in the Legislature by the Baptist and Presbyterian congregations in order, as they said, that "religious freedom be established upon the broad basis of perfect political equality." The Episcopal Church, however, asked for an act of incorporation to manage its political affairs, and the only church incorporation bill brought forward was in response to this request. It provided, among other things, that the clergy when once elected by the vestries should be irremovable otherwise than by sentence of the convocation, and this, as Madison declared, would have been tantamount to "re-establishing their independence of the laity." Even the friends of religious legislation thought the bill too radical and it would have been defeated had it not been for Henry's efforts in its behalf.* Its consideration was postponed till the next session of the Assembly and the interest it aroused was cast in the shade by another and broader proposition.

The Assembly did not have a quorum till May 12, 1784, and the first committee appointed, according to the usual custom, was that on religion, Madison being made one of the members. Among the petitions considered were a number asking that a general assessment be levied for the support of the churches. It was reported favourably, and July 1 the Assembly adjourned till the following November.

The question came up again November 17 upon a resolution "That acts ought to pass for the incorporation of all societies of the Christian religion which may apply for the same." This passed in the affirmative by a vote of 62 to 23. Among the minority with Madison were Wilson Cary Nicholas, John Taylor of Caroline, Alexander White and John Breckenridge. The resolution was followed quickly by one from Patrick Henry—that "the people of the commonwealth, according to their respective abilities, ought to pay a moderate tax or contribution for the support of the Christian re-

* To Jefferson, July 3, 1784, "Works of Madison" (Cong. Ed.), I, 88.

ligion, or of some Christian church, or denomination, or communion of Christians, or of some form of Christian worship," which was adopted by a vote of 47 to 32, and a special committee, with Henry at its head, was appointed to prepare a bill. Petitions favourable to it poured in, one coming from the United Presbyterian Church, and only one appearing against it.* Richard Henry Lee wrote to Madison from Trenton, where he was attending the session of Congress, (November 26, 1784,) "That he considered the bill a measure necessary to morality, that avarice was accomplishing the destruction of religion for want of a legal obligation to contribute something to its support."† This was the ground generally taken by the friends of the bill, and they were, undoubtedly, at this time a large majority of the Legislature and the people of the State.

Almost alone among the leaders of thought in Virginia, Madison saw the fundamental error involved in the proposed legislation. He had endeavoured to make such legislation impossible eight years before when he offered his amendment to the Bill of Rights, with the pregnant words, "And that therefore no man or class of men, ought, on account of religion *to be invested with peculiar emoluments or privileges.*" His argument against the bill was one of the most careful and elaborate ever constructed by him. A skeleton of it has been preserved, in which the line of thought is clearly indicated. He began by laying down the broad proposition that religion was not within the purview of the civil power—that it was something separate, apart and precedent to it—that to establish Christianity by law would lead naturally to a legal establishment of uniformity of belief, and to penal laws to punish violations of belief, and that the history of religious legislation showed this had always been the tendency. The true question was not, Is religion necessary to the well-

* Journal of the House of Delegates.
† Dept. of State MSS.

being of mankind? but, Is the establishment of religion as a part of the civil administration of the State necessary for religion itself? The natural propensity of man was toward religion, and the experience of history showed that religion itself was corrupted by compulsory State establishment. Mr. Henry had shown how States had fallen when religion sank into decay, but these downfalls had happened in States which had religion established as part of their civil policy. Such a general assessment as the bill contemplated had, however, no parallel in history. He instanced the religious freedom of other States,—Pennsylvania, New Jersey, where religious freedom was provided by the early constitution granted her by the proprietaries, Rhode Island, New York and Delaware. He drew the case of the primitive Christianity, of the Reformation, and the dissenters formerly in Virginia, and traced the progress of religious freedom. Coming to a specific discussion of the measure before the House he insisted that it was impolitic, as it would interfere with immigration, which should be untrammelled by fear of taxation for any spiritual purpose, and it would for the same reason encourage emigration as an escape from such taxation. The state of society did not show a reason for the measure. Recent war and bad laws were the cause of the disorganized condition, which was as bad in New England where religious legislation existed as in those States where it did not exist. The true remedy was to be found in continued peace, the passage of laws to cherish virtue, regular and exemplary administration of justice, personal example set by individuals, voluntary associations for religious purposes, the formation of which would be encouraged by the decisive defeat of the pending measure, thus depriving them of any hope of artificial support, and the education of the young. He showed what would be the probable effect of the measure, if it became a law. As the assessment was to be for the support of the Christian religion, the courts would be eventually called upon to decide what was Christianity—whether it was Trinitarianism, Arianism or Socinianism—whether it involved salvation by faith or works; and the whole question of faith, doctrine and creed over which the world had been convulsed for ages and which was beyond the ken of any temporal tribunal would be before the judges. The end would be the definition by the State of what was orthodoxy and what was heresy. Such a condition he declared dishonoured Christianity, and he closed with a panegyric of that religion and an appeal to the real meaning of that clause of the Declaration of Rights which had been moulded from his broader amendment.*

When the assessment bill was nearing its final stages and its passage appeared to be inevitable it was checked by the reintroduction of the bill, which had been postponed from the last session, to incorporate the Episcopal Church. This time, however, it included the laity in its provisions and was thus shorn of the chief objectionable feature that had originally characterized it. Under these circumstances Madison resolved as a strategic movement to vote for it. "A negative of the bill," he wrote to Jefferson, January 9, 1785, "would have doubled the eagerness and pretexts for a much greater evil,—a general assessment,—which there is good ground to believe was parried by this partial gratification of its warmest votaries."† The bill was passed by a vote of 47 to 38, George and Wilson Cary Nicholas being among those who adhered to the opposition.‡

The advocates of religious legislation being placated by this success, it was proposed to them that the assessment bill be postponed, that it be printed and distributed, and the people invited "to signify their opinion respecting the adoption of such a measure to the next session of the Legislature"—an appeal which was reasonable

* "Writings of Madison" (Hunt), II, 88.
† Id., II, 113.
‡ Journal of the House of Delegates.

enough and was acceded to because there was every reason to believe the reply would be favourable to the bill. The Assembly adjourned January 5, 1785, and the discussion was transferred to the people.

The Episcopal clergy generally favoured the bill, and so did the Presbyterian ministers at first, being "as ready to set up an establishment which is to take them in as they were to pull down that which shut them out," as Madison put it. The Presbyterian laity, however, did not generally favour the measure, and their influence was sufficient to finally cause the general convention of Presbyterians to ask for the Act of Religious Freedom.*

The credit for planning the campaign against the bill among the people does not belong to Madison, but to George Nicholas and his brother Wilson Cary Nicholas. In fact, Madison favoured making no campaign, and would have had the counties opposed to the bill take no action against it. On April 22, 1785, George Nicholas wrote to him from Charlottesville that his brother had told him of a conversation with Madison on the propriety of remonstrating and that Madison had advised against it. He was afraid this silence would be construed into assent, as the Assembly had only postponed the measure till it might know if it were agreeable to the people. A majority of the counties was in favour of the measure, but a majority of the people was not, and this would be denied if it did not appear by petition. Some petitions were sure to be sent, and he thought it would help the cause if all held the same language. Would Madison, if he agreed with him, draw up a petition of remonstrance? He was the man best able to do it. Nicholas would attend to its distribution in the counties.

To these entreaties Madison yielded, and on July 7 Nicholas wrote to acknowledge the receipt of the remonstrance not a word of which he could change without

* "Writings of Madison" (Hunt), II, 145.

marring it.* It was printed as a broadside by the Phœnix Press in Alexandria, and copies were sent far and wide throughout the State, receiving thousands of signatures; and when the Assembly met in October the assessment bill was buried beneath the copies of this paper which came from every corner of the State. It was written in fifteen paragraphs and was an unanswerable protest against all religious legislation. It embodied the main arguments which Madison had made in his speech in the Assembly, but the speech had reached only a few scores of hearers, and the remonstrance reached thousands and carried conviction to them.

The bill should be defeated, the remonstrance said, because it was, as the Bill of Rights declared, the right of every man to exercise his religion according to the dictates of conscience, and not according to the dictates of other men. Religion was, therefore, exempt from the authority of society at large, and especially from the creatures of that society, the Legislature. In asserting a right to embrace that religion which we believe to be of divine origin, we must accord an equal freedom to those whose minds have not yet been convinced by the evidence that has convinced us. The Christian religion explicitly disavowed a dependence upon the powers of this world. It flourished without the assistance of human laws,—in spite of every opposition from them. It was plain that if it was not invented by human policy it must have existed before it was established by human policy. To demand support for it would be a confession of weakness, and encourage in those who opposed it a belief that it could not stand on its own merits. When Christianity shone with greatest lustre was before it was incorporated as a civil policy. "Pride and indolence in the clergy, ignorance and servility in the laity; in both, superstition, bigotry, and persecution" had followed church estab-

* Dept. of State MSS. The remonstrance may be found in "The Writings of Madison" (Hunt), II, 183.

lishment.   Contentious rivalry among the various Christian sects would be sure to follow the passage of this bill, and had already become more vigorous in the discussion of it.   If it became a law men would evade it, and it would thus bring other laws into disrespect.

The success of the remonstrance was extraordinary. It put the advocates of religious legislation on the defensive and made them a helpless minority.   From having been in control a few months before, they were now the mere shattered remnant of a party.

The bill to assess the people for the support of the Christian religion sank into the earth beyond the hope of resurrection, and in place of it appeared one of the greatest measures that Thomas Jefferson ever wrote— the Bill for Establishing Religious Freedom in Virginia. He had drawn it in 1779 as a part of his revised code of laws for Virginia, but it lay moribund and unnoticed, till Madison introduced it as a fitting expression of the change in public opinion which his remonstrance had brought about.   It was passed December 26, 1785,* and the battle for complete religious liberty in Virginia was won.

* Hening's "Stats. at Large," 12, 84.

CHAPTER X

HOW THE ANNAPOLIS CONVENTION WAS CALLED

PATRICK HENRY's general expressions in favour of strengthening the Federal Government were a tolerably correct reflection of the attitude of the Virginia Assembly on the subject. It amounted to an admission that something should be done, and specific dissent to every project brought forward to that end. As the session progressed it became evident that the legislation desired by the Federalists could not be secured; even if it could be what chance of concurrence would it have from twelve other State Legislatures? The outlook was gloomy indeed, and impending disaster was only averted by seizing a succession of circumstances and turning them to a purpose different from that which they had been designed to serve. The story of the manipulation of these occasions is the story of how the Annapolis Convention was called.

The boundary between Virginia and Maryland was the Potomac River, and the charter of 1732 to Lord Baltimore defined it as the southern shore.* The Constitution of Virginia confirmed this boundary, but reserved the right of the free navigation of the river. Madison and others feared that this confirmation might be construed into a total surrender of jurisdiction over the river, thus leaving Virginia's commerce wholly at the mercy of such regulations as Maryland might choose to make. A harmonious agreement on regulations for the two States was obviously the best remedy for the threatened evil, and on April 25, 1784, Madison wrote to Jefferson and asked him to sound the Maryland dele-

* "Writings of Madison" (Hunt), II, 41.

gates in Congress on the subject of the appointment of commissioners from that State to meet commissioners from Virginia and draw up joint regulations for the navigation of the whole river, which should be submitted for approval to the Legislature of each State. Favourable promises coming from the Maryland leaders, the Virginia Assembly, on Madison's motion, provided for a commission on June 28; and he, George Mason, Edmund Randolph and Alexander Henderson were named as commissioners, any three of whom should have power to act.

On December 28, the Assembly, again on Madison's motion, gave the Virginia commissioners, or any *two* of them, authority to unite with the Maryland commissioners in representing to the State of Pennsylvania that it was in contemplation to promote the clearing of the Potomac River and extend its navigation from tide water as far upwards as practicable, and open a convenient road from the head of navigation to the waters running into the Ohio, and to ask the co-operation of that State in providing convenient regulations for the use of the route.

Almost simultaneously with the agreement to these instructions an act was passed incorporating the Potomac Company for the purpose of improving the navigation of the river and opening communication with the Western country,* the terms of incorporation being the result of General Washington's personal negotiations with the government of Maryland. He had cherished the project ever since 1754, when he went as a messenger for Governor Dunwiddie to the French forces on the Ohio, and in 1770 he put it into form in a letter to Governor Thomas Johnson, of Maryland, suggesting that extending the navigation of the river by partial portage at its source to the Ohio ought to be taken up as a public measure, "as a means of becoming the channel of conveyance of the extensive and valuable trade of a rising

* Hening's "Stats. at Large," II, 510.

empire."* After the Revolution he urged action by the Legislature of Virginia in a letter to Governor Benjamin Harrison, and his interest in the work on the river was the keenest he manifested in the intervening years between the termination of his military service and his re-entry into public life in a civil capacity.

In the latter part of March, 1786, Mason received word that two of the Potomac commissioners appointed by Maryland would soon be at Gunston Hall, on their way to Alexandria, and would go forward with him to that town, where a meeting of the commissioners from both States was to take place. This was the first intimation Mason had received of his appointment or of the meeting.† The other commissioners, having been in Richmond when the commission was created, were, of course, cognizant of their appointment, and Henderson, by some means or other, heard of the time and place of meeting; but neither Randolph nor Madison received any notification of the meeting, and they remained at home in ignorance that it had been called. The fault was not on the side of Maryland, for the Governor of the State had written to the Governor of Virginia proposing the time and place for the meeting of the joint commission, and no objection having been made the Maryland commissioners presumed the arrangements were satisfactory, and set forth on their journey in full confidence that they would be joined by their Virginia colleagues. The representation from Maryland was complete, and Daniel of St. Thomas Jenifer, Thomas Stone and Samuel Chase of that State, with Henderson and Mason from Virginia, waited for several days in Alexandria for Madison and Randolph, until Mason concluded that, like himself, they had not been notified. He decided, however, to proceed to business, as the Marylanders had travelled a considerable distance in bad weather, and

* See "Washington's Interest in the Potomac Company," Johns Hopkins University Studies. Third Series, 81.

† Mason's Letters to Madison, Dept. of State MSS.

a failure of the purpose of their journey would be due to the carelessness of the Virginia officials. General Washington came to Alexandria while the commissioners were waiting, and showed Mason, who saw it for the first time, a copy of the Virginia resolution of December 28, respecting the application to Pennsylvania. As this gave power to any two of the Virginia commissioners to act, Mason concluded the resolution of June 28, creating the commission, conferred the same power, neither he nor Henderson having a copy of the resolution. They also believed it covered regulations for Chesapeake Bay and the Pokomoke River, as the Maryland commission did.* The supposition was natural for the additional reason that in 1777 Virginia and Maryland had arranged for a joint meeting including in its scope the Chesapeake and Pokomoke, but the meeting never took place.† In reality the Virginia resolutions confined the negotiations to the Potomac and required at least three commissioners to act.

It would appear that General Washington conferred with the commissioners from the start, and for their own comfort and his convenience they moved from Alexandria to Mt. Vernon. The prospective extension of the navigation of the Potomac, in which he was concerned, and the regulations to govern the navigation, were closely allied subjects, and his counsel entered, to a greater or less extent, in the proceedings of the joint commission. At Mt. Vernon, therefore, on March 28, 1785, the commissioners entered into a compact concerning the jurisdiction over the Rivers Potomac and Pokomoke and Chesapeake Bay and the navigation thereof. Freedom of navigation was granted by Virginia to Maryland over Virginia waters, and by Maryland to Virginia over Maryland waters. There was to be free trade between the States. Lighthouses, buoys, etc., on the Potomac and the Bay were to be maintained

---

* Mason to Madison, August 9, 1785. Dept. of State MSS.
† Scharf's "History of Maryland," II, 529.

at the expense of both States, Virginia paying five parts and Maryland three parts.* The discussion and arrangement of these matters naturally led to broader subjects of concern to the States, such as the desirability of uniform export and import duties and regulations of commerce, as well as currency and rates of exchange, and a supplementary report on these points was agreed to.

The Mt. Vernon compact came before the Maryland Legislature and was agreed to November 22, and a final clause was added proposing that resolutions should be sent to the Legislatures of Pennsylvania and Delaware, and that those States be requested to nominate commissioners to meet commissioners from Maryland and Virginia, to agree upon uniform trade regulations for the four States. Pennsylvania and Delaware actually accepted the invitation, and on February 20, 1786, Maryland named her commissioners "to meet commissioners from the States of Pennsylvania and Delaware, for the purpose of considering and digesting the most proper measures for improving the inland navigation of the Susquehannah River, and the waters communicating with it, and for effecting a navigable communication between the Bays of Chesapeake and Delaware, *and also to confer on any other subject which may tend to promote the commerce and mutual convenience of the said States.*"† This action came too late, for Virginia had already passed resolutions of invitation to all the States.

It was not a part of the programme of Madison and his party that a partial uniformity of trade regulations should be effected by agreement among groups of States. They wished the uniformity to prevail throughout the whole country, and to be under the control of the national Congress. It was to this power that the Virginia legislature was unalterably opposed, for it was jealous of the northern marine and believed that national navigation laws would foster northern shipping interests at

* Scharf's "History of Maryland;" II, 531.

† Id., II, 528, *et seq.*

the expense of southern export and import interests. Moreover, the Virginia Assembly furnished no exception to the general rule that no body of men willingly and deliberately lessens its own power and importance. The utmost concession that could be wrung from the reluctant legislators was a proposition to vest the desired power in Congress for not more than thirteen years; but such a partial measure would not be worth urging upon the other States; and when Madison perceived the hopelessness of expecting more he took up the proposition passed by Maryland, November 22, and enlarged it into a request to all the States to appoint commissioners "to take into consideration the trade of the United States; to examine the relative situation and trade of said States; to consider how far a uniform system in their commercial regulations may be necessary to their common interest and permanent harmony; and to report to the several States such an act, relative to this great object, as, when unanimously ratified by them, will enable the United States in Congress effectually to provide for the same." Such a convention, it was hoped, would recommend to the State Legislatures to do what the Virginia Legislature persisted in refusing to do.

The members of the State government always suspected those who had served in the Continental Congress of leaning too much toward Federal power, and of a desire to deprive the State governments of their prerogatives. They were especially suspicious of Madison, the avowed champion of schemes to increase the resources of the continental establishment. He was fully aware, therefore, that if he introduced the amended Maryland recommendation it would be prejudiced from the start, and to avoid this he put it in the hands of John Tyler, a member of the House of Delegates who had never performed continental service, and to whom the suspicion of Federalism did not attach. Tyler introduced it and it lay unnoticed upon the table until January 21, 1786, the last day of the session, when it was substituted for the bill giving Congress power over navigation and commerce. It went through with a rush and without exciting much notice, the minority against it being insignificant.* Dr. Walter Jones, St. George Tucker, Meriwether Smith, George Mason, David Ross, William Ronald, Edmund Randolph and Madison were appointed the Virginia delegates to the meeting; Ronald's name was dropped at his own request. Smith had been one of the few members opposing the measure.† Before it was adopted Madison described it in a letter to Washington, as the natural outcome of the Mt. Vernon meeting,‡ and so it was, but it was an outcome entirely unforeseen by the initiators of the Mt. Vernon meeting. To increase the power of Congress was Madison's greatest object at this time. His Potomac resolution of June 28, 1784, had no such purpose, being meant, as appeared upon its face, merely to secure uniform navigation regulations with Maryland. When the Maryland Legislature proposed to include two other States in the arrangement Madison saw his chance and sprang the proposition to call in all the States. It was a secondary move, and he would have preferred an act directly giving Congress power to make commercial regulations.

There were mighty chances against the proposition for the meeting producing any beneficial results, and Madison looked with despair upon the prospect. First, all the other States were asked to agree to send delegates to the meeting, and all the States hardly ever agreed to anything; second, if the meeting did take place it must agree upon a report to the States, and there was no reason to expect greater harmony in this assemblage than there was in the Continental Congress, where discord reigned; third, if a plan should be agreed upon, under the terms of the call of the meeting every State must accept it before it could become effective, and it

* "Writings of Madison" (Hunt), II, 218.
† Id., (Hunt), II, 223.
‡ Id., II, 198.

seemed preposterous to expect such unanimity from such antagonistic elements. But affairs were rushing to a crisis, and it was clear that something must be done to save the Union from disintegration and America from disgrace. Far-seeing men began seriously to apprehend that soon the people who had won a glorious victory against Great Britain would fall back under the yoke of that or some other foreign power. The most dangerous and demoralizing inclinations of weak human nature were becoming more and more in the ascendancy in the State governments—a tendency to pass laws by which the fulfilment of contracts might be avoided, to stamp paper with figures and promises and call it money, to repudiate debts and avoid the obligations of honest men. "I saw enough," wrote Madison to Jefferson, March 18, 1786, "during the late Assembly of the influence of the desperate circumstances of individuals on their public conduct, to admonish me of the possibility of finding in the council of some one of the States fit instruments of foreign machinations."*

To avert the impending calamity would be more difficult in the future. Kentucky was already asking for admission as a State, and there would be other Western States to follow and "proportionally impede measures which required unanimity," as Madison feared.

---

* "Writings of Madison" (Hunt), II, 229–230.

CHAPTER XI

THE resolution proposing the convention to consider commercial arrangements was almost the last act of the session of the Virginia Assembly terminating January 21, 1786. A quorum of the Virginia deputies elected to the Convention met in Richmond after Madison had left and proposed Annapolis as the place for the meeting and the first Monday in September for the date. The General Assembly when it adjourned had been in session ninety-seven days, and with the exception of the first seven days Madison's attendance had been uninterrupted. Indeed, his capacity for work was inexhaustible, and his labours were never laid aside for pleasure.

The Legislature transacted much business, yet little of it gave satisfaction to the friends of good government. The "itch for paper money," as Madison characterized it, had been only temporarily allayed; but he took pride in the fact that "the ambitious hope of making laws for the human mind" had been "extinguished forever." The collection of the tax for the year had been postponed, and it was agreed that when it came to be collected tobacco might be accepted in payment instead of specie. For this method of payment Madison voted, although he disapproved of it; but he hoped, by allowing thus much to the soft money party, to prevent them from pressing the more dangerous measures they had introduced. The State's quota of $512,000 to the Federal Treasury was ordered to be paid for the year 1786 before May, although the postponement of the tax collections made it certain that there would not be a penny in the treasury with which to make the payment. The State had gained some reputation by paying its quota the year before, but Madison said, "our conduct this (year) must stamp us with ignominy."* Yet the Virginia Legislature was no worse than other State Legislatures and better than some. Madison freely expressed his contempt for its proceedings and tendencies. No session, he declared the day it adjourned, deserved so little applause. There was, he said later, (March 19,) "both ignorance and iniquity to combat," and the best way was "to defeat the designs of the latter by humoring the prejudices of the former."†

The session being ended Madison went back to Orange and found relief from political activity in other studies. Lesiure, in the sense of idleness, he never knew, for his hours were always full of activity, and time was never a weight on his hands. His recreation was merely to change the field of his mental work. There was awaiting him at home "a literary cargo," as he called it, sent by Jefferson, and he plunged into the boxes of books with the keen ardour of the true lover of knowledge for its own sake. Among the volumes were a number of Buffon's "Histoire Naturelle Générale et Particulière," which he had not thus far had time to examine, and he now read them with the care of one to whom natural history was no new study, for he was familiar with the animal life of his State. He even proposed to collect the skins of wild animals in Virginia and have them stuffed, and hoped to send some animals alive to Paris for European naturalists to study. He caged a live oppossum with seven of her young, but they died before he had a chance to make scientific observations of them. He disputed Jefferson's statement in his "Notes on Virginia," in which Buffon agreed, that the fallow and roe deer of Europe were also natives of America, and declared, as the result of inquiry from Western travellers, that the common deer seen in Virginia was the only one indigenous

* "Writings of Madison" (Hunt), II, 219, et seq.
† To Monroe, Id., II, 233.

to this country, being found in the Western woods and as far south as New Orleans. He secured a wounded monax or woodchuck, noted its temperature, and after its death recorded its measurements in comparison with the European marmot, as described by Buffon, and concluded they were the same animal. He treated a mole in the same way, and when a weasel fell into his hands he compiled an elaborate table of its measurements, even to the exact size of the conque of the ear and the nails of each foot, paralleling the figures with the similar measurements in Buffon of the belette and ermine.* In these researches he was, of course, an amateur, and he did not pretend to be more.

He took a like interest in inventions, saw the first phosphoric matches in 1785 with much curiosity, and gave two guineas for a newly invented lamp. He commissioned Jefferson to buy him a curious pocket compass, not much larger than a watch, such as he had recently seen. He hoped to find it useful in case of a pedestrian tour through the Western woods, and for the same purpose desired a pocket telescope to inspect objects which he could not approach. He suggested the making of a walking stick with a microscope and scale of measurement set in the handle.† In later life he drew the designs of a chair with a writing desk attached to the arm. James Rumsey, who in 1784 invented a boat to be propelled by a stream of water ejected by steam power from the stern, was engaged as one of the engineers by the Potomac Company when Madison was active in its affairs,‡ and Madison knew of his experiments, and later he knew John Fitch, who in 1788 begged piteously for his assistance to secure government patronage of his efforts to build a steamboat.§ He encouraged both Rumsey and Fitch without, how-

* "Writings of Madison" (Hunt), II, 239, *et seq.*
† Id., II, 134, *et seq.*
‡ Records of Chesapeake & Ohio Canal Co. MSS.
§ Dept. of State MSS.

ever, piercing the future which their discoveries were destined to revolutionize.

It was efforts such as these, to assist the progress of the human race, that principally concerned Madison, rather than the consummated beauties of nature, but appreciation of the picturesque was not entirely lacking in him. He fed upon splendid scenery from infancy, for the prospect from the little porch, which was all the house in Orange then boasted, was one of surpassing beauty, embracing the mighty range of the Blue Ridge lying across the whole horizon, while around him the lesser mountains and spreading valleys offered a succession of beautiful prospects. In all of picturesque Virginia there is no part more beautiful than that in which the Madisons lived. When Madison left home in the early summer of 1786 to go to New York, instead of taking the usual and more direct route through Fredericksburg and the Northern Neck, he crossed the mountains and went to Winchester in the Shenandoah Valley, to see his relations, and by Harper's Ferry to Lancaster, Pa., and he then saw Harper's Ferry for the first time. The day was unfavourable for the clouds hung low, but he climbed the mountain to see the view, and although he got drenched in a thunder storm, he was able to form some idea of the panorama that lay beneath him.* It was not, however, as an artist that he looked at it; his eye dwelt rather upon the enrichment of the valley by the crops in full maturity, and at the rapids of the Potomac he was principally observant of the progress of the work undertaken by the Potomac Company in opening the bed of the river to make navigation feasible.

The works of men and men in their relations to one another were the great objects of his thoughts, and, of course, the aboriginal Americans came in for their share. He was familiar with the different tribes and admired the eloquence of the chiefs, but of actual contact with the Indians he had little, not being a pioneer and not being

* "Writings of Madison," (Hunt), II, 257.

of an adventurous spirit. They were a reality to him, however, for his great aunt's husband, Jacob Hite, was killed by them in 1776,* and he kept in touch with his friends in Kentucky, to whom Indian warfare was a dreadful fact. In the autumn of 1784, when he was travelling to enlarge his knowledge of the country, at Baltimore he fell in with the Marquis Lafayette, who was coming from a visit at Mount Vernon, and accepted the Marquis's invitation to accompany him to a treaty, as Indian negotiations were called, with the Oneidas at Fort Schuyler, near Albany. On the journey he formed an intimacy with the charming Frenchman and took the measure of his ability and character. "With great natural frankness of temper," he wrote, "he unites much address and very considerable talents. In his politics he says his three hobby-horses are the alliance between France and the U. S., the union of the latter and the manumission of the slaves. The two former are the dearer to him, as they are connected with his personal glory. The last does him real honour, as it is a proof of his humanity. In a word, I take him to be as amiable a man as can be imagined and as sincere an American as any Frenchman can be; one whose past services gratitude obliges us to acknowledge and whose future friendship prudence requires us to cultivate." He intimated, too, that when the Marquis had performed a meritorious act he liked it to be widely known. As he had influence with the French Government Madison improved the opportunity to fill him full of the Virginia position on the subject of the navigation of the Mississippi and the unreasonable attitude of Spain.† It was shortly after this journey that Washington mentioned to Madison the desire of Catharine of Russia to compare the dialects of the natives of her most northeastern possessions with those of the American Indians, with a view to throwing some light, perhaps, upon the vexed question

---

* Records of the Hite family.
† "Writings of Madison" (Hunt), II, 85. See *ante* p. 60.

of the original habitat of the American race. Madison fell in with the idea and procured from an Indian student a vocabulary of the Choctaw and Cherokee dialects which he gave Washington to send to Russia.*

Of more interest than these investigations were his reflections on the pressure of population upon the means of subsistence in a letter to Jefferson written June 19, 1786, twelve years before Malthus's first "Essay on the Principle of Population" was published. Jefferson described to him a walk he took at Fontainebleau in the autumn of 1785, when he fell in with a peasant woman who told him she received, when she was employed, 8 sous a day for wages, which her rent so completely absorbed that she and her family were often without bread. Contrasting her, as a representative of the most numerous class in the community, with the few who were proprietors of large estates and lived in luxury, Jefferson asked himself why so many should be obliged to beg in a country where there was such a large amount of land kept idle for the pleasure of hunting game. It seemed to him a violation of natural right, as the earth was given as a common stock for man to live upon. The letter was in Jefferson's most philanthropic vein, painting the same pathetic picture of social injustice which has moved the hearts of observing men since the world began. Leading into the theory which is now associated with the name of Henry George, Jefferson said it was too soon to say that every man in America who could find uncultivated land should be at liberty to cultivate it, paying a moderate rent, but it was not too soon to provide by every possible means that as few people as possible should be without a little portion of land, as the small landholders were the best part of a population. To these observations Madison replied that the fact that no such poverty was found in America as existed in Europe was due chiefly to the sparseness of our population. A certain degree of misery seemed in-

* "Writings of Madison" (Hunt), II, 320.

separable from density of population, however much the laws might favour division of property. Even if the lands used by the idle rich in Europe were parcelled out among the poor would there not still remain a large number of the latter unrelieved? No problem in political economy seemed to him more puzzling than that of the proper distribution of the inhabitants of a fully peopled country. Let the lands be apportioned among them ever so wisely and cultivated ever so carefully, there must yet be a surplus of people beyond those engaged in agricultural and other productive employments, and to reduce this class was the most necessary reform. A more equal division of property produced a greater simplicity in living and a less consumption of superfluities. Here he broke off, remarking that he must remember that he was writing a letter and not a dissertation.* Later in life he began an essay on the "Symmetry of Nature" which dealt with the same subject. The opening sentence was: "The planetary system, the greatest portion of the universe as yet brought under human observation, is regulated by fixed laws, and presents most demonstrably, a scene of order and proportion." By analogy he concluded that the whole universe, if it were understood, would exhibit proofs of the same arrangement. In animal life each species has a general relation to the other. The faculty of multiplication seemed to be indefinite, yet in all but the human species nature has established a law of proportion setting bounds to the reproductive faculty. Among animals this is maintained by the limited amount of vegetable subsistence provided and by depredations of carnivorous beasts upon herbivorous; among carnivorous by the limited number of herbivorous, by their depredations upon one another, and of man upon the whole. Man has certain peculiar characteristics, being a prey to no other animal and able to multiply the natural supplies of food. What then is to prevent him from multiply-

* "Writings of Madison" (Hunt), II, 246, *et seq.*

ing to an indefinite extent? Would nature permit her favourite offspring to destroy the whole system of proportion? If this had been the design, why should it not have been accomplished long ago? Why should there be on earth anything more than human policy spared for its own use? The history of the human race could be traced for several thousand years, yet there was no evidence that the aggregate population had undergone any material increase, nor was there proof that any species of animal or plant was extinct, although the bones of mammoth animals found recently on the Ohio came near to being evidence against this proposition. His conclusion was that when the secret laws of nature should be more fully understood it would be found that there was a law of proportion in human life as in plant and animal life.*

In the intervals of his other work he continued his study of law, but he now declared he had abandoned his desire of practising it as a profession. Another way of securing a competence, as he hoped, was suggested to him by Monroe, and the two statesmen fell in with the tide and became in an innocent way speculators in land. Apparently they made several ventures, but the chief one was in certain wild lands in the Mohawk region, near the head waters of the Hudson River. They inspected the lands and found them as rich as the soil of Kentucky. Consulting General Washington, who was regarded as an expert, he said the lands were good, and intimated that if he had money to spare and was disposed to buy land he would buy here. So Monroe and Madison bought a tract of about 1,000 acres for one dollar and a half an acre, and confidently expected to grow rich, because land a little lower down the river and inhabited sold for eight or ten pounds an acre. But the preliminary payments Madison was forced to ask Monroe to meet alone, for he had no ready money. So certain were the two speculators of making a handsome

* Dept. of State MSS.

profit that they determined upon a second and larger purchase in the same locality and to associate with them in the scheme their friend Jefferson, not only because they wished to raise the money they needed upon his credit, but because they wanted him to share in their prospective good fortune.   There was no reason, Madison wrote Jefferson, why Jefferson should not avail himself of this opportunity to improve his condition. They proposed to him, therefore, to lend his credit in his private capacity to raise between 4,000 and 5,000 louis, Monroe and Madison being sureties, at an interest of six per cent. per annum.   One reason for the cheapness of the land, Madison explained, was the scarcity of specie, and there would soon be such a fall in the rate of exchange that money drawn by bills from Europe now and repaid in a few years would probably save one year's interest at least.*   Jefferson did not find it feasible to join in the enterprise, and so far as Madison's share in it went it was abandoned.   It is strange that he should have gone as far as he did, for his pecuniary affairs were in a most unsatisfactory state, a condition which appears to have been habitual with him.   He had, as we have seen, a farm of his own,† but he had the use of a part of the income from his father's farm besides, and he assisted in the business management of the whole estate.   In the disordered financial condition of the country payments were irregular and prices fluctuated beyond calculation, and the planters were generally distressed in their circumstances, Madison being no worse off than most of his neighbours.   He wrote to his brother Ambrose, September 8, 1786, that he could not obtain the money due for the tobacco he had sold and that Ambrose must continue to pray their creditors.‡ October 5, 1786, he wrote to Monroe declining further speculations for the present, and thanking him for his

* "Writings of Madison" (Hunt), II, 266.
† Ante. *p* 76.
‡ "Writings of Madison" (Hunt), II, 269.

"very friendly procrastinations of the repayment which ought long ago to have been made."* Part of the money was paid in December.

The great object of Madison's journey north in the summer of 1786 was not, however, to sell tobacco or look for cheap lands which would rise in value, but to sound the leading men at New York, where Congress was sitting, and at Philadelphia, which was the centre of the continent, on the subject of the Annapolis meeting.† He found many men in favour of making it a means of calling a second convention for amending the Articles of Confederation, but he himself did not believe this was possible. In fact, he almost despaired of the convention accomplishing anything, and he was certain that Virginia would take no part in measures to strengthen the Federal power, if the Federal Congress agreed to a treaty with Spain shutting up the Mississippi, as it then seemed probable would be done.

Travelling with one servant Madison arrived in the Maryland town September 5, and went to the tavern kept by George Mann, where he remained eleven days. How he lived is shown by the itemized account of his landlord for £14 7s. 2d. for board and lodging for himself and servant and stabling for his two horses. He always breakfasted at Mr. Mann's, but was charged with dinner for six days only, having on the other days, it is presumed, dined abroad with his friends. He drank wine, punch or porter each day, and his servant had grog. His landlord called him "Colonel" Madison, but this was hardly more than a title of respect in those days, and was frequently applied to Madison as he grew older.‡

When he reached Annapolis he found only two commissioners present. By September 11, Delaware, New Jersey, Virginia, New York and Pennsylvania were represented. Although the Maryland Legislature had

* "Writings of Madison" (Hunt), II, 274.
† Rives, II, 115.
‡ Dept. of State MSS.

taken the action which led to the calling of the meeting, it sent no delegates. Daniel Carroll explained to Madison in March that the Assembly was afraid the convention, if it acted, would try to weaken the powers of Congress, where the right to make commercial regulations really belonged.* North Carolina sent no delegates, because there had been no session of the Legislature since the invitation to the meeting had been received. South Carolina sent none, because she had recently instructed her delegates in Congress to vote for national regulation of commerce for fifteen years, and this seemed to be sufficient to show sympathy with the objects of the meeting. Connecticut took no action, having a prejudice against conventions and being in a spiteful mood, because of tariff wars with neighbouring States. Nobody knew what Georgia had done, the State being remote from the scene, but in reality she had done nothing. New Hampshire, Rhode Island and Massachusetts had each selected delegates, but they did not deem it worth while to attend.† The delegates who were present and constituted the famous Annapolis Convention were not for the most part men of great consequence. Tench Coxe was there from Pennsylvania, a pigmy beside the great men of his State. He was afterwards in the Treasury Department and was a political economist of some ability; but as a public man he was quarrelsome, uncertain and petty, and an importunate office-seeker.‡ Benson was Hamilton's obscure colleague from New York. New Jersey sent Abraham Clark, W. C. Houstoun and James Schureman, but Delaware had two strong men in George Read and John Dickinson, and Virginia had the strongest delegation present in Madison, Edmund Randolph and St. George Tucker. Meriwether Smith, David Ross and George Mason, who had also been elected delegates, did

* Dept. of State MSS.
† "Writings of Madison," (Hunt) II, 262.
‡ Dept. of State MSS. Applications for office.

not attend. Mason would have been an acquisition and was earnestly urged to go, but he was kept at home by an attack of the gout. The veteran of the meeting was John Dickinson. He had served in the protesting Congresses of 1765 and 1774, and in the Revolutionary Congress of 1776, where he wrote the Articles of Confederation, and in subsequent Congresses. He was elected to be president of the Convention, but it was extremely doubtful whether there would be anything for him to preside over, the representation was so slim. New Jersey was the only State whose delegates were empowered to do more than make recommendations for commercial regulations, and in their commission was included recommendations for strengthening the Federal Government. Under the leadership of Hamilton the Convention decided to disregard its ostensible object, and merely to issue an address calling for another convention of delegates from all the States on a broader scale. His experience in New York had been similar to Madison's in Virginia. He had advocated the lodging of the power to make commercial regulations in Congress, and when he saw that the opposition in the Legislature of his State could not be overcome he had thrown his weight in favour of the Virginia proposition for the conference at Annapolis. The address he offered the conference was the only thing it considered, and its unanimous adoption was the only result of its three days' session. The too radical expressions in the draft of the address were toned down at Randolph's insistence. Madison advised Hamilton's acquiescence by saying: "You had better yield to this man, for otherwise all Virginia will be against you,"* Randolph's power in the State then being at its zenith. The address set forth the critical situation of affairs and proposed that the States which the delegates represented "should concur and use their endeavours to procure the concurrence of the other States, in the appointment of com-

* Morse's "Hamilton," I. 167.

missioners to meet at Philadelphia on the second Monday in May next, to take into consideration the situation of the United States; to devise such further provisions as shall appear necessary to render the Constitution of the Federal Government adequate to the exigencies of the Union; and to report such an act for that purpose to the United States in Congress assembled as, when agreed to by them and afterwards confirmed by the Legislatures of every State, will effectually provide for the same."*

Having launched this address the Annapolis Convention adjourned and the members dispersed. Madison had proposed it with small hopes that it would accomplish anything, and Hamilton had gone to it without enthusiastic expectations. It failed signally of the purpose for which it was called, and out of that failure came an unauthorized proposition which brought about the Convention which framed the Constitution of the United States, but that Convention had really been in the mouths of men for some years.

* "Hamilton's Works" (Lodge), I, 319.

CHAPTER XII

PREPARING FOR THE GREAT CONVENTION

To FIND the originator of the project of holding a convention of delegates from all the States to evolve a remedy for the obvious defects of the Government under the Articles of Confederation would be a fruitless search. That existing conditions could not long continue was self-evident, and many men must have formulated plans for a change, the most natural first step towards which would be a conference of all the parties in interest. It is of small consequence, therefore, who first gave expression to a thought which must have been so common. According to Madison, the first person to print the suggestion of a convention was Pelatiah Webster, "an able but not conspicuous citizen," in a pamphlet published in May, 1781;* but Alexander Hamilton made the same suggestion in a private letter to James Duane, September 3, 1780.† The Legislature of New York passed resolutions favouring the plan in 1782 and that of Massachusetts in 1785. In 1784 the President of Congress, Richard Henry Lee, wrote Madison that it was common talk among the members.‡ Madison replied December 25, 1784, that he put no confidence in the continuance of the Union under the present system, and hoped the convention proposition would not be prejudiced by an admission that Virginia did not favour it, although he feared such was the case.§ March 25, 1786, William Grayson, delegate from Virginia,

* "Writings of Madison" (Hunt), II, 402.
† "Hamilton's Works" (Lodge), I, 203.
‡ Dept. of State MSS.
§ "Writings of Madison" (Hunt), II, 100.

wrote that many members of the Congress favoured a convention to revise the Articles of Confederation.*

The initiative could not, however, be expected to come from the Congress itself. The days of glory of that extraordinary body were over, and it was now composed of shifting elements—delegates who came and went and took an interest only in those matters that immediately concerned their respective States. The tone had lowered and the more eminent men of the country did not seek service in a helpless, disintegrating body. The contrast between the Congress of 1783, when Madison's service terminated, and that of 1786, when the Annapolis meeting took place, was significant. In 1783 Wilson of Pennsylvania, Charles Carroll of Maryland, Henry Lee of Virginia, Gerry and Osgood of Massachusetts, Duane of New York, and Boudinot of New Jersey, were his associates; now, there were almost no members of note except Richard Henry Lee, Gorham of Massachusetts and Charles Pinckney of South Carolina. Congress preferred, Madison said, to keep the ship of State afloat "by standing constantly at the pump, not by stopping the leaks which have endangered her."†

It was Alexander Hamilton who saw in the Annapolis meeting a possible means of stopping the leaks, and calling the convention which was in the minds of so many men. The immediate argument was that the Annapolis meeting was for the purpose of considering regulations of trade, but these involved indirectly all other Government regulations, and could not be readjusted unless the other parts of the Government were also readjusted.

The interval between the adjournment at Annapolis and the meeting at Philadelphia was spent in arousing public opinion to the necessities of the occasion, and all the States appointed delegates except Rhode Island.

* Dept. of State MSS.
† "Writings of Madison" (Hunt), II.

That State had refused assent to the proposed revenue system, had taxed her neighbours who were obliged to use her convenient ports, and was having a debauch of paper money and repudiation of debts. "Being conscious of the wickedness of the measures they are pursuing they are afraid of everything that may become a control on them," Madison wrote his father, April 1, 1787.* So the Constitution was made without Rhode Island's help.

Edmund Randolph, who, as Governor of Virginia, was by consent of his colleagues the head of the Virginia delegation to the convention, wrote to Madison, March 27, 1787, proposing that a scheme of government be engrafted upon the Articles of Confederation, and that the Virginia delegates draw up some general propositions to be submitted to the Convention. Madison replied April 8 outlining a plan; but so far as the Articles of Confederation were concerned he said his ideas of a reform struck too deeply and involved too systematic a change to include their retention.† The plan he outlined to Randolph he had previously (March 19)‡ set forth in a letter to Jefferson, and subsequently (April 16)§ he laid it before Washington. He said he conceived that the individual independence of the States "was utterly irreconcilable with their aggregate sovereignty," but that "a consolidation of the whole into one simple republic would be as inexpedient as it was unattainable." The main points which he thought required attention were a change in national representation, giving proportional power to the larger States; that the National Government should be armed with "positive and complete authority in all cases requiring uniformity," such as the regulation of trade, including the right of taxing both exports and imports, "the

* "Writings of Madison" (Hunt), II, 335.
† Id., II, 337.
‡ Id., II, 328.
§ Id., II, 344.

fixing the terms and forms of naturalization, &c., &c. ";
that the National Government should have a right of
negative, such as the King of England had enjoyed
before the Revolution, on all State legislation; that
there should be a supreme judiciary having jurisdiction
"in all cases to which foreigners or inhabitants of other
States may be parties," and in admiralty cases; that
the appointment of National officers should vest in the
National Government; that it should have control of
the militia; that there should be two legislative chambers, one chosen by the people or the Legislatures, the
other holding for a longer term, the members to go out
by rotation, so as always to leave a large majority of old
members; that there should be a council to revise all
laws passed; that there should be a National Executive;
that domestic tranquillity should be guaranteed to the
States; that the National Government should have the
right of coercion over the States; and that the new Constitution should be ratified by the people of the States,
not by the Legislatures.

Early in 1785 (January 6) George Muter of Kentucky
wrote to Madison propounding some questions that
Caleb Wallace, Madison's old college mate at Princeton,
had suggested on the subject of a Constitution for Kentucky,* and August 23, 1785,† Madison replied setting
forth his ideas on the subject of what a State Constitution should be. He thought the Legislature ought
to include a Senate, to give wisdom and steadiness to
legislation. The lower House ought to be expressly
restrained from meddling with religion, abolishing juries,
taking away the right of habeas corpus, forcing a citizen to give evidence against himself, controlling the
press, enacting retroactive laws, at least in criminal
cases, abridging the right of suffrage, taking private
property for public use without paying for it, *licensing
the importation of slaves*, etc. He had formed no final

* Dept. of State MSS.
† "Writings of Madison" (Hunt), II, 166.

opinion whether the Executive should be elected by
the Legislature or the people or should be one man
with a council, or a council simply with a president
primus inter pares. The judges should hold during
good behaviour, and their salaries should not be changed.
The chief courts only ought to be named, giving the
Legislature power to institute the others. Impeachment proceedings he would have tried before the Senate,
the Executive and the judiciary. As for the right of
suffrage, to confine it to landholders would exclude
too many citizens; to extend it to all citizens without
regard to property, or even to all who possessed a pit-
tance, might throw the power into hands that would
abuse it. A good middle course might be found in broad
qualifications for electors to the popular branch of the
Legislature and a narrower suffrage for the Senate.
This might offend the sense of equity, but he saw no
reason why rights of property which bore the chief
burden of government and were so much the object of
legislation should not be respected as well as personal
rights. For the more numerous chamber he supposed
annual elections would be insisted upon, but many
good statesmen favoured triennial. For the Senate
four or five years might be the period. It seemed unnecessary to prohibit an indefinite re-eligibility. With
regard to the Executive, if the elections were frequent
and by the people there could be no objection to re-
elegibility. If they were infrequent there should be a
temporary or perpetual incapacitation of re-elegibility
to the chief magistracy. This letter in conjunction
with those to Washington, Jefferson and Randolph
may be taken as fairly representing Madison's notions
of what a constitution should be before the Federal
Convention met.

He went into that body armed with a practical
knowledge of the needs of the country gained from
as great experience in its government as any member possessed; but in theoretical knowledge of govern-

ment he surpassed all his associates.   He fully realized the tremendous issues trembling in the balance, and he prepared for the convention completely.   After his election as a delegate he arranged his notes carefully. They were the result of profound study begun twenty years before at Princeton and continued unremittingly. He was an omnivorous reader of everything relating to government, and the limited library resources of his neighbourhood were substantially increased by his acquisitions from Paris.   His erudition covered the whole field of experience of mankind in government, so far as it was applicable to conditions in America. He prepared before he went to Philadelphia several memoranda to assist him in the debates as they might arise.   One was on the various confederacies of the world, Lycian, Achæan and Amphyctionic among the ancients, and Belgic, Helvetic and Germanic among the moderns.*   The Lycian Confederacy was an illustration of value, because the members voted in proportion to their pecuniary contributions to the whole government. The Amphyctionic League offered an illustration of a general government which had power to declare war and coerce the cities which were parties to the confederacy.   The Achæan Confederacy was an example of perfect equality among its members, each city sending the same number of deputies to the Senate.   The Federal power could make war, send and receive ambassadors, etc.   The Helvetic Confederacy showed a general diet of united cantons, two deputies from each, with decisions made by a plurality of votes.   The particular cantons had their particular diets for their own affairs, and were really independent commonwealths, bound together by a common instrument of government.   In the Belgic Confederacy, on the other hand, there was an unlimited number of deputies to the central law-making body, but each province had only a single vote.   The deputies held office for different periods of time, some

* "Writings of Madison" (Hunt), II, 369.

for six years, some for three, and some for one year. It was a perpetual union for common defence, and the federal power could levy import and export duties, receive and send ambassadors, and attend to all foreign affairs, the provinces reserving sovereignty within their respective borders, coining money of equal standard, and contributing each a quota to the treasury of the Confederacy. The Germanic Confederacy was interesting, because it had three legislative colleges—the electors, the provinces and the imperial cities. The chief authorities upon which this memorandum was based were Montesquieu's *L'Esprit des Lois* (1784), Ubbo Emmius, the Dutch historian, (in Latin), the *Code d l' Humanité ou Législation*, by Felice, in thirteen volumes, (1778), the *Encyclopædia of Political Economy*, Plutarch's works, the *Encyclopedie* published under the direction of Diderot and d'Alembert, John Potter's *Archæologia Græca*, two volumes, (Oxford, 1688-9), Demosthenes, Grotius' *De Jure Belli et Pacis*, Raleigh's *History of the World*, Gillies' *History of Greece*, Polybe's *General History* (probably the Paris edition of 1609), Stanyan's *Switzerland*, William Coxe's *Voyages*, *Dictionnaire de Suisse*, Sir William Temple's *Remarks on the United Provinces* (1674), Gabriel Bonnot de Mably (1709-1785), and several others.

A more useful paper than the one on foreign confederacies was an indictment he prepared against the existing Government, entitled "Vices of the Political System of the United States."*

The counts were: The failure of the States to comply with Federal requisitions, resulting naturally from the number and independent authority of the States; the encroachments of State upon Federal authority, as instanced in Georgia's treaties with the Indians, the unauthorized compacts between Virginia and Maryland, and Pennsylvania and New Jersey, and the raising of troops by Massachusetts; the violations of the laws of nations and of treaties, the treaty of peace

* "Writings of Madison" (Hunt), II, 361.

and those with France and Holland all having been disregarded; the trespasses of one State upon the rights of another, illustrated in Virginia's laws restricting foreign vessels to certain ports, the Maryland and New York laws restricting their ports to vessels belonging to their own citizens, the issues of paper money and commercial regulations; the want of concert in matters of common concern, as shown in the lack of uniformity of naturalization laws, diverse laws on the subject of canals, etc.; the absence of any guarantee to the States of protection against internal violence, making it possible that a military minority might at any time oppress a majority of the people; the want of sanction by the Federal power to the laws passed by the States, and inability to coerce recalcitrant States; the difference in the form of ratification of the Articles of Confederation by the different States, some having them as a part of their Constitutions and others as having been sanctioned only by the Legislatures, thus making them easy of evasion; the multiplicity of laws, causing a useless and dangerous "luxuriancy of legislation;" their constant changing, causing chronic instability, and the incurable injustice of many of these laws.

CHAPTER XIII

THE GREAT CONVENTION. I.

THE proceedings of the Convention were ordered to be kept secret, so that the members might deliberate uninfluenced by outside applause or criticism, and the people were not permitted to take part in shaping the Convention's work. Of that work Madison imposed upon himself the task of being the reporter. His object, as he stated many years afterwards, was to preserve "the history of a Constitution on which would be staked the happiness of a people great even in its infancy, and possibly the cause of liberty throughout the world." He chose a seat in front of the presiding officer, with the members to the right and left of him, where he could hear all that was said, and he took down each speech on the spot, using abbreviations and a few arbitrary characters of his own. He wrote out his notes each day at his lodgings, being aided in his task by a knowledge of the style of most of the speakers, whom he had heard speak in the Congress. Franklin's speeches were nearly all written, and his colleague, Wilson, read them, Franklin himself being too feeble to stand the fatigue of delivering them himself. They were handed to Madison after delivery and copied by him. When he was writing out Hamilton's chief speech the latter happened to enter his room and reading it pronounced it to be correct. Gouverneur Morris saw Madison's report of one of his speeches and made no changes in it. Not a single day of the sittings of the Convention did Madison miss, and his report was as complete as one man could make it.* It is a remarkable example of

* "Writings of Madison" (Hunt), II, 391.

good reporting and of prolonged concentration upon a laborious task.

The Convention determined at the outset to go beyond the purpose for which it was called. The Annapolis meeting proposed that this purpose should be to render the Government "adequate to the exigencies of the Union," and that the conclusions reached should be reported to Congress and become operative when agreed to by the Legislatures of all the States. But when Congress considered the Annapolis programme, it modified it and appointed May 2 as a day for a meeting of delegates from the several States, to revise the Articles of Confederation and recommend to Congress and the State Leigslatures such provisions as would, when agreed to by the States, "render the Federal Constitution adequate to the exigencies of Government and the preservation of the Union."*

With "a manly confidence in their country," as Madison termed it, the members of the Convention exceeded their commission and wiped the Articles of Confederation out of existence, substituting for them a Constitution which was not to be submitted to the State Legislatures at all, but was to go into effect when ratified by the people of nine States. They trusted to public opinion to support them, being encouraged to do so by recalling the alacrity with which Virginia's proposition for a meeting to consider better trade regulations had been accepted, and how the delegates to the consequent meeting had gone a step further and recommended a general convention, to which all the States but one had sent delegates.†

It was generally agreed that the most radical defect in the Articles of Confederation lay in the power of the States to comply with or disregard, as they saw fit, the recommendations of Congress, and that the most pressing duty before the Convention was to find a remedy

* Journals of Congress (Ed. 1800) XII, 14.
† Federalist, No. XL.

for this evil.*   To do so none of the leaders of the Convention wished to erect a complete democracy.   The
inclinations of a few members lay in that direction,
but they exerted little influence, for the democratic
sentiment of the country was opposed to holding the
Convention, and had not sought to send its champions
as delegates.   The assemblage was looked upon from
the beginning as one of federalists.

In planning the National Congress, therefore, it was
not intended that it should represent population alone,
but wealth also, and the Senate or second chamber,
especially, was designed to represent conservative forces.
John Dickinson of New Jersey thought it should be a
large body, as its influence, "from family weight and
other causes, would be increased thereby."†   Elbridge
Gerry of Massachusetts, afterwards an ardent member
of Jefferson's party, said it should be so constituted as
to render secure "the commercial and moneyed interest."‡   Charles Cotesworth Pinckney of South Carolina said it was meant to represent the wealth of the
country.§   George Mason suggested that no one be
permitted to serve as a senator who was not possessed
of a certain amount of property.¶   Gouverneur Morris
of Pennsylvania and John Rutledge of South Carolina
agreed that the representation should be by wealth, not
by numbers.‖   Abraham Baldwin of Georgia expressed
the same view.**   Charles Pinckney went a step further
than Mason and would have had property qualifications
for all the high offices.   The President should be worth
at least $100,000 a Federal Judge at least $50,000, and
members of Congress a less amount.††   Pierce Butler
agreed with his colleague Rutledge that representation
in both Houses should be according to the wealth of

* Madison to W. C. Rives, October 21, 1833.   Works (Cong. Ed.)
IV, 313.

† "Madison Papers" (Gilpin) II, 817.

‡ Id., II, 819.   ‖ Id., II, 1034-1035.
§ Id., II, 969.   ** Id., II, 998.
¶ Id., II, 972.   †† Id., II, 1283.

the States. It was intended, however, to recognize the "democratic principle" by basing representation in the House upon population as "the only security for the rights of the people," but Madison also declared that in America the fairest way of measuring the wealth of a community was by the number of inhabitants.* In estimating population it was agreed to count all the freemen and two-fifths of the slaves, this being the ratio proposed by Madison in Congress in 1783. The idea was that slaves partook of the nature of both population and property. They were estimated as property in computing the taxable wealth of a community and they had, under the law, certain limited personal rights.†

As both the Annapolis and Philadelphia meetings were held at Virginia's initiative her delegates thought it incumbent upon them to offer the Convention some plan of government as a starting-point for the debates, and they spent three weeks, while waiting for a quorum of delegates to reach Philadelphia, in drawing one up.‡ It contained the features of Madison's ideas of government, as outlined in his letters to Randolph and Washington, but it was Randolph's hand that actually drew up the resolutions known in the Convention as "the Virginia plan," and as Governor of the State and a fluent and persuasive speaker the distinction of presenting it to the Convention fell to him. This he did on May 29, when eight States had assembled, in an exhaustive and able speech pointing out the evils of the existing system and explaining the general principles of the substitute he offered.§ It was not expected that this substitute would come forth from the crucible of debate in the form in which it went in, and the Virginia delegates were not themselves bound to adhere to it. It was, however, not only the point from which the debate started, but the pivot about which it revolved.

* Gilpin, II, 1074.
† Id., II, 1083.
‡ Rowland's "Life of George Mason," II, 101
§ Gilpin, II, 727, *et seq.*

The plan comprised fifteen declaratory resolutions of principles which ought to be applied in the Government of the United States:

There should be two branches of the National Legislature, the members of the first to be elected every year, and all the power vested in the old Congress should belong to the new one, beside the right of legislating wherever the separate States were not competent, or "the harmony of the United States" might be "interrupted" by State legislation. There should be a National Executive, and a judiciary to consist of one or more supreme tribunals, and of subordinate tribunals to be instituted by the Legislature, jurisdiction to extend to piracies and felonies on the high seas, captures from an enemy, cases in which foreigners might be interested, or which respected the collection of the national revenue, and questions involving "the national peace and harmony." A republican form of government should be guaranteed to every State, and the proposed articles of union should be submitted for ratification to assemblies of representatives of the people in the several States, especially chosen for the purpose. These features of the Virginia plan finally appeared in the Constitution.

But the plan further proposed that the members of the "second branch of the National Legislature," or Senate, should be elected by the members of the popular branch "out of a proper number of persons nominated by the individual legislatures," and that the National Legislature should have power to call forth the force of the United States against any State failing to fulfil its duties to the Union, and to negative all laws passed by the several States contravening the articles of union or any treaty; also that the National Executive should be chosen by the Legislature and be ineligible for reelection. Provision was made for a Council of Revision composed of the Executive and "a convenient number" of the National judiciary, to pass upon all laws coming from the National Legislature. If the Council disapproved of any act it was not to become operative, unless it was passed again by a vote of — members of both Houses of Congress. Under the same conditions State legislation not negatived by Congress could be vetoed by the Council. These features of the Virginia plan did not appear in the Constitution. Several of them were especially favoured by Madison,—(1) A representation in both branches of the Legislature proportioned to the wealth and population of the respective States; (2) the right of negative of State acts by the National Congress, and (3) the Council of Revision to negative improper laws.

As Madison explained in *The Federalist* (No. XXVII) the chief opposing forces in the Convention were the larger States, which wished a participation in the National Government proportioned to their importance, and the smaller States, which were tenacious of the equal representation they enjoyed under the Articles of Confederation. They fought their battle over the question of representation in the Senate, the delegates from the smaller States being a unit in insisting that it be equal for each State, and asserting positively that they would sign no instrument of government which made it otherwise. Luther Martin of Maryland, Gunning Bedford of Delaware, a former college mate of Madison's, who was under positive instructions from the Legislature of his State to accept no scheme of government destroying State equality, Oliver Ellsworth of Connecticut, and John Dickinson of New Jersey, were the chief speakers on the side of the smaller States.

In Madison's first speech in the Convention (May 30) he proclaimed as his central idea that a National Government ought to be established and not a "federal one among sovereign States."* Later, in the course of debate, he said an equal voice in government by unequal portions of the people would infuse mortality into a Constitution which ought to be so constructed as

* Gilpin, II, 752.

to last forever. He would preserve the State rights "as carefully as the trial by jury," but the new government was not to operate upon the States, but upon the people directly, and equal State representation might easily come to mean government by the minority. The smaller States threatened to disrupt the Union, unless they had their way. What, then, Madison asked, would be their position? They would be a prey to the larger States, who would be under no obligations to protect them.

On the other side Oliver Ellsworth said he depended for domestic happiness as much on his State government as an infant upon its mother for nourishment.* Dickinson said Madison pushed the small States too far; that some of their representatives wished for two branches in the National Legislature and were friends to a' strong National Government, but that they would rather submit to a foreign power than be deprived, in both branches of the Legislature, of equality of suffrage, and thereby thrown under the domination of the larger States.† Bedford coincided in this view, and the members were shocked to hear in the heat of debate sentiments of disloyalty to the American Union.‡

Madison contended strenuously that there was no real difference between the interest of the smaller and larger States. The real opposition of interests lay, he explained, between slave States and free States. He was so much impressed with this fact that it had occurred to him as a fair plan to apportion the votes in one House of Congress according to the number of free inhabitants only, and in the other according to the whole number, counting the slaves as equal to freemen. By this arrangement the South would have the advantage in one House and the North in the other.¶ The proposition met with no favour, for the delegates from the smaller States believed an adherence to their position

* Gilpin, II, 1014.
† Id., II, 863, n.
‡ Id., II, 1014.
¶ Id,, 1088.

to be absolutely necessary to their existence. The question thus became a simple one. It was whether the Convention should break up or surrender the point to the smaller States, and the committee that drafted the compromise in effect recognized this condition of affairs. To save appearance it was stipulated that money bills should originate only in the House of Representatives, but as the right of proposing amendments was finally given to the Senate this apparent concession amounted to nothing. The smaller States were not, however, ungrateful to the larger States, and in return for the vital point yielded them they voted steadily afterwards for those propositions which gave increased power to the General Government.*

If Madison's plan had prevailed the boundaries of the several States would not have been destroyed and they would still have had complete control over their local affairs, but the idea of State sovereignty would have been killed beyond the hope of resurrection. This idea, was, however, stronger with the small States than their desire for the Union.

The concession of equal State representation in the Senate was the most important of the so-called compromises between opposing interests made in the formation of the Constitution. Another one was effected towards the end of the Convention's sitting hardly less one-sided, but happily not permanent in its provisions. This was the bargain by which the slave trade was permitted to continue for twenty years for the benefit chiefly of South Carolina and Georgia, and taxation upon exports was prohibited for the benefit generally of the Southern States, in return for the power given Congress to pass navigation laws by a majority vote, which it was supposed would prove profitable to the Eastern States. Broadly speaking, the interests of the country were divided into those of the plantation at the South and of commerce at the North. More minutely,

* Bancroft VIII on Madison's authority.

the fisheries and West India trade concerned New England; New York's interests lay in free trade, as her chief port was an entrepôt; the staples of Pennsylvania and New Jersey were wheat and flour; tobacco was the staple of Virginia, Maryland and North Carolina; rice and indigo were the staples of Georgia and South Carolina.* It was argued that these different interests would be a source of oppression to each other if navigation and trade regulations might be made by a bare majority in Congress.

Accordingly, the draft of the Constitution reported by the committee on detail August 6 contained an article providing that no navigation act should be passed by Congress, except by a two-thirds vote; also that no tax or duty should be laid on exports, nor upon the importation of such persons as the States chose to admit.† The last clause would have tied the hands of Congress forever so far as regulating or stopping the slave trade was concerned, leaving the matter wholly within the control of the separate States. It was obnoxious to both Southern and Northern members, and strange to say, the defence of the proposition that the States should deal with the question came from Eastern men.‡ Gouverneur Morris, seeing the trend of sentiment, said; "These things may form a bargain among the Southern and Northern States;" and on August 22 the slave trade and navigation clauses were both referred to a committee of one member from each State, Madison being selected as the member from Virginia.¶ He was in favour of giving Congress the right to tax exports, not only for revenue but for protective and political purposes. "A proper regulation," he said, "of exports may, and probably will be necessary hereafter and for the same purposes as the regulation of imports: viz., for revenue, domestic manufactures, and projecting equitable regulations from

* C. Pinckney's Speech, Aug, 29, Gilpin III, 1450.
† Gilpin II, 1233.
‡ Id., III, 1389.   ¶ Id., III, 1396.

other nations. An embargo may be of absolute necessity and can alone be effectuated by the general authority." He also held that navigation and trade regulations could properly be made by a majority vote in
Congress and that they would benefit the South as well
as the North.* The disadvantage to the South of a
navigation act lay, he said, in a temporary rise in freights.
It would be followed, however, by an increase in Southern
shipping and the emigration to the South of Northern
seamen and merchants. The agricultural interests would
be powerful enough to prevent an adverse combination
in Congress. New Jersey and Connecticut were really
agricultural States and agricultural industries predom-
inated in the interior of all the States. Material accession to agricultural forces might soon be expected
from the West. At any rate a greater maritime
strength would result in a generally increased national security in the benefits of which all sections would
share.

Madison had nothing, therefore, to do with the bargain which Morris predicted. The parties to it were
Georgia, South Carolina and North Carolina, on one
side, and Massachusetts, Connecticut and New Hampshire on the other, this making a majority of the States,
for Hamilton was the only delegate from New York
and the State had no vote. The committee proposed
that there should be no slave importations after the
year 1800, and the first step in fulfilment of the bargain
came August 25, when it was moved and carried that
the date be extended to 1808. Virginia, New Jersey,
Pennsylvania and Delaware voted in the negative.
George Mason had already made his noble speech against
the "infernal traffic,"† and Madison said: "Twenty
years will produce all the mischief that can be apprehended from the liberty to import slaves. So long a
term will be more dishonourable to the American charac-

* Gilpin, III, 1384.
† Id., II, 1390.

ter, than to say nothing about it in the Constitution."*
Concerning the proposition to lay a tax on the import
of slaves, he said he thought it "wrong to admit in the
Constitution the idea that there could be property in
men."†

On August 29, Charles Cotesworth Pinckney said that,
considering the "liberal conduct" of the Eastern States
towards South Carolina, he would vote that the commercial regulations which the Eastern States desired
might be made by a majority vote in Congress instead
of the two-thirds vote required as the clause then stood.
He acknowledged that he had come to Philadelphia
with a prejudice against New England men, but he had
been met by them in such a spirit of accommodation
that his opinion had changed. He found them "as
liberal and candid as any men whatever."‡

So the bargain was completed. Slaves were to be
imported freely for twenty years; there was to be no
possible way, except by amending the Constitution
itself, of preventing the trade. There was to be no taxation of exports, and trade and navigation acts could be
passed by a majority vote in Congress. Georgia, South
Carolina and North Carolina cared primarily for slaves,
for in them they thought their wealth lay, and they
wished to increase it by further importations. Their
attachment to slavery was a stronger feeling than was
their opposition to navigation acts. The desire for
navigation acts was, on the other hand, very strong in
New England, and several delegates from that section
declared the Union was not desirable to them unless
they could have national legislation to foster their commerce. The selfish cupidity of this section thus allied
itself with the perverted morality of South Carolina,
Georgia and North Carolina, and the coalition probably
saved the Constitution from rejection.

* Gilpin, II, 1427. ‡ Id., II, 1451.
† Id., II, 1430.

CHAPTER XIV

A NUMBER of the lesser provisions of the Constitution were incorporated on Madison's motion. These were: The power of the Federal Government to grant copyrights and patents for inventions; to dispose of the public lands and provide temporary government for them; to acquire, with the consent of the States, lands for Federal forts, arsenals, etc., and to regulate intercourse with the Indians. He was the author of the clause conferring exclusive jurisdiction in Congress over a seat of Government, when one should be chosen, and of the article specifying how amendments might be made.* He was in favour of the election of the President by popular vote,† and accepted as approximating this end the intermediate agency of the electoral college which Wilson suggested.‡ It proved at the first election to be only a vehicle for registering the public will, and has never been anything else. Upon Madison's motion a member of Congress was made ineligible for appointment to an office created, or the emoluments of which had been increased, during his term of Congressional service. He assisted in putting the final touches to the Constitution, being a member of the committee on style, the last one appointed by the Convention. His colleagues were Johnson, Hamilton, Gouverneur Morris and King. They were selected as the most polished scholars and the best masters of the English tongue in the Convention.

The most brilliant man of this galaxy had, however,

* Gilpin III, 1353.　　　　　　‡ Id., II, 1200.
† Id., II, 1148.

little to do with the actual framing of the Constitution.
Alexander Hamilton's title to fame rests upon his participation in events before and after the Federal Convention, for his services in the Convention itself were
not transcendant. There his State presented a sorry
spectacle, for his colleagues, Lansing and Yates, were
anti-federalists, and they left Philadelphia in the middle
of the proceedings and went home to endeavour to pave
the way for unfavourable action in their State against
the frame of government which they forsaw would be
proposed to the people for adoption.* As long as they
remained in the convention they were a living argument
against the acceptability to the people of New York of
Hamilton's ideas of government.

These ideas he brought before the Convention immediately after the Paterson, or "Jersey plan," as it
was called, had been presented, and after the Virginia
plan had been under discussion for three weeks. The
Jersey plan was intended to conserve the Articles of
Confederation by making certain additions to them.
The complete sovereignty of the States was to be maintained and a single Congress was to be continued, but
the General Government was to have revenue from
imposts, stamps and the post office, and there was to
be a plural Executive removable by Congress.†

On June 18 Hamilton presented his plan and made
his great speech. He said he was unfriendly to both
the Virginia and the Jersey plans, but especially to the
latter, for he regarded the success of a new Government
as impossible while the States were left in possession of
their sovereignty. As long as this continued they
pursued their own interests, and their tendency was to
regain the powers they delegated. Their inhabitants
were more anxious to prevent a dissolution of the State
government, as the State government was a necessity
immediately surrounding them. "All the passions,

* Leake's "Life of John Lamb," 305.
† Gilpin, II, 862, *et seq.*

then, we see, of avarice, ambition, interest, which govern most individuals, and all public bodies, fall into the current of the States, and do not flow into the stream of the General Government." He thought the general power must swallow up the State powers or be swallowed up by them. He did not mean to shock public opinion by proposing an extinguishment of the State governments, but they ought to be extinguished. The difficulty of securing the best talent to manage the National Government in a country so large as the United States was, however, a great problem, and made him almost despair of a republican government being possible over so great an extent. The British government was the best in the world, and he doubted whether anything short of it would do in America. It seemed to have been admitted that a good Executive could not be established on a republican basis. He was aware that his plan went beyond the ideas of most members. It could not be adopted out of doors, but neither could the Virginia plan be adopted at present. He saw signs that the people were being cured of their fondness for democracy and that they would in time be unshackled from their prejudices. He submitted his sketch, therefore, chiefly as a suggestion of the amendments he would probably offer to the Virginia plan. His scheme provided for two legislative chambers and a Supreme Executive and judiciary, as in the Virginia plan, but the Senators and the Supreme Executive were to hold office during good behaviour, and the Governor of each State was to be appointed by the General Government. The Supreme Executive was to have absolute power of negative of all laws about to be passed, and each Governor was to have similar power over all laws about to be passed in his State.* Much of Hamilton's speech was prophetic, and but little of it was of immediate application. It commanded the admiration of all,†

* Gilpin, II, 828, *et seq.*
† Yates' Report, Elliott's Debates, XI.

and George Read of Delaware openly expressed his approbation of the plan, stating that he wished to see the States wiped out of existence.* Probably Gouverneur Morris also agreed with him,† as he held a government of the people in contempt; but not a single speech was made in Hamilton's support.

When the Constitution was finally framed, he said he did not approve of it generally, but would accept it as preferable to anarchy. He did not believe it would prove to be durable, but one element of its durability he comprehended better than many of his colleagues did.

The article in the Constitution concerning the powers of the supreme judiciary excited, in the course of the debate, but little opposition of sentiment, and did not apparently arouse a deep or widespread interest. The Virginia plan contemplated a court having a very restricted jurisdiction, chiefly, as we have seen, over admiralty and prize cases, and those involving "the national peace and harmony;" but the article finally adopted went many leagues beyond this. In *The Federalist* (No. LXXVIII) Hamilton said "some perplexity" had arisen respecting the right of the Supreme Court to declare an act of the National Legislature unconstitutional. He thought, however, nothing was clearer than that every act of delegated authority contrary to the tenor of the commission was void, and, consequently, that no act of the Legislature contrary to the Constitution would be valid. It was the business of the court, therefore, to ignore such an act, whenever, as he explained in a later number (LXXXI), there was "evident opposition." Luther Martin, the most extreme State rights man in the Convention, as Hamilton was the most extreme consolidationist, wrote a letter to the Legislature of Maryland, June 28, 1788, opposing the ratification of the Constitution, and stating as one of the deprivations of State power for which it provided,

---

* Gilpin, II, 990.   † Rives, II, 352,

that the Federal judges could determine whether any laws were contrary to the Constitution, and the States would be bound by the decision.*   In the Convention Gouverneur Morris said: "A law that ought to be negatived will be set aside in the judiciary department, and, if that security should fail, will be repealed by a national law." George Mason, James Wilson and others held the same opinion.   John Francis Mercer, of Maryland, and John Dickinson, on the other hand, expressed their disapprobation of the doctrine that judges had authority to declare a law void.   That there should have been perplexity on the subject was not strange, for the delegates had no precedent in England or America to guide them.

The Articles of Confederation† made provision for a Federal Court of Appeals in admiralty cases, and for the settlement of disputes between any two States by the mutual appointment, upon petition, of commissioners or judges to constitute a court to hear and determine the question at issue.   If the States in interest could not agree on the judges Congress might select them. Pennsylvania and Connecticut, in a controversy over lands on the Susquehanna River, applied for such a court and the case was the only one ever tried.   A similar court was organized to hear a dispute between Georgia and South Carolina, and Madison was one of the judges, but it would appear the case never came to trial.

In Virginia in 1782 Chancellor Wythe, speaking *obiter dictum* from the bench, expressed the opinion that the court had a right to declare void an act of the Assembly contrary to the Constitution of the State.‡   In May, 1787, when the Federal Convention was sitting, the Superior Court of North Carolina so declared a certain act of the Legislature of that State, this being the first

* Elliott's Debates, I, 380.
† U. S. Reports, 131, appendix by the reporter, J. C. Bancroft Davis.
‡ Rives, II, 264.

judgment of the kind under a written Constitution.*
The Supreme Court of Rhode Island had, however,
already made a similar judgment under an unwritten
Constitution, and the judges were removed from office
in consequence.† It was to this case that Madison
referred in the Convention when he said (July 17);
"In Rhode Island the judges *who refused to execute an
unconstitutional law* were displaced and others substituted, by the Legislature, who would be the willing
instruments of their masters."

In urging the clause of the Constitution providing
for its adoption by the people and not by the State
Legislatures, he said ratification by the Legislatures
would make it a treaty and a law violating it "might
be respected by the judges as a law, though an unwise
and perfidious one. A law violating a Constitution
established by the people would be considered by the
judges as null and void." Evidently the remark was
intended to apply to State legislation, for Roger Sherman
in concurring said a law *of a State* contrary to the Constitution would be invalid. In the last stages of the
Convention the judiciary article was moulded into this
form: "The jurisdiction of the Supreme Court shall
extend to all cases arising under the laws passed by the
Legislature of the United States." This was amended
so as to extend the jurisdiction to all cases arising "under
the Constitution and the" laws passed by Congress.
Madison promptly suggested that this went too far—
that the court's jurisdiction ought not to extend "generally to cases arising under the Constitution." It
should be "limited to cases of a judiciary nature. The
right of expounding the Constitution in cases not of this
nature, ought not to be given to that department."
Johnson, of Connecticut, who moved the amendment,
explained that he did not mean to include a general
jurisdiction and the clause was agreed to, "it being

* Coxe on The Judicial Power, 248.
† Id., 298.

generally supposed," as Madison reports, "that the jurisdiction given was constructively limited to cases of a judiciary nature." The Dred Scott decision rendered seventy-five years later, was, as it happened, the first case in which a Federal statute declared by the Supreme Court to be unconstitutional did not relate to the judiciary.*

Madison, as we have seen, earnestly advocated the granting to Congress of power of negative over State acts, but this was not inconsistent with granting the Supreme Court power to declare such acts void. He wished to provide for some degree of harmony in State legislation and to avoid the necessity of applying coercion to arrest the operation of an unconstitutional law after it had gone into effect. Such extreme measures would, he said, be considered an act of war by the coerced State and a dissolution of all existing contracts, and would involve a disruption of the Union, all of which would be avoided if unconstitutional laws could be strangled at birth.

On the other hand he would hardly have advocated, as he did, the Council of Revision, with some of the Federal judges as members, to pass upon National legislation, if he had seen in his mind's eye the possibility that when on the bench these members might be called upon to pronounce, not upon the construction of the law, but upon the question whether it should not be stricken from the statute books. It would be an unnatural assumption to say he supposed that a National law which had gone through the Council of Revision might be declared void by the judiciary. It must be remembered, however, that if the judiciary article in the Constitution did not mean to Madison all that it subsequently developed into, he was not alone. Some members doubtless thought the power of declaring a State law contrary to the Constitution void was lodged in the Supreme Court, but not the power of so declaring

* Coxe on The Judicial Power, 20.

an act of Congress; others thought this power also existed; and yet others accepted the article and did not speculate as to what its effect would be.

Gouverneur Morris and James Wilson were the only two members who spoke in the Convention oftener than Madison. Morris exerted an influence over the proceedings by his fearless criticism of the various propositions offered, but Wilson brought a conservative intellect and far-seeing statesmanship to bear upon them, and much of the credit for the result belongs to him. As the days and weeks went by, however, and step by step the Convention got forward towards its goal, the fact became generally recognized that the first man of the assemblage was James Madison. William Pierce, a delegate from Georgia, described him in the notes he took in the Convention:* "Mr. Maddison is a character who has long been in public life; but what is very remarkable every Person seems to acknowledge his greatness. He blends together the profound politician, with the scholar. In˚the management of every great question he evidently took the lead in the Convention, and tho' he cannot be called an Orator, he is a most agreeable, eloquent, and convincing speaker. From a spirit of industry and application which he possesses in a most eminent degree, he always comes forward the best informed Man of any point in debate. The affairs of the United States, he perhaps has the most correct knowledge of, of any Man in the Union. He has been twice a member of Congress, and was always thought one of the ablest Members that ever sat in that Council. Mr. Maddison is about 37 years of age, a Gentleman of great modesty,—with a remarkably sweet temper. He is easy and unreserved among his acquaintances, and has a most agreeable style of conversation."

He represented the largest, richest, and most influential State in the Union, the one which had led in the great events culminating in the Convention. In the

* American Historical Review, VII, 331.

progress of debate it became apparent that his distinguished colleagues, Mason and Randolph, were so strongly
opposed to some of the articles of the Constitution that
they could not be depended upon to advocate its adoption. Madison, however, kept the majority of the Virginia delegation with him and spoke for the State. He
was willing to sacrifice some of his opinions in order to
gain a result approximating his desires. He had no
unique scheme of government which he had personally
evolved and to which he was irrevocably attached.
He wished to frame a government strong enough to
preserve the Union, to fulfil its obligations, and to
command obedience at home and respect abroad. He
attended to the business before him with untiring devotion and was more continuously present at the sittings
of the Convention than any other prominent member.
He was uninfluenced in his course by any selfish motives.
He wished primarily to see a measure drafted that would
stand a fair chance of adoption by the people, and this
feeling fortunately was dominant in the Convention.

The result was a work coming from "men in a world
of men," and not from youthful idealists nor beings of
perfect wisdom. As it was obtained by mutual sacrifices of individual preferences it was wholly satisfactory
to none, although moderately satisfactory•to nearly all.
Pierce Butler said: "We must follow the example of
Solon, who gave the Athenians not the best government he could devise, but the best they would receive."
Wilson said that one reason why the Constitution should
be submitted to the people and not the State governments for ratification was that the State governments
would be certain to oppose it.* But the people themselves knew hardly anything more than State governments and had for the most part only State ideals. Madison, Hamilton, Rutledge and the other great leaders
could look beyond State borders and see a great future
for a new American nation; but how would the people

* Yates.

generally receive a Constitution that destroyed some and crippled other of the powers of the States? In these States centred all the material interests and most of the sentimental feelings of their inhabitants. As Story has said, "The wonder, indeed, is not, under such circumstances, that the Constitution should have encountered the most ardent opposition, but that it should ever have been adopted at all by a majority of the States."

CHAPTER XV

FORMING THE LINES

MADISON was now thirty-four years old and was still a bachelor. His blood flowed temperately, but not coldly, and in 1786 he was so attentive to some lady whose identity has been lost that there were rumours that he was about to be married. General Henry Lee, who told him he "loved and respected" him, congratulated him with enthusiasm and expressed the hope that the condition on which he was about to enter would soften his political asperities. The report penetrated to Kentucky and Caleb Wallace also sent his felicitations.* How near consummation the affair was, or why it failed, there is now nothing to show.

As the statesman left youth behind him his health improved and his body filled out, but he was not robust and suffered often from digestive troubles. He still dressed soberly, but less like a parson than in the earlier days. He affected, we are told, a springing, rising step, probably to overcome his defects of stature; and the somewhat rustic bearing which had marred his manner in early manhood had disappeared.† Blessed by Heaven with a ready sense of humour, which official cares did not destroy, he was a genial companion and enjoyed personal popularity. His social circle was large and the best in America, and in it his rank was high, with every promise of increasing importance in the future. In his county his neighbours and large family connection looked up to him with pride; but among the people at

* Dept. of State MSS.
† "Virginia Convention of 1788" (Grigsby) Virginia Historical Collections, IX, 96.

large,—the crowd that is,—he was not well known and
had no following, for he had none of the showy qualities
of the popular leader. He had the homage of men of
his class, the respect of all good men, the affection of a
chosen few, and the personal hatred of none. It is
probable that his dominant personal sentiment was his
affection for Thomas Jefferson, and in turn Jefferson
treated him with extraordinary confidence and respect. He
was entrusted with the education of Jefferson's nephews
during their uncle's absence and selected their schools.
The library at Monticello was free to him, but that at
Montpelier was growing larger every day, many of the
books being sent over by Jefferson at Madison's request.
Jefferson gave him a watch, and in 1785 urged him to
buy a small farm near Monticello, so that they might
look forward to an uninterrupted companionship. He
begged him to visit him in Paris, but Madison was obliged
to decline. He had in 1783 refused an appointment as
Minister to Spain. His development was, therefore,
unassisted by foreign travel, but he knew Italian, in
which language Mazzei and Bellini usually corresponded
with him, beside the Spanish and French which he had
learned in his childhood.

While the warmest affection and intimacy existed
between Jefferson and Madison they did not co-operate
in public affairs either immediately before, or during,
or immediately after the formation of the constitution
of the United States. The philosopher was enjoying
himself in Paris and following out trains of thought that
sometimes led him to absurd conclusions. He loved
liberty so ardently that he seriously doubted, he wrote,
whether men were not best off without any government at all, as some of the Indians lived; at any rate
he was quite sure that "a little revolution now and then"
was a good thing to have in a free State.* He seemed
oblivious of the cold fact that unless something were
speedily done to save it his country would soon have

* "Writings of Jefferson" (Ford) IV, 362.

no government and a "little revolution" that would probably undo the work of the great Revolution. While he was indulging his fancy Madison was at work in earnest.

Soon after the Constitution was published there arose throughout the country a formidable opposition to its acceptance. It came chiefly from three classes: first, those who looked upon the Federal authority as foreign authority that had merely taken the place of Great Britain and who consequently feared an enlargement of it would lead to oppression; second, those who were willing to give the Federal Government a few additional powers, but wished a continuance of the Articles of Confederation, thinking that a more centralized government would wipe out the State governments; third, those who wished the Union to break up and hoped that three or more separate confederacies would emerge from the wreck, this being the smallest class of all, and the most silent, for it did not work by direct arguments. As New York was the Capital, the opposition was most active there, in hope of producing an impression on Congress before the Constitution went to the people. To counteract this opposition, Alexander Hamilton and John Jay determined to print a series of papers defending and explaining the Constitution, and they invited Madison to co-operate. Jay had not been in the Convention that framed the Constitution, and Hamilton's views had not prevailed there. Madison, therefore, had an easier task than either of his associates, for he had merely to recast arguments already made. The first papers appeared over the signature "A Citizen of New York," and were designed for circulation in that State, but afterwards the pseudonym "Publius" was adopted, and the papers were intended for the whole country. Jay falling ill, Hamilton and Madison wrote nearly all the papers, not in collaboration but separately, twenty-nine of the eighty-five coming from

Madison's pen.* The tenth of the series, which was his first, was on the Union as a safeguard against domestic faction. It was followed by his answer to the allegation that the country was too extensive to exist as one confederacy; his familiar illustrations that the cause of the downfall of all previous confederacies was their lack of cohesion; an exposition of the difficulties encountered by the Convention and the impossibility of framing a perfect plan, urging that its virtues be studied and its defects not magnified; an explanation that the scheme intended a republic not a democracy; a defence of the powers of the Convention; a general view of the powers of the Union; an argument against the supposition that the Union would be dangerous to the State governments, in which he stated that if the sovereignty of the States could not be reconciled with the happiness of the people the sovereignty of the States ought to be sacrificed; an explanation of the distribution of government powers, and essays on the House and Senate. As to the representation in the Senate he said it was a necessary compromise and a lesser evil. He would have the people contemplate the advantages that might arise from the clause as it stood, rather than anticipate the possible mischiefs.

As the papers of *The Federalist* appeared they were sent throughout the country and gained many converts, especially among the most influential class of citizens. Rev. James Madison, of William and Mary, for example, one of the most liberal churchmen and scholars of his day, wrote his cousin soon after the Convention adjourned that he considered the Constitution "the *chef d'œuvre* of continental wisdom," but he feared the institution of a single Executive and Senate, both prob-

* Rives, II, 482, *et seq.*

Jacob Gideon, Jr., wrote to Madison, Washington, January 19, 1818, that he intended to print a new edition of *The Federalist* and wished to know the name of the author of each number and Madison returned the edition sent him with the names affixed (Mad. MSS.) The author has used the Gideon edition.

ably to hold for life, would lead to aristocracy and tyranny; but a few weeks later (Feb. 9, 1788,) he said the letters of "Publius" had well-nigh worked a conversion in him. George Nicholas, who had a minute knowledge of public opinion in Virginia, distributed the letters in the disaffected portions of the State, especially in Kentucky; but it required more than *The Federalist* to overcome the opposition in that State.*

Of the Virginia delegates to the Philadelphia Convention Randolph and Mason refused to sign the Constitution. Randolph wished to hold himself free to follow whatever course should seem best and would not tie his hands. He hoped to secure a second Convention to formulate amendments before ratification; at least this was his attitude when he left Philadelphia. Mason disapproved of too many features of the Constitution to commit himself to support the whole. When he left Philadelphia there was small prospect that he would not be in the opposition. Jefferson once spoke of Randolph as a chameleon constantly changing his hues, but it would be fairer to say he had a hopelessly impartial temperament and so easily saw both sides of a question that he was never quite sure that he was on the right side. Public affairs were not George Mason's first interest. He lived on his plantation and knew little of what went on at Philadelphia or New York. He failed, therefore, just as Jefferson did, to realize the dangers impending, and Madison's efforts to arouse him to a sense of the approaching crisis in 1785 came to naught. He was not a man whom others could influence. He lived in a little world of which he was the head and he was accustomed to have his own way. He did not have it at Philadelphia, and he determined to try to have it in Virginia. When he first returned he was reported to have said of the Constitution that he was willing to take it all rather than lose it all, but criticisms of his course in refusing to sign it reached his

* Dept. of State MSS.

ears and embittered him. Some of his admirers, too, encouraged him to believe that he could frame a Constitution himself, that he had influence enough to have it approved by Virginia, and that Virginia was powerful enough to compel its acceptance by the other States.*

His protest against the Constitution printed in October, 1787, in a folio broadside, was the briefest and most cogent of the papers of the kind emanating from the anti-federalists.† The absence of a bill of rights, insufficient representation in the House, the overwhelming power of the Senate, the absence of a Council of State as a check upon the President, the too great power of the President and Congress, the permission of the slave-trade—these were the chief grounds of his objection. The measure would, he said, result in a monarchy, or a corrupt and oppressive aristocracy.

There was another man in opposition who wielded a greater power than Mason. Patrick Henry was selected as one of the Virginia delegates to the Federal Convention, but declined to go, "being too distressed in his circumstances." This was the reason he gave the Governor, but it was generally suspected that he wished to be free to oppose or approve the result of the Convention's labours, as he saw fit. Up to this time he was supposed to be of the Federalist party, but he had never given any real assistance to the efforts made to strengthen the General Government. He was now classed by the more ardent Federalists as a disunionist. Henry Lee wrote in December, 1787, "Henry is the leader of this band." George Nicholas wrote April 5, 1788, that Henry had become almost avowedly the enemy of the Union and would oppose any plan to strengthen it, and that those who then followed him would leave him if his real designs were known to them. Rev. John Blair Smith, a Presbyterian minister, president of Hampden-Sidney College, wrote June 12 that

* George Nicholas to Madison, April 5, 1788, Dept. of State MSS.
† Ford's "Essays On the Constitution."

Henry had resorted to lower means to poison the minds of the people against the Constitution than he had ever exerted before. He had written to Kentucky that ratification would mean the closing of the Mississippi, and was busy persuading the people that it would carry with it church establishment.* Archibald Stewart, a member of the Assembly, wrote December 21, 1787, that on every available occasion Henry gave the Constitution a side blow.† Edward Carrington, a member of Congress, reported February 10, 1788, that he had been travelling in the track of Henry and the people were disposed to follow him blindly, that he specified no amendments that he wanted, and it was believed aimed at dismemberment of the Union. There was danger, Carrington said, that weak men, no matter what their views might be before, would be led away by his eloquence when the Convention to consider ratification should meet.‡

Henry was making the fight of his life. When the question of providing for the ratification Convention came before the General Assembly, the majority was not hostile to the Constitution. Henry moved (October 25), that the Convention should be vested with power to propose amendments to the Constitution, this being intended as a quasi-instruction to make amendments the condition of ratification, but John Marshall offered a substitute providing "for full and free investigation and discussion" and this was passed. In a month Henry turned the majority to himself, and November 30 introduced a bill to pay the expenses of delegates to another constitutional convention if one should be determined upon, and for a delegation to visit the other States and consult on amendments. To the terror of the Federalists this effort to prejudice the action of the coming Convention was carried by a majority of fifteen votes.¶

* Dept. of State MSS.
† To Madison, October 21, 1787, Dept. of State MSS.
‡ Dept. of State MSS.   ¶ Rives, II, 532, *et seq.*

Richard Henry Lee was also in the opposition. He was willing to do no more than extend the powers of Congress under the existing system, and wrote to the Virginia delegates in this sense when the Philadelphia Convention met. After it adjourned he planned, as we shall presently see, to alter it in the Continental Congress of which he was a member. A proud, passionate man, who lived like a petty prince, he received his tone from no one, as Washington said. Nevertheless, he loved popularity and courted applause, and it was hinted that this fact influenced his action.* Fortunately he decided not to enter the Virginia Convention, being in bad health, but before it met (October, 1787), he wrote a series of letters over the signature "The Federal Farmer," and they had great popularity among the anti-federalists.

William Grayson, also a member of the Continental Congress, was at first barely neutral and then actively hostile. James Monroe, whose star was slowly rising, General Nelson, lately Governor, whose star was sinking in old age, but who still had weight with the people because of his eminent services in the past, and Benjamin Harrison, also an ex-Governor, a tough veteran of rugged power, were among the opponents of the Constitution. From over the water there came not a word of assistance to the friends of the measure from the great leader who had written the Declaration of Independence. On the contrary he damned it with faint praise and criticism and desired its ratification without Virginia's assistance, having an ill-defined notion that if this were accomplished the State could subsequently force amendments as the price of her ultimate accession to the Union.

Dr. William McClurg, one of the Virginia delegates at

* Benjamin Hawkins, a friend of Madison's, Warrenton, February 14, 1788, reported the following questions from an illiterate wheelwright who had been reading the Constitution and Lee's criticism of it: "Is Mr. Lee thought to be a great man? Is he not a proud, passionate man? Was he one of the Convention? * * * Is he fond of popularity? Is he an enemy to General Washington and Docr. Franklin?". Dept. of State MSS.

Philadelphia, where he made but two speeches and always voted with Madison, returned to Richmond in October and canvassed the state of public opinion with reference to the Constitution.* When it first reached the people, he said, nearly everybody liked it; then they began to examine it closely and, of course, found flaws in it. Their chief objections were to the combined powers of appointment lodged in Senate and President, the extraordinary power the latter might exercise over the House of Representatives, and the power of Congress over the time and manner of choosing representatives. To these George Lee Turberville, a member of the Assembly and a warm Federalist, added as prevailing objections: The absence of a bill of rights, the absence of a Council of State, the power given the judiciary which would eventually destroy the State courts, the inhibition of any State from raising revenue by taxing exports, the permission to import slaves for twenty-one years, and that treaties could be ratified without the consent of the House of Representatives.† Even the advocates of the Constitution came to the conclusion that its ratification would not be possible without a concession to the widespread desire for amendments. These, they insisted, however, should be recommended for adoption in the way prescribed by the Constitution itself.

Shortly after the Federal Convention adjourned Madison received a letter from Carrington‡ in Congress earnestly requesting him to come to New York at once, as the Virginia delegation was hopelessly split and Richard Henry Lee unopposed by Grayson was concerting measures against the new Constitution. Carrington for himself confessed that he did not like every part of it, but said he saw not how he could ever combine his strength and interests with others without

* McClurg to Madison, Richmond, October 31, 1787. Dept. of State MSS.
† To Madison, December 11, 1787. N. Y. Public Library (Lenox) MSS.
‡ Dated September 23, 1787. Dept. of State MSS.

sacrificing some of his personal opinions. Responding to this appeal Madison hastened to New York and he and his party succeeded in suppressing the hostility to the Constitution in Congress and having it referred for consideration to conventions of the States as the Federal Convention planned.

His first idea was that it would be more becoming if those who had framed the Constitution should not attend the conventions called to ratify or reject it, but he heard that Mason intended to stand for election in Virginia and he yielded to the importunate entreaties of his friends and determined to seek an election himself. Andrew Shepherd, one of his influential neighbours, wrote December 22, 1787,* to say there would be no difficulty in securing the election in Orange county, but Henry Lee seemed to doubt this, and suggested that there were several counties in Kentucky which would be glad to choose him if Orange county did not.† Archibald Stewart, who had seen Henry change a favourable to an unfavourable majority in the Assembly, wrote "for God's sake do not disappoint the anxious expectations of y^r friends & let me add y^r country!"‡ Two delegates were allowed for each county and in Orange county, beside Madison, Gordon, Parker and Thomas Barbour were candidates, the two latter being avowed anti-federalists, who made such an industrious contest that Madison's friends and his father were alarmed for the result, and wrote to him that the voters were wavering and his presence was necessary. The Baptists especially, of whom there were many in the county, had been influenced by Henry's arguments.¶

Madison returned the day before the election and made but one speech, but he won a number of necessary votes by good luck. While riding about fifteen miles north of Montpelier, he stopped to refresh himself and his horse

* N. Y. Public Library (Lenox) MSS.
† December, 1787. Dept. of State MSS.
‡ Richmond, Nov. 2, 1787. Dept. of State MSS.
¶ Madison to Madison, Orange, January 20, 1788. Dept. of State MSS.

at a place called Gum Spring, and accidentally fell in with
Rev. Mr. Leland, one of the chief Baptist clergymen of
that section of the State.   The conversation immediately
turned upon the new Constitution and Madison and the
parson argued it point by point for some hours, the
final outcome being the parson's conversion and a change
of heart on the part of the Baptist voters. Madison
was elected the next day by a reasonable majority, his
colleague being James Gordon, also a federalist.   The
general result of the elections was supposed to be favourable to the ratification, but definite predictions could
not be made, for the delegates were not pledged and
many had not made up their minds.

General Washington, thinking he could be of more
service to the cause outside, decided not to enter the
Convention.   Chancellor Wythe, one of the delegates
at Philadelphia, from which city he had been called
away soon after the Convention met by the illness of
his wife, also lent his influence on the side of the Constitution.   So did John Blair, a silent delegate at Philadelphia, but a man of importance in the State, and Dr.
McClurg.   So did Edmund Pendleton, now old and
crippled by a fall from his horse, but still among the
most respected of the Virginians, and George Nicholas,
Edward Carrington, Henry Lee and Francis Corbin.   Edmund Randolph, when he returned from Philadelphia,
was coldly received by his Federalist friends.*   As
Governor he laid the Constitution before the General
Assembly and accompanied it with a letter explaining
and excusing his refusal to sign it.   Carrington declared the letter helped the Federalists, but it was not
until the eve of the Convention that Randolph distinctly
arrayed himself with that party.   Mason and his friends
considered him an apostate, and after the ratification
was carried Mason wrote of him (December 18, 1788,) as
the "young A——ld" (Arnold).†

* Archibald Stewart to Madison, Richmond, November 2, 1787.
Dept. of State MSS.
† Rowland's "Mason," II, 308.

CHAPTER XVI

WHEN the Virginia Convention met the Constitution had been ratified by eight States,—Delaware, Pennsylvania, New Jersey, Georgia, Connecticut, Massachusetts, (by a bare majority,) Maryland and South Carolina. In the New Hampshire Convention there was a hostile majority, but the Federalists succeeded in obtaining an adjournment, and there was a meeting in June for the second time. In New York, also, the majority was hostile, and Hamilton declared the Constitution could not be ratified unless Virginia took favourable action. The adoption thus really depended on Virginia. New Hampshire, it is true, took favourable action before Virginia did, thus completing the nine States necessary under the Constitution to put it into effect, but if Virginia had acted unfavourably, New York would also have done so, and with North Carolina's help measures could have been concerted to cause a reconsideration by some of the States, which had ratified in the belief that all the other States would do the same.

The Virginia Convention was called to order the first Monday in June, 1788, in the State House at Richmond; but the hall being inadequate to hold comfortably the 170 members and numerous spectators an adjournment was taken to the "New Academy on Shockoe Hill," a building erected by the Chevalier Quesnay for a French-American University. It stood on the north side of Broad Street between Twelfth and Thirteenth, in the square where the monumental church now is. There was some dispute over the elections from Accomack,

Franklin, Cumberland and Westmoreland counties, but it occupied little attention, and on June 4, two days after the first meeting, the Convention resolved itself into committee of the whole and proceeded to its main business.* A week later Henry, in writing to General John Lamb in New York, said that the parties in the Convention were almost evenly divided, but that four-fifths of the people of the State were opposed to the Constitution.† The latter statement he repeated in debate, and it was an exaggeration; but it is, nevertheless, true that a direct vote of the people on the Constitution would probably have been unfavourable to it. The plan of the opposition in the Convention was to break down the Constitution by showing its weak spots and loading it with amendments. The Federalists wished to debate it article by article, when it could be successfully defended, and then to agree to recommend amendments for the first Congress to take up in the manner provided by the Constitution itself.

Pendleton was chosen president and Wythe chairman of the committee of the whole, but this was merely a recognition of their ability as presiding officers and meant no preference for their views.‡

The leaders of the Federalist forces were Madison, Pendleton, George Nicholas, John Marshall, Innes, Henry Lee and Francis Corbin. Their chief opponents were Patrick Henry, George Mason, James Monroe, William Grayson, Benjamin Harrison and John Tyler. It was a battle of the giants, the like of which was never seen before, but the strongest man among the giants was the delegate from Orange county, and this because no other man was so completely armed and so familiar

* "Journal of the Convention of Virginia," Virginia State Library MSS.

† Henry's "Henry," II, 335, et seq.

‡ "The Debates and Other Proceedings of the Convention of Virginia "(Robertson) Petersburg, 1788, is reproduced in "Elliott's Debates," Vol. III. Grigsby's "Virginia Convention of 1788," Virginia Historical Collections IX, is an interesting and valuable narrative account of the proceedings of the Convention and its leading characters.

with the methods of attack and defence as he. He had spent his life preparing for the Philadelphia Convention, he had done more than any other member to frame the plan it submitted, he had already spoken often on every phase of the plan, he had heard every conceivable argument that could be brought against it and all the answers, he had defended it point by point with pen and speech. Mason, who was his chief opponent in logical argument, had not given a tenth part as much attention to the subject as Madison had. Moreover, Mason was now opposing some provisions in favour of which he had argued at Philadelphia, and he lost his temper, which was a serious handicap. Next to Madison, Edmund Randolph and George Nicholas made the most effective speeches, but Randolph was an object of easy attack because of his previous vacillation.

In the beginning the debate was allowed to roam at will over the whole field, and being a contest of declamation the chances were favourable to Henry's party; but after ten days spent in this way the Convention began on June 14 to consider the Constitution article by article, and the tide turned. On this day Madison spoke thirteen times and in the three succeeding days twenty-two times. The arguments used in this great debate are now mere curiosities. Time has shown that the fears of Mason and Henry were absolutely unfounded. Mason's arguments were generally such as he had outlined in his broadside six months before; but the country has suffered nothing from the omissions in the Constitution which caused him so much concern, the representation in the House of Representatives has been found to be adequate and increases sufficiently, the Senate has developed no tyrannical power, the Supreme Court acts automatically to keep the necessary balance of powers, the President created an advisory council for himself at the very beginning.

Henry's arguments were general, their chief cornerstone being that the new Government would eventuate

in consolidation, the obliteration of State lines and loss
of liberty. He would have had the Constitution begin
"We, the States," etc., instead of "We, the people," etc.
Ten years later he was telling the people with perfect
satisfaction that Virginia was to the Union what Caroline
County was to Virginia!

Madison's first great speech was made June 16, 1787,
immediately after a long and elaborate argument by
Randolph. He was in striking contrast to his colleague,
for Randolph was a large man of great personal beauty,
with a full musical voice, a ready flow of richly ornamented language, and an easy graceful gesticulation.
During the whole time the Convention sat Madison
was ill and feeble, and for two days he was absent from
his seat. When he rose to speak he usually carried his
hat in his hand, as though he had not intended to make a
set speech. His thin voice was hardly audible when
he began and often sank so that it failed to reach the
reporter's desk. He gesticulated but little, and as he
warmed with his argument his body swayed to and fro
with a see-saw motion. So small was he beside the
other delegates who were nearly all large men, that
when he rose to speak he could with difficulty be seen
from all parts of the hall. He usually carried notes of
his speech, written upon slips of paper in a microscopic
hand, and they were a complete skeleton of his argument. He used simple and direct language without any
ornamentation, and he indulged in no verbal flights.
He spoke only for the purpose of explaining, defending
and convincing, and seemed to be indifferent to applause. John Marshall was listening to him and in
after years said, "If convincing is eloquence he was the
most eloquent man I ever heard." An outline of his
first speech will serve as an indication of the others he
made.

To quiet the fears that tyranny would follow because
of the powers given government by the Constitution
he declared an examination of history would show that

abuse of power by the majority trampling on the rights of the minority had produced turbulence, factions and consequent despotism more than anything else. He ridiculed Henry's statement that the country needed no change, being then in repose, and asked how if this were so, it happened that deputies from all the States but one had been sent to the Philadelphia Convention? Henry's fear of the provision concerning the militia was unfounded as the new plan only allowed the General Government to control it for the specific purposes of executing the laws, suppressing insurrections and repelling invasions. As for the dreaded power of raising armies he wished it were not necessary, but must not the General Government have power to defend the United States, if a foreign country should make war against it? Would not the knowledge that no such power existed stimulate foreign countries to fall upon us? Henry had instanced Switzerland as a confederacy of independent States which were happy, but, Madison suggested, if he had looked a little further he would have found in several of the cantons the vilest aristocracy that ever existed. As for amendments, if one State proposed them others would do so, and they would be hopelessly diverse in character.

He then explained the Constitution. It stood by itself. In some respects it was Federal; in others it was of a consolidated nature; yet it was neither completely. The parties to it were the people, that is, the people as composing thirteen sovereignties. If it were completely consolidated a majority of all the people could ratify it, but a majority had already pronounced for it. As a matter of fact, however, no State was bound by it without its own consent. It was intended to be a Government established by the thirteen States, acting by their people—not by their legislatures. It was in this regard totally different from the existing Government, which was derived from the dependent authority of the Legislatures of the States. Then, the

House was elected by the people at large in proportion to population, but the Senate by the States in their equal and political capacity. It was thus a complicated scheme of government, which he hoped would avoid the evils of consolidation and of confederation as well. Henry had satirized the powers proposed to be given the General Government, but he submitted that power to collect taxes was an absolute necessity, especially in time of war. That the General Government would swallow up the State governments seemed an absurdity, when it was remembered that the representatives must depend upon the people of the States for their election and the Senators upon the State Legislatures.

It was during the last week of the Convention that Henry attempted a trick of great adroitness which came near being successful. We have seen how before the meeting he had sedulously spread the report in Kentucky that the Constitution, if adopted, would result in the closing of the navigation of the Mississippi. If the fourteen Kentucky delegates voted against ratification Henry would carry the day, and they would be certain to vote against it, if they could be brought to believe it would result in closing the river. Henry, therefore, without premonition of his intention made this argument: "There is no danger of a dismemberment of our country, unless a Constitution be adopted which will enable the Government to plant enemies on our backs. By the confederation, the rights of territory are secured. No treaty can be made without the consent of nine States. While the consent of nine States is necessary to the cession of territory, you are safe. If it be put in the power of a less number, you will most infallibly lose the Mississippi. As long as we can preserve our unalienable rights, we are in safety. This new Constitution will involve in its operation the loss of the navigation of that valuable river.

"The honourable gentlemen cannot be ignorant of the *Spanish transactions*. A treaty had been nearly entered into with Spain to relinquish that navigation. That relinquishment would inevitably have taken place, had the consent of seven States been sufficient."

He repeated the statement the next day and challenged Madison to say whether or not it was true.. Several days afterwards (June 12), Madison replied, and his words had weight, for no one had done so much as he to keep the navigation of the river free. He showed how the State had itself once been willing to abandon it and had been opposed by Northern and Eastern States. Since the peace matters were somewhat reversed, and there were some members of Congress from Northern States who were willing to surrender the right of navigation for a time in return for certain commercial advantages. He did not favour this, and he insisted that the adoption of the Constitution would be favourable to preserving the right of navigation. Emigration to the Western country would increase; it would be from the North as well as from the South and the advocates of free navigation would be more numerous.

When Henry returned to the charge Madison said our weakness precluded any treaty, and that he honestly believed there would be better chances under the new than the old system. He then made the important disclosure of the actual state of affairs in Congress. Seven States were not now disposed to surrender the river. New Jersey had instructed her delegates not to surrender it, and Pennsylvania had the same sentiments. A few days later he brought the matter to a close. "Were I at liberty," he said, "I would develop some circumstances which would convince this house that this project will never be revived in Congress, and that, therefore, no danger is to be apprehended."

Henry denied that he was "scuffling for Kentucky votes," but his purpose was too apparent, and only failed because of Madison's bold statement, which led most of the Kentucky delegates to vote for ratification. It was carried June 25 by a vote of 89 to 79, the Convention having been in session twenty-three days. The greatest orator of his time, the master who could sway Virginia audiences as no other man could, who had become habituated to success with them and had on this occasion exerted his marvellous powers as he had never exerted them before, had suffered defeat from a thin-voiced, feeble scholar who never aroused the enthusiasm of an audience in his life. Henry neither forgot it nor forgave it, and we shall presently see how deeply he resented it.

CHAPTER XVII

BEFORE the Virginia Convention met, Cyrus Griffin, one of Madison's correspondents in New York where he was representing Virginia in Congress, summed up the chances of adoption of the Constitution, as they appeared to him (March 14, 1788):

"The adjournment of New Hampshire, the small majority of Massachusetts, a certainty of rejection in Rhode Island, the formidable opposition in the State of New York, the convulsions and committee meetings in Pennsylvania, and above all the antipathy of Virginia to the system, operating together, I am apprehensive will prevent the noble fabric from being erected."*

The friends of ratification in New York hung expectantly upon the proceedings in Virginia. May 19, 1788, Hamilton reported to Madison that Clinton was in absolute control and "inflexibly obstinate," but his followers might be shaken if nine States ratified before New York acted. Hamilton declared he had positive information that Clinton had, on several occasions, expressed an opinion of the "inutility of the union." It was a matter of vast importance that Virginia and New York should keep up "an exact communication," and the instant Virginia should take decisive action he wished Madison to send him the news by express, at all possible speed, changing horses. He would pay all expenses liberally.†

The New York Convention to consider the question of ratification of the Constitution met at Poughkeepsie, June 17, 1788. According to Hamilton the Anti-Federal-

* Dept. of State MSS.
† Id.

ists had a majority of two-thirds in the Convention and
four-sevenths in the State. The leaders were, he believed,
Disunionists, but were afraid to reject the Constitution
at once, as they were not prepared for the crisis. They,
therefore, proposed a long adjournment, till the following
spring or summer, which would give the State a chance
to see how the new government worked. If all went
smoothly New York would come into it; otherwise it
would be easy to finally reject it, as the augmentation
of taxes would be a fatal argument against it.* William
Duer wrote, June 23, 1788: "If you adjourn without
doing anything we will do the same."† The next day
an express arrived at Poughkeepsie conveying intelligence
of New Hampshire's ratification, and this lent some
encouragement to the Federalists, but Hamilton said
it was "a gleam of hope" only if similar news came from
Virginia. This arrived a few days later, and the prospects of the Federalists brightened. The opposition
was unable to agree upon a programme, some being
for amendments as a condition of ratification, and others
for amendments as a condition of staying in the union.
Hamilton asked Madison whether he thought a con-
ditional ratification would be acceptable, and Madison
replied that it would not.‡ A compromise was effected
and ratification was finally forced through with a
clause expressing "full confidence" that certain amendments would be accepted and proposing a second convention to formulate them. A circular by "unanimous
order" was adopted to be sent to the other States,
inviting their co-operation. North Carolina co-operated
and remained out of the union for more than a year.
Rhode Island also demanded the second convention,
to revise a system which she had never deigned to consider. The concurrent efforts of the Federalists in Virginia and New York saved New York from rejecting the

* Dept. of State MSS.
† Id.
‡ Id.

constitution, but the efforts of the Anti-Federalists of the two States, in the opposite direction, narrowly missed causing unfavourable action in Virginia. When the New York delegates to the Philadelphia Convention, Lansing and Yates, returned to their State in July they formed, with a number of other Anti-Federalists, the Association of Federal Republicans, with General John Lamb, formerly of the Revolutionary Army, as chairman, the object being to open correspondence with the leading Anti-Federalists throughout the country, and concert measures to defeat the ratification of the Constitution; but although they began operations before the Constitution had issued forth from the Convention, a fatal procrastination or extraordinary coincidence of accidental delays characterized their subsequent movements and defeated their purpose. By the time they began correspondence several States had ratified the Constitution, and they concentrated their efforts upon New Hampshire, North Carolina, and Virginia, their chief strength lying, of course, in New York, the headquarters.

Their correspondents in Virginia were Henry, Richard Henry Lee and Grayson, but letters to them did not arrive until the convention of ratification had been in session a week, and it was then too late to send and receive letters from New York before an adjournment would take place.*

It will be recalled that before the Convention met Henry carried a motion in the Assembly to pay the expenses of a delegation, if one should be deemed advisable, to consult with the other States on the subject of amendments to be proposed to the Constitution. A copy of this resolution Edmund Randolph, as Governor, transmitted to Governor Clinton in a letter dated December 27, 1787, but strange to say it did not reach Clinton till March 7, 1788. The Legislature was then about to adjourn and consequently took no action, and

* See Leake's "Life of General John Lamb," 305, et seq.

Clinton replied to Randolph explaining this fact, but added that the State Convention called for June 17 would be glad to hold communication with Virginia as to the subject of the letter. If Clinton's letter was unofficial, then Randolph, who was a supporter of ratification when he received it, was not bound to use it. If it was official his duty was to present it to the Legislature by which it could be sent to the Convention. He took the advice of his council which decided that it was official. The General Assembly of the State obtained a quorum June 24, and the letter was laid before it, but it was unnoticed till the following day, after the final vote in favour of ratification had been taken in the Convention. Had it been in Henry's hands before that time it would have been a powerful, though not necessarily a successful argument, at any rate for delay. How Randolph's letter of December 27 was so long in reaching New York is only explicable on the supposition that it was the victim of the uncertain mails of the time, not having been sent by express or private conveyance, the usual means employed in communications of importance.

The Constitution having been adopted by the Convention June 26, Henry did not abandon his fight against it. Soon after the adjournment Madison was re-elected a member of the Continental Congress by the General Assembly and departed for New York. Why was this honour conferred without Henry's opposition by a body over which he held all-powerful sway? Perhaps he was indifferent, perhaps he did not venture to oppose himself to the strong sentiment in Madison's favour, but rumour had it that he was actuated by less worthy motives. "I do verily believe," wrote Turberville to Madison, November 13, 1788,—"I do verily believe that Mr. Henry voted for you to Congress this time with no other view but to keep you from (your) country until some more favour'd man, some minion of *his* or of *his* party shall have had an opportunity to supplant y^r interest." *

* N. Y. Public Library (Lenox) MSS.

It is not necessary to believe this, but it was, undoubtedly, a great convenience to Henry to have Madison out
of the way while he played his game. The opening for
the first move was afforded by the New York circular
inviting co-operation for a second Federal Convention
to propose amendments to the Constitution. George
Nicholas and Marshall were busy practising their profession, Pendleton and Wythe had returned to their
duties on the bench, Henry Lee was with Madison in
New York, and Randolph was not regarded with much
fear by the Anti-Federalists or with much confidence by
the Federalists. Corbin alone of the leading Federalists in the Convention was in the Legislature, and Henry
had on his side Grayson, Monroe and Harrison. "I am
under painful apprehension," wrote Washington to
Madison, September 21, 1788, "from the single circumstance of Mr. Henry having the whole game to play
in the Assembly of this State." It was believed that, as
Randolph had originally favoured a second Convention,
he would be selected to now bring the proposition forward. Francis Corbin wrote to Madison, October 21,
1788:

"He will injure his political Reputation by his doub-
lings and turnings. He is *too Machiavellian* and not
Machiavellian Enough—I wish, I sincerely wish, he would
be advised and would take advice—but this, I fear, is out
of the question. We Virginians are too much accustomed
to solitude and slavery—too much puff'd up with our own
foolish pride and vanity ever to entertain any other idea
than that we alone are wise and all the rest of the world
Fools."*

Carrington, writing about the same time, said the
Governor was in favour of the second Convention,
and would come into the Assembly; but he was
mistaken, for Randolph did not come into the
Assembly and under no circumstances would he have
introduced such insidious resolutions as Henry drew up.

* Dept. of State MSS.

Henry brought them in himself on October 27. They set forth that "Many of the great, essential, and unalienable rights of freemen, if not cancelled, were rendered insecure under the Constitution," and in order to quiet the people and prevent "those disorders which must arise under a government not founded in the confidence of the people," application should be made to the new Congress, as soon as it should assemble, "to call a second convention for proposing amendments to it." A substitute providing that Congress should itself be asked to propose the amendments in the regular course was voted down by 85 to 39—more than two to one. Henry, as chairman of the committee appointed for the purpose, drew up the address to the other States transmitting the resolution and it was adopted by a vote of 72 to 50. Corbin, Richard Bland Lee, afterwards a Member of Congress of some prominence, Zachariah Johnson and Turberville led a hopeless minority and realized that they were overmatched. "Would to Heaven you were here," wrote Turberville to Madison the day the resolutions were introduced; and later (November 10) he wrote: "It would glad my very soul to see you in this city before the session rises—your very presence would sink into nonentity almost—those aspiring assassins who now triumphing in their calumnies of absent characters, have belittled themselves even in the estimation of their adherents."*

In the hands of an Anti-Federalist representation in the first congress Henry's resolutions could cause the new Constitution to commit suicide at the outset, Madison said. Henry's next move was to endeavour to secure such a representation.

Edward Carrington paid a visit to Washington in the autumn of 1788, and reported to Madison (October 19) that he found the General much alarmed over the probability that Anti-Federalists would represent the State in the first Senate. Henry and Richard Henry Lee would

* N. Y. Public Library (Lenox) MSS.

stand for election, he presumed, and as it would be impossible to exclude the former, Lee would be carried through by his influence, "Unless a Federalist very well established in the confidence of the people can be opposed. He is decided in his wishes that you may be brought forward on this occasion."*   Madison's own preference was for an election to the House, but when Carrington mentioned this Washington expressed the opinion that Madison could be more useful in the Senate, as there would be much depending on that branch unconnected with the other. Carrington himself said (October 22), that it would be idle to bring forward any other Federalist than Madison. The other candidates were Grayson (in place of Henry who refused to serve) and Richard Henry Lee, and they were elected by a few votes only, many delegates who had voted with Henry voting now for Madison. The vote stood 98 for Lee, 86 for Grayson and 77 for Madison. Madison's friends declared that his strength had grown up to the day of the balloting and that if the election could have been postponed for a few days longer he would have won.†   His defeat was due to the opposition of one man and that man held the Legislature in the hollow of his hand. Henry Lee wrote (Alexandria, November 19, 1788): "Mr. Henry on the floor exclaimed against your political character, and pronounced you unworthy of the confidence of the people in the station of Senator. That your election would terminate in producing rivulets of blood throughout the land."‡   A cruelly false rumour spread that he advocated a surrender of the Mississippi; it originated in a remark of Grayson's which was misinterpreted. Another false report was that he was opposed to amendments to the Constitution under any circumstances, and this was generally believed because it originated with Henry, although Madison took

---

*Dept. of State MSS.

† Turberville to Madison, Nov. 10, 1788, N. Y. Public Library (Lenox) MSS.

‡ Dept. of State MSS.

the trouble to write and. contradict it.   The day after
the election Theodorick Bland congratulated Lee on his
triumph over the "non-emendatorys."* Madison's defeat
was taken much to heart by his friends.   Henry Lee
wrote that his wife shared his mortification, and Rev.
James Madison said he felt it sensibly.   Whatever disappointment Madison himself felt he did not disclose,
and it may be doubted whether he ever expected to
succeed, for he had in estimating political probabilities
a perfectly impartial temperament uninfluenced by his
personal desires.   Even in the Virginia Convention,
when he was in the thickest of the fight, he was able to
go to his room and write letters to Washington estimating
the chances of ratification as impersonally as if he had
been a mere looker on.

Having defeated him for the Senate, Henry tried to
prevent his election to the House.   "The object," wrote
Turberville, November 13, "of the majority of to-day
has been to prevent y^r election in the House of Representatives as demonstrably as if they had affirmed it—
first, by forming a district (as they supposed) of counties
most tainted by Anti-Federalism in which Orange is
situated—& then by confining the choice of the people
to the residents in the particular districts—Mr. Henry
without argument—or answering a single reason urged
ag^t it—launched into a field of Declamation—brought
all the imaginary horrors of the new government upon
us—& carried a decided and large majority with him—
how unfortunate is it for Virginia that you are not on the
floor with us."†

The district thus formed comprised seven counties
besides Orange and the delegates from five of these
had voted against ratification in the recent convention,
while the sixth had divided its vote.   There would then,
apparently, be little probability of Madison's election
from his own district, while the law for the first time

*Bland to R. H. Lee, Nov. 9, 1788. Lee MSS., University of Va.
† N. Y. Public Library (Lenox) MSS.

forbade a candidate from seeking an election in any other district than that in which he lived. This was so radical a departure from the established custom that its constitutionality was not believed in, and several other districts offered to place Madison in nomination,   He decided, however, to stand in his own county. James Monroe was selected as his opponent. "Let me apprize you," wrote Carrington, November 18, 1788, "that you are upon no occasion of a public nature to expect favours from this gentleman."*

The contest was, however, a perfectly friendly one. Madison first met Monroe at Richmond in 1782, and they served in the Congress together. Until the question of the adoption of the Constitution arose their political views had harmonized, and their personal friendship had become permanent. Monroe's opposition to the Constitution had at first not been pronounced, but he was now distinctly of the Anti-Federal party.

That party, however, was not in the ascendancy throughout the State. The Legislature was a body to register Henry's will, but the voters were more independent. Although George Mason thought Monroe would defeat Madison, others who made a closer study of the situation said the district was probably Federal, and that Madison could carry it if he conducted an active campaign in person. Monroe wrote "hundreds of letters," and Henry's statement that Madison had said not a letter of the constitution could be altered was freely repeated to Madison's detriment.† George Nicholas advised him to issue a statement defining his position on this subject, but he declined to do it. That he should be elected was looked upon as all-important by his friends, as the other States would take his defeat as an indication of hostility to the Constitution on the part of Virginia.

* Dept. of State MSS.
† Turberville to Madison, Dec. 14, 1788, N. Y. Public Library (Lenox) MSS.

Madison reached Virginia in the dead of the winter, the election being ordered for February 2, and made a tour of his district addressing the people, he and Monroe often engaging in joint debate. In his old age he described one of the meetings to his friend N. P. Trist:

"We used to meet in days of considerable excitement and address the people on our respective sides; but there *never was an atom of ill-will* between us. On one occasion we met at a church up here (pointing toward the Northwest). There was a *nest of Dutchmen* in that quarter, who generally *went together*, and whose vote might very probably turn the scale. We met there at church. Service was performed, and then they had music with two fiddles. They are remarkably fond of music. When it was all over we addressed these people, and kept them standing in the snow listening to the discussion of constitutional subjects. They stood it out very patiently—seemed to consider it a sort of fight of which they were required to be spectators. I then had to ride in the night, twelve miles to quarters; and got my nose frost-bitten, of which I bear the mark now (touching the end of his nose on the left side)."

This injury he used to point to humorously as the scar of a wound received in battle for his country.

Henry's invention of districting a State for partisan purposes has since been often imitated. It received the name of Gerrymander in 1812, when Gilbert Stuart drew his grotesque map of Massachusetts showing how the districts were marked off when Elbridge Gerry was Governor. It failed its inventor, however, miserably, for Madison was elected over Monroe by a considerable majority, and seven out of nine of his colleagues were also Federalists. There was great joy among the friends of the Constitution, for now it would start fair in the hands of its friends. Rev. James Madison, in sending his congratulations and sympathetic encouragement to his kinsman and namesake, indulged himself in a forecast of the coming grandeur of the country which had the inspiration of true prophecy. "If they [the laws to be enacted] sh^d fortunately, as I trust they will have the evident stamp of wisdom and of Justice, they may gradually eradicate opposition, and then in its stead establish in ye affections of the people, ye strongest attachment to ye General Gov^t, and perhaps within ye Period of one Century, ye World may see a *Republic* composed of at least sixty millions of free men—for such will be the Population of America within that Time, provided it continues nearly at ye rate it hath hitherto observed—The only Chain by which such a multitude will be bound together is that of wise and just Laws. May your Beginning promise such a Blessing."

But in the midst of the triumphant tone sounded by the letters of the Federalists were a number asking Madison's influence with the new Government to procure offices for the writers. In the Constitutional Convention neither he nor any other member foresaw that the unchecked distribution of the lesser offices of Government would prove a greater and more enduring evil than any other that the Government under the Constitution could be called upon to withstand.

CHAPTER XVIII

THE LEADER OF THE HOUSE

ALL the time the Convention was sitting in Philadelphia framing a new charter of government, the Congress provided for under the old charter was in session in New York. Many members were absent, being delegates to both bodies, but routine business was transacted. The attendance was so light that the Secretary was ordered to write to the Governors of the States and ask them to urge the representatives to attend, as important business was to be transacted. The report from Philadelphia might arrive at any moment, but there were fewer members present every day. Sometimes there was a quorum; sometimes only six States were represented, sometimes only five, sometimes only two.*

On September 28 the report from the Constitutional Convention was read. It submitted the Constitution of the United States and requested that it be sent to the several State Executives to be by them submitted "to a convention of delegates, chosen in each State by the people thereof, under the recommendation of its Legislature, for their assent and ratification; and that each convention assenting to and ratifying the same, should give notice thereof in Congress assembled."

If nine States ratified it, Congress was to name a day for the inauguration of the new Government.

Richard Henry Lee, in the ardour of his opposition, offered sundry amendments to the Constitution, hoping that they would be considered by Congress, and those that were agreed to submitted with the Constitution to the

---

* Journals of Congress (Ed., 1801) XII, 53, *et seq.*

several States. This effort to prejudice and embarrass the verdict in the States was not unexpected, and was met with so general an opposition that he abandoned it, the amendments being neither considered nor entered upon the journal. By a unanimous vote the course recommended by the Convention was followed,* but beyond this Congress would not go, and Lee was able to boast that there was "a bare transmission of the Convention plan, without a syllable of approbation, or disapprobation on the part of Congress."

On October 8 Madison returned from Philadelphia and took his seat. He found the attendance so thin that he doubted whether there ever would be a quorum again. February 25 Alexander Hamilton joined him as a member for a brief period, and they were the only men of note in the Congress. In the spring both left and Madison went to Virginia to be present at the elections for the first House of Representatives. In July he came back. The congress languished during the summer and the light of its life feebly flickered in the autumn. November 3 only two members attended. November 15 Cyrus Griffin of Virginia was the only member present; from then on a few members would have their names recorded as present each day. On March 2 Philip Pell of New York attended alone, and the Congress was dead. It never adjourned, and had no formal dissolution. The faithful Secretary, Charles Thomson, wrote the last entry in the Journal, and he and the forgotten Mr. Pell were the sole spectators of the end.† People had forgotten that the Congress still lingered, for attention was concentrated upon the new Congress called to meet March 4th.

To appreciate the importance of this, the first session of the first Congress, it is only necessary to reflect upon the force of precedence in the affairs of men and especially in government affairs. How the new Government was started would determine how it would be conducted for

---

* Journals of Congress (Ed., 1801) XII, 110, *et seq.*
† Id., XIII, 193.

years to come, and its duration would be influenced by the trend it received in the beginning. Serious blunders would be costly indeed, for they might cause the experiment to end quickly or even violently.

The first communication received by the Senate from the House of Representatives was delivered by Madison, and stated that the House had agreed that the Senate should notify the President and Vice-President of their election. The day before, April 6, the arrival of Richard Henry Lee, Madison's successful rival for Senatorial honours, had made a quorum.* Yet in the next five years, until 1794 when the Senate ceased to sit in secret session, that august chamber was as silent as the grave, exerting little influence upon the people, and those who served in it were buried from public sight, while the public interest was entirely in the House. In preventing Madison from being a Senator, Patrick Henry had unwittingly placed the man whom he dreaded in a position of real power.

The House had secured a quorum five days before the Senate and on April 2 named its first committee, that on rules, with Madison as a member. On April 8 the House resolved itself into Committee of the Whole on the state of the Union, and the first member to address the chair was Madison. His programme for the work of the body of which he was the undisputed leader included three things of pressing necessity: to provide revenue with which to run the Government, to create the necessary executive machinery, and to submit amendments to the Constitution which would unite the people in its support by satisfying the most serious objections which had been made to it.

The revenue bill which he introduced took as a system ready at hand, which could be quickly passed, the old impost measure of 1783, which had already been fully discussed and generally acquiesced in.† It contemplated

* Annals of Congress, 1st Cong., 18.
† Rives III, 193, *et seq.*

specific duties on importations of liquors, molasses, wines, tea, pepper, sugar, cocoa, and coffee, and ad valorem duties on all other articles. He added to the bill three paragraphs providing for discriminating tonnage dues on shipping,—a low rate for ships built and owned in the United States, a higher rate for ships belonging to the subjects of Powers with which we had treaties of commerce and a still higher rate for ships belonging to the subjects of Powers with which we had no treaties.

The day after he presented his bill, (April 9), Fitzsimmons of Pennsylvania moved to add a few manufactured articles for specific duties, and Hartley of the same State in supporting his colleague said the object was to encourage home manufactures, which had sprung up since 1783 and were rapidly increasing.* To this encouragement Madison did not object. In the Constitutional Convention, in discussing the question of export duties, he said they might be necessary, "and for the same purposes as the regulation of imports, viz: for revenue, *domestic manufactures*, and providing equitable regulations from other nations." He now stated his position more fully on this subject and did not, in fact, deviate from it afterwards. "I own myself the friend," he declared, "to a very free system of commerce, and hold it as a truth, that commercial shackles are generally unjust, oppressive, and impolitic; it is also a truth, that if industry and labour are left to take their own course, they will generally be directed to those objects which are the most productive, and this in a more certain and direct manner than the wisdom of the most enlightened Legislature could point out." There could be no profit, he said, in a man furnishing himself with everything he needed; he exchanged with other men. In the same way town and country exchanged their products to mutual advantage, and one part of a country with another, and one nation with another.

* Annals of Congress, 1st Cong., 105, *et seq.*

Some manufactures would spring up naturally; there were others already established with State assistance, which ought not to be allowed to perish for want of a continuance of protection under the new Government, and he was willing to make them an exception to his general rule. An embargo in time of war was another exception which required no defence. The argument that a country should produce everything it needed, so as to be independent in time of war, was, he thought, overdrawn. We were now a nation, and could obtain supplies abroad when we needed them. But a discriminating tonnage tax was a different matter, because other nations discriminated against us, and if we treated all equally we were in effect discriminating against our own ships. Incidentally, we should encourage means of transportation, and enlarge our markets.*

Two days after this speech, April 11, Smith of Maryland presented a petition from tradesmen, manufacturers and others in Baltimore, reciting the prevailing poverty, and praying that duties be laid on all foreign articles that could be made in this country, so as to give a preference to American labour.† Several other petitions of similar purport followed. Fisher Ames of Massachusetts introduced into Madison's schedule wool cards, because they were "manufactured to the eastward as good and cheap as the imported ones."‡ A few days later Clymer of Pennsylvania showed how a steel furnace was in progress in Philadelphia, and with a little aid from the Legislature had made three hundred tons of steel in two years and now made two hundred and thirty tons annually; with further encouragement it would supply the American market.¶ Steel was then put in the schedule without serious opposition. Theodorick Bland, an extreme Anti-Federalist, objected, be-

* Annals of Congress, 1st Cong., 210, *et seq.*
† Id., 115,
‡ Id., 124.
¶ Id., 148.

cause "then certainly you lay a tax on the whole community, in order to put the money in the pockets of a few, whenever you burden the importation with a heavy impost."*

He did not raise the Constitutional argument against protective duties, nor was it heard at this session of Congress, although eight of the fifty-nine members had served in the Constitutional Convention. The debate finally centred about the items in the schedule laying a duty on rum and molasses from which rum is made. Madison desired to avoid an excise tax, which he knew would be unpopular, and yet indirectly collect it by a duty on molasses, and a higher duty on rum, of which a great deal was imported from the West Indies, the difference in duty being intended as a protection to the American rum manufacturer.† Massachusetts in particular, and New England generally, vigorously resisted the proposition. Goodhue of Massachusetts said rum was a necessity of life among the poorer classes. To make it Massachusetts imported from 30,000 to 40,000 hogsheads of molasses annually. Ames said the tax would be paid almost exclusively by Massachusetts.‡

April 21 Madison's proposition for discriminating tonnage dues came up, and he explained its provisions.¶ The tax was intended for political purposes primarily; it was a revenue measure only incidentally. The commerce between Great Britain and America was much greater than that between America and all other countries. The actual figures as furnished by the Treasury Department nine months later (December, 1790,) ‖ showed that from 1789 to October, 1790, about 766,000 tons of shipping paid tonnage dues, of which the United States had, including vessels in the coastwise trade, five hundred and eight and eight-tenths thousand and Great

* Annals of Congress, 1st Cong., 168.

† Id., 129.
‡ Id., 138.
¶ Id., 181.
‖ Dept. of State MSS.

Britain two hundred and fifty-five and two-tenths, the other nations having an insignificant amount, France leading with thirteen and four-tenths. The American tonnage was thus nearly two-thirds of the whole, the British nearly one-third, and the rest about one-twentieth. This made the British six times as great as all the rest of the foreign tonnage, yet Great Britain utterly refused to negotiate a commercial treaty with us. An advantage over Great Britain, Madison agreed, should be given to those countries with which we had treaties, notably France. Perhaps Great Britain would then come to terms. At any rate the deplorably one-sided conditions in force should be stopped. American ships were absolutely excluded from British West Indian ports, and into other British ports they might enter only if they carried nothing but American products, and yet British ships entered our ports on an equality with American ships and might carry the products of the world. Madison declared he believed in freedom of commerce, but when it had, by force of circumstances, fallen into the hands of one country, artificial measures were necessary to place it where it naturally belonged, and he wished to see our shipping increase, furnishing a nursery for seamen and a foundation for an American navy. Discriminating duties, he declared, were a great power, which ought to be invoked in the beginning. If the experiment could be tried without injustice, he would like to see the importation of West Indian rum forbidden until we should be allowed to carry to the West Indies, in our own vessels, the produce which necessity obliged the West Indies to take from us. He would have the Government show the power and the will to injure, and thereby compel foreign nations to treat us with that respect which our former feebleness had failed to command. He would tax brandy lightly because it came from France, with which nation we had a treaty, and would prepare for a commercial war with Great Britain. Otherwise she would shut us out com-

pletely from her ports and make us tributary to her.
"The produce of this country," he said, "is more necessary to the rest of the world than that of other countries
is to America. If we were disposed to hazard the experiment of interdicting the intercourse between us and
the Powers not in alliance, we should have overtures
of the most advantageous kind tendered by those nations."*

His theory of government was thus made plain
enough. By a system of commercial retaliation and
reciprocity he would render the probability of war as
remote as possible. He did not succeed in his programme. The impost measure was passed and became
a law, but the Senate rejected the discriminating tonnage dues, and the House was compelled to yield in
conference.

The revenue bill being out of the way Madison introduced resolutions to establish three executive departments of the Government,—Foreign Affairs, Treasury,
and War,—the Secretary of each to be removable by
the President.† The interest of the debate was on the
question of removability. There being no word of
guidance in the Constitution, four theories were advanced: (1) that Congress had the power to confer
the right of removal upon the President, (2) that a removal could be accomplished only by impeachment proceedings, (3) that the Senate must advise and consent
to a removal, as it was required to do to an appointment,
and (4) that the President already had the power of
removal. The convention that framed the Constitution
had never considered the question. The founders of
the Government believed that those who filled executive
offices would constitute a set of permanent officials, not
changing as the President changed. Madison thought
the President should have the power and responsibility
of removals, and that the Senate should have as little

* Annals of Congress, 1st Cong., 204, *et seq.*
† Id., 368, *et seq.*

agency in executive matters as possible. The President would, he said, be restrained from removing worthy officials by fear of the public odium he would incur, by the restriction on filling their places which the Senate would exert, and by his own impeachability for misconduct. An unjust removal would constitute such misconduct in Madison's opinion.* No one then foresaw that under the third administration of the Government the party to which Madison belonged would be clamouring for the removal from office of those who belonged to the opposite party, and that no serious obstacles would lie in the way of the use of the public offices as spoils of party warfare. Had the framers of the Constitution conceived such a condition of affairs to be possible they would have devised measures to prevent it, and the opponents of the adoption of the Constitution, if they had foreseen it, would not have overlooked the omission in their arguments against the Constitution. The spoils system was an unthought of evil when Madison introduced his strengthening amendments to the Constitution in the first Congress.

On May 4, Madison gave notice that he would soon bring up the subject of these amendments,† but when he introduced them on June 8 there was strong opposition to considering them, until the Government should be more thoroughly organized. He admitted the reasonableness of the objection, so far as it applied to taking action on the amendments, but insisted upon the importance of putting them before the House and the people at once. He would have preferred their consideration as the first business of Congress, because then its other measures would have been more generously supported. He wished to make friends for the new Government, disarm the opposition in North Carolina

* " The Department of State; its History and Functions" (1893) 44, *et seq.* Madison to Randolph, June 17, 1789, "Works" (Cong. Ed.) I, 476.

† Annals of Congress, 1st Cong., 247, *et seq.*

and Rhode Island, and bring those States into the Union. Only eleven States had ratified the Constitution, and five of these—Massachusetts, South Carolina, New Hampshire, Virginia and New York—had expressed in their acts of ratification a desire for amendments and a confidence that they would be made. North Carolina had refused to ratify until the amendments were made. Not only, therefore, was the Union incomplete, but in every State which had ratified the Constitution there was a hostile minority and in some States its proportions were considerable. He himself thought amendments providing for greater security of rights could be engrafted upon the Constitution without marring it. Above all things it was necessary that it should have behind it a people united in its support. Many people, he said, opposed it because the President had no council, because the Senate had judicial power in impeachment trials and was in other respects so powerful, and because generally the Federal Government had taken too much authority from the States. These objections were ill-founded and he would not yield to them. In meeting others which appeared to him to rest upon a valid foundation he considered that he would fulfil a tacit promise made to the ratifying conventions by the friends of the Constitution that amendments would be offered. He, therefore, proposed nine, each one of which he said was proper in itself, or because there was a wide popular demand for it. These amendments included the less radical propositions of the five ratifying States which had demanded amendments. Two of them were not adopted by the Legislatures of two-thirds of the States —that requiring a greater representation in the House, and that forbidding an increase by any Congress of its own emoluments. His proposed amendment forbidding an appeal to the Supreme Court in suits involving less than a certain sum of money and requiring that a fact triable by jury, according to common law, should not be otherwise examined into, was thrown out by the

Senate. His other amendments, guaranteeing religious freedom, freedom of the press, the right of bearing arms, trial by jury, etc., freedom from unreasonable search, from the quartering of troops in time of peace, from excessive bail, and reserving to the States and the people powers not granted by the Constitution, were agreed to by Congress, submitted to the States, and incorporated into the fundamental law.

During the debate on the amendments some members privately discussed a project for repealing the Constitution and adopting an improved one, but there were only a few opponents of the Constitution in Congress, the real strength of the party lying within the States, where they were hatching measures to destroy the new system of government before it could well get into operation. The Virginia Legislature at Patrick Henry's instance called upon the other States to join in demanding a second convention to consider amendments, and the day after Madison's notice that he would introduce amendments to Congress (May 5) Bland presented the Virginia petition asking for the convention and moved its reference to the Committee of the Whole. Boudinot of New Jersey, supported by Madison, raised the point that, as the Constitution provided that amendments must originate in Congress or be requested by two-thirds of the States, the House could not properly consider one petition. Bland was forced to acquiesce and to content himself with simply having the petition entered upon the Journal.*

Madison's prompt action in favour of amendments was received with great favour in Virginia where it reduced opposition to the Constitution to a single point, that of the power of laying direct taxes; and Henry Lee warned Madison that it would not be safe to exercise this power. Before the amendments were offered the opposition had been so radical that there were murmurings against Grayson, Bland and other Anti-Federalists

* Annals of Congress, 1st Cong., 251s.

in Congress for permitting anything to be done in advance of the desired amendments.*   In North Carolina,
also, the effect was excellent, and gave the needed
strength to the Federalists in the new convention† called
for November, 1789, when the Constitution was ratified
and North Carolina joined the rest of the States, instead
of attracting some of them to leave the Union and join
her, which at one time seemed possible. The appearance of the amendments killed beyond hope of resuscita-
tion the efforts to secure the second Constitutional Convention, ostensibly to improve the work of the first, but
in reality to undo it.   Those who favoured it were Patrick
Henry, George Clinton and other opponents of the adoption of the Constitution, but New York alone responded
favourably to the Virginia invitation. The Virginia
Legislature of 1790 had as members Edmund Randolph,
Henry Lee and John Marshall, and was no longer a body
to register Patrick Henry's will.‡ He realized that
the Constitution which he had opposed so bitterly was
now too strongly intrenched to yield to attack.   Accordingly he left the field to the victors and soon afterwards
changed his own position completely, becoming in the
closing years of his life as extreme a consolidationist as
he had in the trying period of the adoption of the Constitution been an advocate of State sovereignty.

* Dept. of State MSS.
† Id., W. R. Davie to Madison, June 10, 1789.
‡ See Henry's "Life of Patrick Henry."

CHAPTER XIX

AUGUST 28, 1789, a memorial and petition from public creditors in Pennsylvania praying that provision be made for the public debt was presented to Congress and referred to a committee of which Madison was chairman. September 10, he reported that it highly concerned the honour and integrity of the United States to make an early provision in favour of the creditors of the Union, and that the House ought to take the subject up early at its next session. September 21, the Secretary of the Treasury was requested to prepare a plan for supporting the public credit. The next session began January 4, and on January 14 Alexander Hamilton's great report was received. It treated the subject exhaustively and with consummate power. It recommended the funding of the domestic debt and the acceptance of the certificates of indebtedness issued by the old Government from those who held them, without reference to any equitable rights in their increased value by those to whom they had originally been issued and who had parted with them. The report provided for the assumption by the Federal Government of the debts contracted by the States during the Revolutionary War. A well-funded national debt was described as a desirable asset to government, as it served most of the purposes of money in exchanges and was an addition to the active capital of the nation. It had in addition a political virtue as its tendency was "to cement more closely the Union of the States."

The debt of the United States comprised the foreign debt, which with interest amounted to nearly $12,000,-

ooo; the liquidated domestic debt, being certificates of indebtedness for services rendered, money loaned and supplies furnished during the war, amounting to about $40,000,000; and the unliquidated domestic debt made up of Continental bills of credit, which at the rate of exchange agreed upon by Congress (40 to 1) amounted to $2,000,000 more; the whole debt being about $54,000,-ooo. The State debts to be assumed were estimated at $25,000,000 principal and interest. On the subject of the foreign debt there was no difference of opinion. It should be paid according to agreement, and provision for that purpose was in due season passed by a unanimous vote. But the question of the domestic debt allowed for a wide difference of opinion. The disordered condition of the national finances had offered a fine field for speculation, and the certificates issued by the old Congress had been bought and sold upon a speculative basis. If Hamilton's plan was adopted these certificates and the evidences of State indebtedness would be worth more than they had ever been before, and there was consequently a rush to buy them from those who, because of their distance from New York, were ignorant of the prospects of their enhanced value. When Hamilton's report came up for debate January 28, Jackson of Georgia said:

"Since this report has been read in this House a spirit of havoc, speculation and ruin has arisen, and been cherished by people who had an access to the information [by living at the capital] the report contained that would have made a Hastings blush to have been connected with, though long inured to preying on the vitals of his fellowmen. Three vessels, Sir, have sailed within a fortnight from this port, freighted for speculation; they are intended to purchase up the State and other securities in the hands of the uninformed though honest citizens of North Carolina, South Carolina and Georgia."*

There was no denial of the charge. Boudinot ad-

* Annals of Congress, 1st. Cong., 1223, *et seq.*

mitted that "speculation had risen to an alarming height," and it was believed that some Members of Congress were themselves speculating in the probable rise of the value of certificates. Madison himself, who was slow to attribute corruption to others, believed that such was the case.

On February 11 he made a speech defining his position. He said the domestic debt was a supreme obligation upon the new Government which took upon itself the full responsibility for all acts of the old Government. The only question was to whom the payment was due. There were the original creditors who had never alienated their securities, the present holders of these securities, and the intermediate holders through whose hands the securities had passed. The last named he would not consider, as it would be impossible to determine who they were and how much they had lost; moreover, they had acquired and parted with the securities on their own responsibility and gained by the speculation. The two classes of real concern were the original and the present holders. The former had never been paid the value of their service or of the property advanced by them. The certificates were forced upon them, and they were compelled to accept them without regard to their depreciation. We must, however, admit the claims of the holders of the certificates. But it would obviously be unfair to pay both the original and present holders, so he would pay the present holders the highest market price and the balance between this amount and the face value of the certificates he would pay to the original holders. This was a simple scheme. It would only be necessary to know who the present holders of the certificates were, and who were the original holders, which the office documents would show.

In taking this ground he was compelled to defend himself against the charge of inconsistency, for in 1783, in the address to the States on the funding of the debt, he had rejected any distinction between original and purchasing holders of public securities, but he insisted that at that time the transfers had been confined to one limited class of certificates and that the original holders had suffered little loss. It was a different proposition when the transferred certificates were a large proportion of the whole debt and the loss to the original holders had been enormous.

Boudinot replied with a few facts which really demolished Madison's argument. He said that when a man parted with his certificate he put another man in his shoes, and there was no reason why the Government should disown the act of the party himself. Logically carried out, Madison's plan would compel the Government to go back and compensate all who had received Continental money and parted with it for less than it was now worth. Moreover, the plan was impossible of execution as the issuing office did not have all the names of the persons for whom the certificates were really issued. For convenience they had frequently been made out in the names of people who got them for others. Many of them were thus issued in the names of the clerks in the loan office, and it often happened that a man going to the loan office carried money for his neighbours and had the certificates made in his own name. Boudinot had himself once got $10,000 of certificates in this way for ten different people, and it all stood in his name.

A few days later Sedgwick pointed out that if the original holders of the certificates really had an equitable right in their enhanced value they could sue and recover in the courts. The reasoning was one-sided and against Madison, and the funding plan as outlined by Hamilton was agreed to by a safe majority.

That part of Hamilton's scheme which provided for Federal assumption of State debts aroused a far deeper and more acrimonious opposition. The argument in favour of the measure was: the States had taken up arms in a common cause in the Revolution and had been bound to contribute to the best of their ability. Debts contracted by an individual State were thus the same as if contracted by all. Those States which had been exposed to the enemy's ravages had been forced to make greater exertions than the others, and by equal taxation all should help to pay. As matters stood, the sources of revenue of some States were much less than they had been before the new Government was adopted. Massachusetts and South Carolina, for instance, would find it impossible to pay their debts now that they were deprived of the right of levying import duties. Everybody admitted that the debts incurred by the States must be paid, and it could be done more economically by one government and one set of revenue officers than by two sets.

The argument against the measure was: the debts had been incurred by the States wholly upon their own credit and no more than this stood behind the securities when they were marketed. If it had been intended that these separate debts should be assumed by the new Government the Constitution would have so stated, as it had been done with reference to Continental debts. A general assumption would be unjust, because the States which had made effective efforts to provide for their debts would be obliged to shoulder the burdens of other States which had made less efforts. An increase of taxation would be inevitable. As the assumption was not expected by the creditors it had not been generally demanded, South Carolina being the only State which had asked for it.* A list of the debts to be assumed showed that half of the aggregate amount came from Massachusetts, Connecticut and South Carolina.

The arguments for and against the assumption continued to be repeated for weeks, and strongest among the opponents was Madison, who declared his unqualified dissent to Hamilton's proposition that a public debt was a benefit. He thought it was an evil to be got rid of as soon as possible.

* See Tucker's "Life of Jefferson," I, 319, *et seq.*

March 12 the assumption proposition won in Committee of the Whole by a majority of five votes only, and was reported favourably to the House; but before the House took it up on March 23, the new North Carolina members arrived and were admitted. They voted against the assumption, and a motion to recommit was carried by a majority of two votes. The next day the assumption party succeeded in having the funding provision also recommitted, their object being to keep the two measures together and help the unpopular assumption scheme by the less unpopular funding scheme. April 12 the assumption was defeated by a vote of 21 to 29. Its friends then resorted to dilatory tactics, and for a time prevented the House from going into committee. An attempt of Roger Sherman to secure acceptance of a modified form of assumption was defeated, and a bill was ordered to be brought in providing for the foreign and domestic debt without it. The new bill was reported May 6, taken up in Committee of the Whole, May 19, and after several days' debate Gerry moved as an amendment an assumption clause. The assumption had been accepted once and defeated twice, and it was now thrown out again, the bill being passed without it June 2. It had, however, been offered in a separate form the day before and laid on the table. Among those who were opposed to the assumption were four members who deserve to be noticed — Alexander White and Richard Bland Lee from Virginia, and Daniel Carroll and George Gale from Maryland. White was the most active of these opponents and introduced a resolution calling upon the Secretary of the Treasury to report to Congress the ways and means by which he expected to provide for the $25,000,000 of State debts he was so anxious to assume.* The motion was intended to cause delay or embarrassment to the assumption party. Madison supported it, but it was defeated by a tie vote of 25 to 25. White came from Rappahannock County, through which the Potomac

* Annals of Congress, 1st Cong., 1404.

River runs, and his colleague Lee from Alexandria, the chief port on the Potomac, while Daniel Carroll came from the Maryland side of the same river.* Gale was an obscure member who had apparently no personal interest in the river. On July 26, the question of the assumption was before the House again, and Madison, of course, voted against it, but when the vote was announced, it appeared that White, Lee, Carroll and Gale had voted with the assumption party, and the measure was carried by 34 votes to 28. It was by no new argument that this result had been brought about, nor had their opinions changed with their votes. Influences had been brought to bear upon them outside of Congress, and they gained by changing their votes something they wished for more than they wished to defeat the assumption proposition.

The opposition to the funding scheme came chiefly from the South, and there the Federal assumption of State debts was generally disapproved of, except in the State of South Carolina, whose debt was so large that its assumption by the general Government was an alternative for its non-payment. The Legislature accordingly instructed the members to vote for the measure, but the instructions were unnecessary to William Smith and William Tudor Tucker, the two members who represented the broad Federalism then dominant in South Carolina. Ædanus Burke, the third member, represented the extreme type of Anti-Federalists, and when the bill first came up he promptly expressed his alarm at "the political consequences" to the State Governments of such a measure, but he changed his attitude the next day in view of the exigencies of his State.†

In Virginia the funding provision was not generally liked, and the assumption provision was almost universally condemned. Edward Carrington, who had been

---

* This was Daniel Carroll of Upper Marlboro, who should not be confounded, as he usually is, with Daniel Carroll of Duddington, whose lands were embraced in the District of Columbia.

† Annals of Congress, 1st Cong.

one of Madison's staunchest supporters in favour of the formation and adoption of the Constitution, and who was always a strong Federalist, wrote to Madison from Richmond March 27, 1790, that he did not agree with him about the payment of certificates. It was a melancholy truth, he said, that the public rewards with respect to the public debt had been transferred from those who had earned them to those who had paid but little for them. The purchase had often been made "under a dishonourable conduct," but between the public and the original creditors there was no fraud. There was neither law nor equity for paying to another any part of a claim which the present possessor openly and fairly acquired. The soldiers who were the chief sufferers were not now complaining. The assumption proposition, on the other hand, Carrington thought, was a wise measure on principle, but an iniquitous one under actual conditions, and involved a grievous burden on those States which had paid part of their debt. Later (April 7), Carrington reported that the assumption measure was generally unsatisfactory. The Anti-Federalists were naturally opposed to it, and so were many of the Federalists, who considered it as leading to consolidation. It would have a bad effect in alienating the people from the Constitution. Governor Beverly Randolph wrote, July 12, 1790, that it was thought it would produce "a perfectly consolidated government," and a great ferment would result. He believed not a single advocate could be found to support it.*   Bland voted in favor of it, having completely changed his views,† and was liberally censured in the State in consequence. The rest of the Virginia delegation stood solidly against it. Edmund Pendleton, Edmund Randolph and James Monroe were also opposed to it. Rev. James Madison, of William and Mary, wrote congratulating Madison on his proposition concerning the certificates.‡   Henry Lee thought

* Dept. of State MSS.
† Henry's "Henry," III, 418.
‡ Dept. of State MSS.

the bill was "abhorrent to political wisdom and not strictly consonant to justice." He was unalterably opposed to a funding system. National debts gave an undue control to a moneyed class. Madison's motion for the payment of certificates was, he said, pleasing to the country interests and displeasing to those of the towns. As the debate progressed Lee became more pronounced in his views. April 3 he wrote that all of Patrick Henry's dark predictions about the Constitution were coming true. He would rather see the Union dissolve than submit to "the rule of a fixed insolent Northern majority." "Is your love for the Constitution," he asked, "so ardent, as to induce you to adhere to it, though it should produce ruin to your native country?"* George Nicholas said the assumption was unjust and exceeded the power of Congress.

Jefferson arrived too late in New York to take part in the battle then in progress. Probably on Madison's representation he was opposed to the bill as it stood, but he did not take much interest in the pending questions. "I do not pretend to be very competent to their decision," he wrote George Mason, June 15, 1790.† He concluded that the acceptance of a modified assumption bill was preferable to the complete loss of a funding measure; it was certainly preferable to a crash of the Government which was threatened.‡

The Virginia Legislature taking the bill into consideration after it had passed presented the first remonstrance of a State against a Federal act. It was written by Henry¶ and came from a committee of eleven members, seven of whom had advocated the ratification of the Constitution in the convention of 1788, the chairman being Madison's coadjutor, Francis Corbin.‖ The remon-

* Dept. of State MSS.
† Writings (Ford), V, 184.
‡ To Thomas Mann Randolph, June 20, 1790, "Writings" (Ford) V, 186.
¶ Henry's "Henry," II, 456.
‖ Rives, III, 149, *et seq.*

strance denounced the funding act as against good policy, justice and the principles of the Constitution. The restriction against the redeemability of the public debt would create a moneyed class against an agricultural class and was borrowed from England. The assumption act was denounced as unjust to the States which had provided for their debts, and especially to Virginia, which had "redeemed a large proportion of her debt by the collection of heavy taxes levied on her citizens," and would now have an additional burden laid upon her. This measure also transcended the fairly-interpreted powers of Congress under the Constitution. Congress was urged to modify the funding provision and repeal the assumption provision. The resolutions coming after Congress had acted were not entirely approved by the Federalists in the State.

CHAPTER XX

THE Constitution gave authority to Congress to accept from the State or States ceding it a district not to exceed ten miles square, to be exclusively under the jurisdiction of the National Government, for a permanent seat of Government. The provision came from a resolution offered in the Convention on August 3 by Madison that "the Legislature shall at their first assembling determine on a place at which their future sessions shall be held." In his speech supporting the resolution Madison said it would be more important under the new Government than it had been under the old, that the capital be in a central location, because the new Government would be more numerous, and as it would exercise many functions not now pertaining to the Federal Government more people would be obliged to resort to the capital than had hitherto done so. The first Congress under the Constitution was, therefore, in a measure obliged to take up the question of locating a new capital as one of its manifest duties. How the question became involved with that of making provision for the public debt, so that the settlement of the one meant the settlement of the other, is a story of trading of votes in Congress and of a bargain struck between Alexander Hamilton and Thomas Jefferson. The actuating motive of the voting was a desire to secure sectional advantages, and this desire was so apparent that it is clear that there was little of a broad national spirit among the members of the first Congress. To them neither the assumption of the State debts nor the choice of a site for the capital involved any deep principle. The assumption was a part of Hamilton's carefully laid plan for arranging the national finances and it was necessary for the completion of the plan that it be carried. But its most earnest supporters were Representatives of those States which would suffer a grievous financial burden if it failed, and its most earnest opponents were from the States which would gain if it failed. The Constitutional argument was not seriously invoked and influenced no votes against it; it was regarded as a measure of expediency by its friends and opponents. In the form in which it appeared it was, however, a new question, whereas the choice of a permanent site for a capital was an old question which had been fought over for years.

In the autumn of 1783 mutinous soldiers of the army hooted at the doors of Congress and demanded their pay, and as the authorities of Philadelphia were unable to afford protection the Government fled to Princeton. This humiliating incident had borne in upon Congress the necessity of having a home of its own, under its exclusive jurisdiction, and there then began a struggle to secure the capital of the United States which continued with little abatement for the next seven years.

New York offered a tract of land at Kingston. The Virginia delegates promptly wrote to the Governor of their State proposing that joint action be taken by Virginia and Maryland to offer a site on the Potomac River near Georgetown. The prevailing sentiment was then, however, in favor of two capitals, and examination was made of sites near the falls of the Delaware and the falls of the Potomac. Until buildings should be erected it was proposed that Congress sit alternately at Trenton and Annapolis.* Jefferson favoured a floating capital and in writing to Monroe, June 17, 1785,† said that Congress could go to Georgetown from New York and then somewhere else. The idea of two capitals was soon

---

* Sumner's "Financiers and Finances of the American Revolution," II, 235, *et seq.*

† "Writings" (Ford) IV.

abandoned, however, and on December 20, 1784, a resolution passed in favor of erecting buildings at only one place.   Three days later it was voted to go to New York for the present, the result being accomplished by a union of New England and New York members.   February 10, 1785, it was agreed to lay out a town for a permanent residence on the Delaware and commissioners were appointed for the purpose.   They took no steps, however, but merely arranged for the accommodation of Congress at New York.

In Virginia there had been a movement in favor of Williamsburg, and the Rev. James Madison, urged its consideration upon his kinsman, who, however, advocated the joint offer of a Potomac site by Virginia and Maryland, and wrote July, 1783, recommending that Maryland abandon her efforts for Annapolis.   May 10, 1787, a few days before the Constitutional Convention met, Richard Henry Lee offered this resolution in Congress:

"Whereas, The convenient and due administration of the Government of the United States requires, that a permanent situation most central to all parts of the Union be established for holding the sessions of Congress; Resolved, That the Board of Treasury take measures for erecting the necessary public buildings for the accommodation of Congress at Georgetown, on Potowmack River, so soon as the soil and jurisdiction of the said town are obtained, and that on the completion of the said buildings, Congress adjourn their sessions to the said Federal town."*   Congress declined by a vote of five States to four to take the subject up.   After the ratification of the Constitution the idea of starting the new Government in New York was bitterly opposed by the Virginians. New York was, Madison said,† too remote to both South and West.   The West was already prejudiced against the East because of its advocacy of the abandonment

* Journals of Congress (Ed. 1801) XII, 51.
† "Works of Madison" (Cong. Ed.) I, 409, *et seq.*

of the navigation of the Mississippi. It was being tampered with by Spain and must be placated instead of being offended by a choice of the enemy's country for the new capital. The Southern prejudice against the East, also, would be fed, and the Anti-Federalists' statement that the East would have a preponderating influence under the new Government would be believed. There was, he added, another and a highly important reason against sitting in New York. The first year or two of the new Government would see all the great arrangements made affecting its tone for all time, and these would be influenced by its location. Philadelphia was better than New York. If the new Government met in the former city a deliberate choice of a permanent seat might be made, but Southern and Western members coming all the way to New York would be apt to vote precipitately for a change which, he feared, would be to a site north of the Potomac. He was positive this was the hope of the advocates of New York. The only chance for the Potomac was to form a coalition between the Southern and Eastern States, or secure a delay for a few years, by which time the growing Western population would make its voice heard for the Potomac. A vigorous protest against New York was accordingly made in the last hours of the Congress under the Confederation.* A motion by Williamson of North Carolina, in favour of some place farther south than New York was lost, and by one vote Philadelphia shared the same fate. By the same slender majority Baltimore was selected, but set aside August 16, and New York substituted. The argument advanced for New York was simply that the new Government ought to be free to choose a place of residence for itself. August 26, Wilmington, Delaware, was proposed and rejected, Madison voting against it, but on September 2 he voted for Lancaster, Pa. The next day he voted against Annapolis, and September 2 seconded Edward Carrington's motion for a more central

* Journals of Congress (Ed. 1801) XIII, 62, *et seq.*

point than New York. It became apparent that the
new Government would sit in New York or not sit at
all; for while there was a sufficient number of votes to
prevent the selection of that town they could not be
concentrated on any other place. The opposition yielded
and New York was selected. Madison thought the
result fatal to the prospects of the Potomac, and predicted that the site ultimately chosen would not be
farther south than the Delaware or Susquehanna.

When the new Congress met Alexander White of
Virginia laid before it on May 15, 1789, an act passed
by the General Assembly of his State, December 27, 1788,
offering ten miles square of any portion of its territory
for a new Federal district. The next day Seney of
Maryland offered a similar act from Maryland, both
States having acted in the hope that the site selected
might include the soil on either side of the Potomac
River.*

On August 27, Scott of Pennsylvania offered a reso-
lution† that the permanent seat of Congress ought to
be at the territorial centre of wealth and population and
convenient to the navigation of the Atlantic, as well
as easy of access to the Western country.‡ This he
meant as a description of the banks of the Susquehanna,
and September 3, Goodhue of Massachusetts offered
a supplementary resolution in favor of remaining in
New York until removing to that river. It was hoped
to thus secure the support of New York to the Susquehanna, by leaving the capital at New York longer than
it reasonably had a right to expect. Only the Eastern
States were contented to meet in New York, and it was
conceded that it could not possibly be chosen as the
permanent capital. Any place in the East was out of
the question for geographical reasons, so the Eastern

---

* "Locating the Capital," Annual Rept. Am. Hist. Assoc'n. 1895,
289.

† Rives, III, 50, *et seq.*

‡ Annals of Congress, 1st Cong., 786.

members were free to cast their votes as they might advance their interests in other matters before Congress.

Richard Bland Lee, seconded by Daniel Carroll, offered a substitute for Goodhue's motion, providing for the selection of a site most convenient to the Atlantic and to the Western country. In order to attract the Eastern members Madison suggested that the adoption of this motion need not interfere with the ultimate consideration of Goodhue's proposition,* but it was in reality intended to prejudice it, because if it were adopted it would be shown that the banks of the Potomac was the only site satisfying the description. Lee's motion was lost by a vote of two to one, and defeat stared the Potomac party in the face. A combination had been formed by the East and Pennsylvania, and Madison declared that the question had evidently been settled out of doors. His pleadings for delay—even for a day—in order to present reasons against choosing the Susquehanna were disregarded, the House refusing to postpone the question by a vote of 27 to 23. Madison declared the Potomac party faced "a determined and silent majority." Burke of South Carolina said: "A league has been formed between the Northern States and Pennsylvania." Wadsworth of Connecticut wanted to finish the business. He said he "must either give his vote now or submit to more bargaining. He was willing that the whole business of bargaining should be exposed; he would not excuse himself; he did not dare to go to the Potomac. He feared that the whole of New England would consider the Union destroyed. Since the matter had been so prematurely brought on, since members had been forced and, as it were, dragged by the throat to this business, he hoped it was now finished." In an exceedingly angry mood the House adjourned.

The complaints of the Southern members at the bargaining were due to their chagrin at the failure of their own efforts to form a coalition. The Eastern and North-

---

* Annals of Congress, 1st Cong., 840, *et seq.*

ern members had in the beginning of the session endeavored to decide on a location, but disagreeing had made overtures to the South by offering the Susquehanna if Congress might remain for the present at New York. If the South would not agree to this they might expect Trenton to be chosen.* The threat was ineffective and the South offered the temporary location to Philadelphia in return for Pennsylvania's support of the Potomac for a permanent site. The combination promised to be effected when there was an unexpected reunion of Pennsylvania, New York and the East on the basis of fixing the permanent seat on the Susquehanna.

Discussion was resumed in the House, September 4, and the question of the central location of the proposed sites was debated, Madison arguing that the point was of the utmost consequence because as many people as possible should be made friendly to the Government by its proximity to them. He admitted that by the test of the present population of the country the centre was on the Susquehanna, but insisted that it was certainly moving toward the Southwest. He proposed that the question be narrowed to the Susquehanna *or the Potomac*, but the motion was voted down. A few days later he reiterated the charge that the Southern members were being "disposed of." Wadsworth replied for the Eastern members that they had not bargained until they were assured bargaining was in progress for the Potomac.

Vining's endeavor to secure consideration of the Delaware site failed, and so did a motion by the Potomac party that no place should be chosen except upon the banks of a river offering unobstructed navigation to the sea. It was well known that such navigation did not exist on the Susquehanna and did on the Potomac. Another dilatory motion by Madison was swept aside, and September 22 the bill providing for the Susquehanna was passed and went to the Senate. Madison had expressed privately the hope that it would be amended

* Madison to Pendleton, Sept. 14, 1789, "Works" (Cong. Ed.) I, 491.

by that body and his expectations were realized, for the New York and Pennsylvania combination was strong enough to change the place to the eastern side of the Delaware, so as to include Germantown, this being tantamount to the choice of Philadelphia itself. On Saturday, September 26, the bill thus amended came before the House and an effort to postpone its consideration was lost. On Monday, when it was on the point of final passage, Madison called attention to the fact that no provision was made for the continuance in the new district of Pennsylvania law, until Congress should provide some other law. If the omission was not supplied the new district would be left without any law at all. The point could not be ignored and the amendment offered by Madison remedying the evil was agreed to. This compelled the return of the bill to the Senate, and the next day Congress adjourned with the bill unpassed. Madison had saved the rejection of the Potomac site by a hair's breadth.

Before the members of Congress separated to go to their homes Madison and Robert Morris had a private conversation on the subject of the capital, and Morris held out hopes of a satisfactory arrangement between Pennsylvania and the South, but Madison was embittered by the wearisome contest and had little faith that his party would ultimately win the victory. He did not credit the friendly protestations of Morris, who had been chief of the forces in the Senate opposing the Potomac site.*

At the next session the first motion on the subject was made June 10, 1790, when it was proposed that the next Congress meet at Philadelphia. This was agreed to by the House, and the resolution was pending in the Senate, when the funding bill, shorn of the assumption feature, also came up from the House. On June 8, the Senate rejected Philadelphia as a temporary capital

* Madison to Washington, Nov. 20, 1789, "Works of Madison" (Cong. Ed.) I, 495.

and took up in its place a bill for a permanent seat of Government, and immediately Ellsworth offered a new assumption bill. Thereafter the two measures were kept side by side and played against each other. The Southern and Pennsylvania coalition was effected again. "We are sold by the Pennsylvanians," wrote Fisher Ames, June 11, 1790, "and the assumption with it. They seem to have bargained to prevent the latter, on the terms of removing to Philadelphia. It becomes necessary to defeat this corruption."

The House accordingly passed a resolution in favour of holding the next session at Baltimore, but the Senate on June 28 passed a substitute bill providing for a permanent seat of Government on the Potomac River between the Eastern Branch and Connogocheague Creek. By a vote of 32 yeas to 29 nays this bill was agreed to by the House a few days later, and became a law. Success was thus finally substituted for a succession of failures. The story of how it was accomplished can best be told in the language of the chief actor.

Thomas Jefferson came back to the United States from France in December, 1789, and on March 21, 1790, went to New York, to enter upon the duties of the office of Secretary of State. He found public affairs in an alarming state. When the House rejected the assumption scheme, so bitter were the feelings of the two parties that they could not do business together and Congress adjourned from day to day. If the tension was not lessened there was danger that the whole fabric of Government would break. In *The Anas* Jefferson records how the situation was relieved:

"Hamilton was in despair. As I was going to the President's one day I met him in the street. He walked me backwards and forwards before the President's door for half an hour. He painted pathetically the temper into which the Legislature had been wrought, the disgust of those who were called the Creditor States, the danger of the secession of their members, and the separation of the States. He observed that the members of the Administration ought to act in concert, that tho' this question was not in my department, yet a common duty should make it a common concern; that the President was the centre on which all administrative questions ultimately rested, and that all of us should rally around him and support with joint efforts measures approved by him, and that the question having been lost by a small majority only, it was probable that an appeal from me to the judgment and discretion of some of my friends might effect a change in the vote, and the machine of Government, now suspended, might be again set in motion. I told him that I was really a stranger to the whole subject; not having yet informed myself of the system of finances adopted, I knew not how far this was a necessary sequence, that undoubtedly if its rejection endangered a dissolution of our Union at this incipient stage, I should deem that the most unfortunate of consequences, to avoid which all partial and temporary evils should be yielded. I proposed to him, however, to dine with me the next day, and I would invite another friend or two, bring them into conference together, and I thought it impossible that reasonable men, consulting together coolly, could fail, by some mutual sacrifices of opinion, to form a compromise which was to save the Union. The discussion took place. I could take no part in it but an exhortatory one, because I was a stranger to the circumstances which should govern it. But it was finally agreed that, whatever importance had been attached to the rejection of this proposition, the preservation of the Union and of concord among the States was more important, and that therefore it would be better that the vote of rejection should be rescinded, to effect which some members should change their votes. But it was observed that this pill would be peculiarly bitter to the Southern States, and that some concomitant measure should be adopted to sweeten it a little to them. There had been before propositions to fix the seat of

Government either at Philadelphia, or at Georgetown on the Potomac, and it was thought that by giving it to Philadelphia for ten years, and to Georgetown permanently afterwards, this might, as an anodyne, calm in some degree the ferment which might be excited by the other measures alone. So two of the Potomac members (White and Lee, but White with a revulsion of stomach almost convulsive) agreed to change their votes, and Hamilton undertook to carry the other point. In doing this the influence he had established over the Eastern members, with the agency of Robert Morris with those of the Middle States, effected his side of the engagement, and so the assumption was passed, and 20,000,000 of stock divided among favoured States, and thrown in as pabulum to the stock-jobbing herd."

Jefferson also relates that he had Hamilton and Madison to dine with him, and that Madison there agreed that if the assumption bill came up again he would leave it to its fate and while opposing it would not obstruct its coming to a vote. Perhaps this conference is a mistake of recollection on Jefferson's part; but if it occurred it was after the fateful feast when the real bargain was effected.

Hamilton performed his part of the contract first. The act locating the permanent seat of Government on the Potomac was passed in the middle of July. July 23 the amendment to the funding bill providing for the assumption of State debts was agreed to by a vote of 32 ayes to 29 nays. It was approved August 4, 1790. The only Southerners voting for it, except the South Carolina members, were White and Lee of Virginia, and Daniel Carroll and George Gale of Maryland.

As for the part Madison played in a consummation so consonant with his desires in one respect and so contrary to them in another, he had nothing to do with the main bargain, as the first dinner was necessarily arranged for without his knowledge. Afterwards he must have known of the agreement reached, and White and Lee in all probability told him of their intention to vote for the assumption bill. When it came up he played an inactive but a highly important part, for he permitted it to pass without putting in its way any of those parliamentary obstructions which he could use so skilfully when it suited him, and which he had so successfully applied against the bill locating the capital on the Delaware. A year later when the smoke of battle had cleared away, Jefferson declared he had been duped by Hamilton and made his tool in lending his aid to the assumption bill, and that of all the errors of his political life he regretted this the most.* He was not familiar with the pending financial questions, he said; but Madison was perfectly familiar with them and had been fighting against them, and he permitted the consummation of the bargain between Hamilton and Jefferson because he believed it to be for the public interest. The East was determined to have the assumption bill; the South was determined to have the capital. The bitterness of the Southern opposition to the assumption was taken away by the "concomitant measure," as Jefferson called it, which gave it the capital, and Madison's correspondents wrote from Virginia that public sentiment in that State had been appeased. In neither section does it appear that there was serious condemnation of the manifest trading of votes which had brought about an accommodation of interests. A good-natured raillery was indulged in, but none of those who did the bargaining, nor even of those who had changed their votes, suffered in his reputation or received punishment from his constituents.

* Randall's "Jefferson," II, 78.

CHAPTER XXI

THE IMPLIED POWERS

NOT only were the funding and assumption bills opposed by Madison, but Hamilton's bank bill also. It came before Congress, February 2, 1791, and was promptly passed by the Senate. In the House, however, it met with a well-managed opposition of which Madison was the body and soul.* In the course of the debate Elbridge Gerry described him as the original stock from which all other arguments were grafts. "If the trunk fell, its appendages must fall also," he said; so the forces in favour of the bill concentrated their efforts against him. He thought it undesirable that there should be one great bank in America, as there was in England where the object was to concentrate wealth in London. Such an institution would banish the precious metals from use, substituting other mediums to perform their office, and individuals might suffer grievously if there should ever be a run on the bank. But his chief argument against the bank was that the Constitution did not warrant its creation. Certain rules should be observed in construing that instrument. It could not properly be so interpreted as to destroy the nature of the Government. When its meaning was clear it must be interpreted without regard to the consequences which might follow; but when its meaning was doubtful the consequences should be considered. In controversies over its meaning the intention of the framers was a proper guide, if it could be ascertained, and concurrent and contemporary expositions were reasonable evidence of the intention. In admitting or rejecting constructive

* Annals of Congress, 1st Cong. 2d Sess., 1895, *et seq.*

authority the incidentality and importance of the authority were to be considered, as upon this would depend the probability or improbability of the authority being left to implication. Under these rules he could find no place for the bank. The power to provide for the "common defence and general welfare" must be understood as limited by the particular enumeration of powers in the Constitution. To understand otherwise would be to render the enumeration nugatory, and the powers reserved to the State Government would be entirely superseded. It was enough to point out that the words were copied from the old Articles of Confederation. Even if the bank did not interfere with the powers of the States, it would still be unconstitutional, if Congress were not given authority by the Constitution to create it. If a bank might be incorporated by Congress, so might anything else be—canal companies, manufactories and religious societies for instance. A certain set of arguments had been used to explain the Constitution and secure its ratification, and it could not now be administered by another set. It was idle to say that, if there was unwarranted exercise of power by Congress the judges would rectify the mistake. Suppose the judges also should be guided by motives of expediency? He thought the bill "was condemned by the silence of the Constitution; was condemned by the rule of interpretation arising out of the Constitution; was condemned by its tendency to destroy the main characteristics of the Constitution; was condemned by the expositions of the friends of the Constitution, whilst depending before the public; was condemned by the apparent intention of the parties which ratified the Constitution; was condemned by the explanatory amendments proposed by Congress themselves to the Constitution; and he hoped it would receive its final condemnation by the vote of this House."

Ames, Sedgwick, Gerry, Boudinot, Vining and Smith of South Carolina crowded to the defence of the bill.

They took the ground that "every Government from the instant of its formation has tacitly annexed to its being the various powers which are essential to the *purposes* for which it was formed." Ames said: "Congress may do what is necessary to the end for which the Constitution was adopted, provided it is not repugnant to the natural rights of man, or to those which they have expressly reserved to themselves, or to the powers which are assigned to the States." There then began the battle over the implied powers of the Constitution and the general welfare clause which has waged without intermission ever since.

The bank bill passed the House by a vote of 39 to 20, nearly all the Southern members voting against it. Washington doubted seriously whether he ought to sign it. He complained in his conversation with Madison in 1792, of an "unfitness to judge of legal questions and questions arising out of the Constitution," and this was doubtless one of the occasions to which·he alluded. Accordingly, he asked Jefferson and his Attorney-General, Randolph, for their opinion and they advised him against the bill, and Madison, at his request, prepared a veto message for him to use if he desired. Hamilton, however, successfully replied to the objections and the bill became law.

At the end of the year (December 5,) Hamilton's famous report in favor of a protective tariff for the development of manufactures was laid before Congress, and a schedule of duties on imports was introduced to take the place of Madison's temporary schedule adopted at the first session of Congress. On January 21, 1792, Madison wrote to Pendleton to say he considered Hamilton's reasoning on the general welfare clause to be subversive of the fundamental principles of the Government, and "as bidding defiance to the sense in which the Constitution is known to have been proposed, advocated and adopted." A few days later a bill was introduced for the encouragement of the cod fisheries by providing bounties, and he elaborated the arguments he had used against the bank bill to show that bounties on exports were unconstitutional.* The effect of the speech was that the word "bounty" was withdrawn and "drawback" substituted for it and Madison voted for the bill thus amended. The principle involved had not, of course, been altered in the slightest degree by this change, and Hamilton made the contemptuous comment that Madison was afraid to vote against the bill because he saw it was popular and would pass.

Enough has been said to show the irreconcilable difference between the two parties which had now formed, the one accepting the Constitution conservatively with reference to the old conditions, the other using it to form a mighty programme of radical innovation. Political conditions had changed and especially in Virginia. When the State stood as an independent entity under the Articles of Confederation, those who favoured a stronger Federal Government and those who opposed it were almost equal in numbers; but the Constitution had been adopted, and the amendments offered to it by Madison caused nearly everybody to accept it. Many former opponents found themselves now in agreement, and Henry Lee, who had advocated the ratification of the Constitution so zealously, found himself advocating the selection for a vacancy in the Senate, caused by the death of William Grayson, of Patrick Henry, who had moved heaven and earth to have the Constitution rejected. It was even proposed by the friends of Madison to send him to the Senate and force Henry to take Madison's place in the House.† George Mason made overtures of reconciliation with Madison. "I had no occasion" Jefferson wrote to him, February 4, 1791,‡ "to sound Mr. Madison on your fears expressed in your letter. I knew before, as possessing his sentiments fully on that

* Annals of Congress, 2d Cong., 385.
† Dept. of State MSS.
‡ "Writings" (Lodge) V., 276.

subject, that his value for you was undiminished. I have always heard him say that though you and he appeared to differ in your systems, yet you were in truth nearer together than most persons who were classed under the same appellation. You may quiet yourself in the assurance of possessing his complete esteem." The following year the great author of the Bill of Rights died, and there is no doubt that he and Madison were again in substantial agreement on public questions as they had been when their struggle for liberty began.

The truth is that when the new Government began operations national feeling did not predominate with public men and still less with the mass of the people. There had been no national feeling before the Revolution, and although it had been called into being by that momentous struggle it had quickly subsided after the peace. An agreement to try a new form of Government could not simultaneously evoke an affection for that Government, or change the habits of men's thoughts. A Virginian's country was Virginia; next he was a Southerner; last of all he was an American. The new Government had been in existence seven months when Edmund Randolph, a man of far broader patriotism than most men, wrote to Madison that he thought he might leave Virginia. It would, he said, be "the course of expatriation (you see I am not yet a strict American)"* When the representatives of the States came together to run the new Government they met one another with some suspicion, and when a number of measures passed through Congress supposed to favour Northern rather than Southern interests the Southern States manifested jealousy and ill-nature. Everybody was over critical towards the acts of Government. Men who were all-powerful at home found their importance neutralized by so many other powerful men at the capital, and they judged severely, because their agency and responsibility in Government were diminished under the new order

* Conway's "Randolph," 130

of things. "On their estates they were like big ships in a river, while in London they were the same ships in the sea," is the quotation invoked by Tucker, Jefferson's biographer. Tucker's description of the parties was drawn from contemporary sources, one of them being Madison, and is especially interesting. One party, he says, believed that the most imminent danger to the country was in disunion; and that popular jealousy when inflamed by ambitious demagogues would withhold from the general Government the power necessary to insure good order and safety. The other believed that the danger most to be apprehended was in too close a union, and that those who most strongly favoured it wished a consolidated, and even a monarchical, form of Government.*

On May 5, 1792, Madison had a conversation with Washington on the subject of the latter's retirement, which he argued would be unwise, and he explained to him what was the existing political situation. There were a few men, Madison said, who had been opposed to the adoption of the Constitution and who still wished to destroy it, but they had no following. There were others who were unfriendly to republican Government, and who probably aimed at a gradual approximation to a mixed monarchy. Public opinion was, however, so much against them that they would not long retain a dangerous influence. From this it may be inferred that Madison thought they then had such an influence.

Jefferson records in *The Anas* that when he came to New York from France he was shocked at the conversations he heard at dinner parties. "Politics," he says, "were the chief topic, and a preference of kingly over republican Government was evidently the favourite sentiment." Even at the present day similar sentiments may be heard at dinner parties, but they are not taken seriously. Their importance was exaggerated by Jefferson, but there were enough monarchists in the country

* Tucker's "Jefferson," I, 306, *et seq.*

to justify some alarm rather because of what they had said in the past than of what they did at the present.

The man against whom was levelled the full force of the accusation of being a monarchist was Alexander Hamilton, and his record made him dreadfully vulnerable. In the Constitutional Convention he made a speech, June 18, 1789, in which he said he anticipated the time when his colleagues would agree with Necker in thinking the British Constitution the one Government "which unites public strength with individual security." The House of Lords, he declared, was a "most noble institution," forming "a permanent barrier against every pernicious innovation, whether attempted on the part of the Crown or of the Commons." "The hereditary interest of the King was so interwoven with that of the nation, and his personal emolument so great, that he was placed above the danger of being corrupted from abroad, and at the same time was both sufficiently independent and sufficiently controlled to answer the purpose of the institution at home." While the Convention was sitting, Hamilton wrote to Washington from New York, July 3, saying that in New Jersey and New York he had taken pains to find what the public sentiment was in the matter of Government. "A plain, but sensible man" had in conversation with him said the present Government would not answer, and for it must be substituted "something not very remote from that which we have lately quitted." "I am more and more inclined to believe," said Hamilton, "that former habits of thinking are regaining their influence with more rapidity than is generally imagined." He was convinced that "no motley or feeble measure" would finally receive public support. The "former habits of thinking" of the people were those of loyal subjects of a king; the "motley or feeble measure" then under consideration in the Convention became the Constitution of the United States. When Hamilton became an officer of the Government and offered a plan of finance having for its avowed purpose the strengthening of the central power, it was not unreasonable to attribute to him a desire to shape events towards the model which he had proclaimed as the best.

Hamilton regarded Madison as a factor necessary to the success of the new Government. He wrote to him, November 23, 1788, to say he was glad he was going into the House, where his presence would be needed, especially as Wilson, King and Gouverneur Morris would not be there.* Soon after he became Secretary of the Treasury he asked him (October 12, 1798,) to aid in preparing the plan which must be submitted to the next session of Congress for increasing the public revenue and taking care of the public debt.† Apparently, Madison's reply was not a definite one, and when Hamilton's plan was offered in Congress, Madison opposed every feature of it. The disappointment and chagrin of the Secretary of the Treasury knew no bounds. He unbosomed himself in a long confidential letter to his friend Edward Carrington, March 26, 1792. "When I accepted the office I now hold" he said, "it was under full persuasion, that from similarity of thinking, conspiring with personal good will, I should have the firm support of Mr. Madison in the general course of my administration. Aware of the intrinsic difficulties of the situation, and of the powers of Mr. Madison, I do not believe I should have accepted under a different supposition." Madison had not, he went on, expressed to him any change in the views he advocated in 1783 on the subject of the State debts, and during the sitting of the Constitutional Convention had said he favoured the assumption. Hamilton had, therefore, told him he counted on his support for his financial measures in Congress, but Madison alleged, as a reason for a change of views, that the recent alienation of the certificates of debt by the original holders had altered the situation, and that the assumption he favoured was of State debts

* "Hamilton's Works" (Lodge) 8, 205.
† Id., 210.

as they existed at the peace, before any of the States had themselves provided for them. Hamilton believed his opposition to be sincere, but stories had since been brought to him that Madison and Jefferson were at the head of a faction hostile to him, and that on one occasion in private conversation Madison had used language unfriendly to him. He was forced to believe this, because Freneau, who was employed in Jefferson's department and was a friend of Madison's, had been systematically defaming him in his newspaper. Therefore Hamilton had changed his opinion of Madison. His character was "one of a peculiarly artificial and complicated kind." Hamilton accused him of having opposed the motion to request of Hamilton a report on ways and means to carry out the Western expedition against the Indians, because he knew that if the motion failed Hamilton would feel so slighted that he would resign. He had in debate made insidious insinuations calculated to give the impression that the public money had been so applied as to give advantage to speculators. Madison, Hamilton admitted, had an excuse for his enmity, for before this Hamilton had declared openly his "determination to consider and treat him as a political enemy." As for the cry that there was a monarchical party, Hamilton declared by all that was sacred that he did not favour a monarchy, and that he was affectionately attached to a republic. "A very small number of men," he said, "indeed may entertain theories less republican than Mr. Jefferson and Mr. Madison, but I am persuaded that there is not a man among them who would not regard as both criminal and visionary any attempt to subvert the republican system of the country. Most of these men rather fear that it may not justify itself by its fruits, than feel a predilection for a different form; and their fears are diminished by the factions and fanatical politics which they find prevailing among a certain set of gentlemen and threatening to disturb the tranquillity and order of the Government." The danger to the country lay with those men who fostered the spirit of faction and anarchy with sinister motives. He did not include Madison among them, but Thomas Jefferson was "a man of profound ambition and violent passions."

Edward Carrington, to whom this letter was written, was appointed Marshal for the District of Virginia, September 26, 1789, and was one of the few Virginia Federalists who did not join the opposition to Hamilton's measures; yet before Hamilton wrote to him he had written to Madison, April 20, 1791: "I confess myself staggered upon the measure of the Bank and wish it had been let alone. I have read with attention your reasoning on the subject, and do not think it is refuted by the arguments on the other side—I am however unwilling to be converted to your opinion, being much prepossessed in favour of Banks, and think if it is unconstitutional for the Federal Gov't. to establish institutions of the kind it is a defect."* It was probably he who informed Hamilton that the people in Virginia were almost unanimously against him, for, August 16, 1792, Hamilton wrote to John Adams: "I have a letter from a well-informed friend in Virginia who says 'All the persons I converse with are prosperous and happy, and yet most of them, including the friends of the Government, appear to be much alarmed at a supposed system of policy tending to subvert the republican Government of the country.'"

Edmund Pendleton published observations against the bank bill. Patrick Henry, who was so prejudiced against Madison that he generally disagreed with him on principle and who was soon to turn into an extreme consolidationist, wrote the remonstrance of the Virginia Legislature against the assumption act, and declared Hamilton's report on manufactures meant "subserviency of Southern to N——n interests."† The State was almost a unit in its opposition to Hamilton's policy.

* Department of State MSS.
† Henry's "Henry," II, 456.

What was Madison's real belief? He was a self-contained man, and the hidden current of his hopes, fears and ambitions he disclosed to no one, and we must judge him by what he said and did and by his surroundings. He knew Hamilton well,—knew his genius, his force, and his inflexible devotion to a Government of strongly centralized power. He knew also that Hamilton's system was repugnant to a great majority of the people of America, whose attachments were local or sectional. In opposing Hamilton Madison secured the favour of the people of Virginia as he had never secured it before, and he now stood for the first time upon the firm ground of a public man who has behind him a constituency practically undivided in its support of him. But his position was a perfectly natural one, and if base motives of expediency must be attributed to him, because he declined to follow Hamilton's lead, the same odium must attach to the former Federalists, in Virginia who now acted with him, as they had before acted with him when they demanded the Constitutional Convention and the ratification of its results. Further than this, the same odium must be visited upon all the former Federalists in the South who were now the preponderating force in the Anti-Federal party. It is true this party included as members those who had opposed the adoption of the Constitution, but they now accepted it. At the present day it is possible for a man who is a member of the Democratic party to be esteemed, even by those who do not agree with him, as an honest patriot, and no violent mental effort should be necessary to attribute political integrity and patriotic motives to the leaders who founded the Democratic party more than a century ago.

Did Madison believe the charges levelled by his party against Hamilton? How did it happen that he countenanced the methods of party warfare which Jefferson instigated and which no one can now excuse? These charges and these methods were not Madison's, but no protest against them came from him, and he must share in the censure history pronounces against them. The truth is that Madison now had a party chief. This chief neither directed nor suggested Madison's opposition to Hamilton's consolidation policy, but his political conduct was now influenced by Jefferson's stronger personality and extraordinary power of attracting men to him. To this must be attributed the fact that Madison at this period of his career often found himself in a position foreign to his former political habits. In the heat of political conflict men say and even believe things of their opponents which at calmer times they would not sanction. This must be remembered in extenuation of Madison's attitude toward Hamilton. It is a merciful interpretation which ought to be accepted by the partisans of Hamilton, in exchange for like charity extended towards their own hero, who also sadly needs it.

CHAPTER XXII

WASHINGTON yielded to the requests of the leaders of both parties and determined to hold the Presidency for a second term, but the Anti-Federalists endeavored to defeat the re-election of John Adams to the Vice-Presidency. At Hamilton's request* Madison had given his aid to Adams' first election, and had opposed George Clinton, whom Patrick Henry favoured and who was regarded as the arch-conspirator against the Constitution. Clinton was now, of course, reconciled to the Constitution, and was put forward against Adams, who, it was alleged, was of aristocratic tendencies.† In reality no well-informed man believed him to be a real aristocrat, but he was a Federalist and his party would suffer by his defeat. John Beckley, clerk of the House of Representatives, was the active agent of Madison, Monroe and other Southern leaders in the endeavour to compass Adams' defeat. He wrote to Madison, October 17, 1792, from Philadelphia, the letter to be opened by Monroe if it did not find 'Madison at Fredericksburg where he was supposed to be, reporting that he had conferred with Melancthon Smith, who acted for the Republicans in New York, and an authorized representative of the party in Pennsylvania, and they had decided to drop Aaron Burr for the Vice-Presidency and vigorously press the candidacy of Clinton. It was hoped Henry would win over North Carolina, and some electoral votes could even be counted upon from New England. Beckley spoke bitterly of Hamilton, whom he hated and feared.

* Dept. of State MSS.
† Rives, III, 311, *et seq.*

Hamilton was working against Clinton, he said, but his zeal would in the end betray him, for Beckley had a clue to "something far beyond mere suspicion" about him, which at the proper time he would disclose. Hamilton's hand, Beckley said, could be seen in the proceedings of the Virginia Legislature, for he desired the re-election to the Senate of Richard Henry Lee.* The author of the letters of the Federal Farmer, who had endeavoured to strangle the Constitution in the old Congress before it could reach the people, who had opposed its ratification bitterly and had been sent by Patrick Henry to the Senate where he could oppose it in its operation, had turned Federalist and was now Hamilton's friend. Beckley said Hamilton worked with "closeted friends," and that he was "an *extraordinary* man, with a comprehensive eye, a subtle and contriving mind, and a soul devoted to his object."

The scheming of the Virginians was so far successful that at the Presidential election in 1792 Virginia, which cast a larger electoral vote than any other State, cast it solidly for Clinton for Vice-President and carried North Carolina and Georgia with her, while New York also voted for him and he had one vote from Pennsylvania. His total was, however, only fifty votes, while Adams received seventy-seven.

Madison had become as bitter a partisan as Jefferson himself, and like him he called the Federalists "Monocrats" or "Anglicans." He was a party to the schemes to expose what he called the "mal-administration of the Treasury," and joined in the cry that money raised to pay the French loan was being diverted from its purpose and lodged in the United States bank "to extend speculations and increase the profits of that institution." The cruel resolution introduced into the House with Madison's full knowledge and approval by his colleague Giles to investigate the Treasury Department, was to his blinded eyes "a pretty interesting scrutiny," for

* Dept. of State MSS.

with some, he said, suspicions were carried very far.* The truth was that Hamilton had not paid an instalment of the French debt, for the very good reason that he was not sure he could safely do so. The revolutionists were in control of the Government, but the stability of their régime was a question of grave doubt, and if he paid the money to rebels would he not have to pay it over again if the legitimate Government were restored? Madison ridiculed this idea. The vain argument, he said, might be made that the Government of France had not yet arrived at the age of stable maturity, "yet it must be evident to all the dispassionate part of mankind that the revolution was sufficiently established to insure it against the danger of a retrograde movement."

When Thomas Jefferson left Paris liberty was the talk of fashionable French society, to which it meant little more than did those dinner party conversations in favour of monarchy which alarmed him so much when he arrived in New York. It was not until the cry for liberty coming from the great heart of the common people moved them to action that it became a force, and when the Bastile fell a passionate sympathy was felt with the French by many Americans. It seemed to them that the American Declaration of Independence was destined soon to become a living truth in the old world as it was in the new. There appeared to be every moral reason why America should support the revolutionists in France, and when war broke out between England and her allies on the one side and France on the other it became evident that a strong hand would be needed in America to check overt acts of hostility to England. Now, if Madison and Jefferson had had the question to decide, they would have decided for neutrality, for war was a hateful thing to them and they spent their lives searching for the undiscovered secret of how to conduct a Government on a basis of everlasting peace. Never-

* To Edmund Randolph, February 23, 1793. "Works" (Cong. Ed.) I, 575.

theless, the proclamation of neutrality which Washington issued, April 22, 1793, did not suit them, because it was not worded as they would have wished it to be. It was too strong, Madison said, and violated our moral obligations. It declared the disposition of the people to be one of neutrality, but the President had no right to speak on this point. The French sentiment was "warmly right," and executive politics were now of an "Anglified complexion."*

The coming of Genet, the first Minister from republican France, was looked forward to as offering an opportunity for the people to show their displeasure at the tone of the proclamation. Madison hoped Genet would be received in such a way as would counteract the official coolness manifested towards France, but the enthusiasm of his greeting and his manner of reciprocating it were more than Madison or any other leader of the French party had bargained for. French privateers were fitted out in American ports, where French prizes also were brought. Genet being officially informed that these things could not be permitted, declared he would appeal from the officers of the Government to which he was accredited to the people who were the masters of the officers and superior to them. He was given his passports and those who had heralded his coming with so many hopes found themselves in a ridiculous position. There was a large defection from the French party. "The only antidote for this poison," wrote Madison, "is to distinguish between the nation and its agent; between principles and events; and to impress the well-meaning with the fact that the enemies of France and Liberty are at work to land them from their honourable connection with these into the Government of Great Britain,"† but it was too late, for the poison spread and with it the bitterness of the French party grew.

It would be easy to bring many incidents to show

* "Works" (Cong. Ed.) I, 584.
† To Jefferson, "Works" (Cong. Ed.) I, 596.

that the rancorous enmity of the Federalists towards the Republicans was as great as that of the Republicans towards them, but one circumstance will serve as a sufficient example. The question of the Presidential succession came up in Congress and a motion that the office should descend in the event of the death of the President and Vice-President to the Secretary of State was voted down, because Jefferson was the Secretary of State, and it was desired to put a slight upon him. Accusations of base partisan motives were bandied about freely and intruded into almost every debate in Congress, and even figured in the debate on the bill to naturalize aliens.

When the first Congress met the disposition was to accord naturalization readily in order to add to the population and obtain emigrants to the West. Madison opposed this, saying that brute numbers was not what was needed, but good citizens. He would not exclude from American citizenship any man of good fame, but he would not admit any who would not add to our wealth and strength.* The utmost that he could accomplish, however, was an extension of the probationary period of residence from one year, as it then was, to two years, with an additional requirement that no one should be naturalized who was not of "good character." In the Congress of 1794 he introduced a bill extending the obligatory period of residence before naturalization to five years and requiring proof that the applicant was a man of good moral character "attached to the Constitution of the United States, and well disposed to the good order and happiness of the same," and a clause was added requiring him to renounce any title of nobility he might have had as a foreigner. The last requirement precipitated a remarkable debate, which turned, as everything at that time did, upon foreign politics.† Ames said, "The convention of another nation (France)

* Rives, III, 479, *et seq.*

† Annals of Congress, 3d Cong., 1032.

had indelibly disgraced themselves by legislating upon trifles, while matters of importance stood by. What would be the sense of America upon our spending day after day in debating about such a frivolous thing?" This taunt Madison answered by the absurdest argument that ever fell from his lips. No man, he said, could say how far the revolution in Europe would extend. If it took place in Great Britain, as he expected it would, the peerage of that country would flock to the United States. He would welcome them, but he would not admit them to citizenship, until they had renounced their titles.

In the course of the debate Dexter of Massachusetts declared there was no more reason for the rule proposed than there would be to hinder His Holiness the Pope from entering the United States. He went on at some length to ridicule the tenets of the Catholic Church and the ranks and titles it observed. It was Madison's old self, the champion of religious liberty, who rebuked him. "He did not approve," he said, "the ridicule attempted to be thrown out on the Roman Catholics. In their religion there was nothing inconsistent with the purest republicanism. In Switzerland about one-half of the cantons were of the Roman Catholic persuasion. Some of the most democratic cantons were so; cantons where every man gave his vote for a representative. Americans had no right to ridicule Catholics. They had, many of them, proved good citizens during the Revolution."*

The Federalists returned to the charge. If one man must renounce his titles before being admitted to American citizenship, they said, why wouldn't it be as just to compel another under the same circumstances to renounce membership in a Jacobin club? Again: you want to hold us up as aristocrats. Very well, we will hold you up as slave-dealers, and an amendment was offered that no one owning slaves should be admitted to citizenship. Nevertheless, the clause requiring the renunciation of titles of nobility before securing natural-

* Annals of Congress, 3d Cong., 1035.

ization was retained in the bill, and the useless provision is a part of the naturalization laws at the present time.

Not even could Hamilton's retirement from the Administration be accepted by Madison without bitterness. His last recommendations as Secretary of the Treasury were "an arrogant valedictory report," and of his return to the practice of law he said: "It is pompously announced in the newspapers that poverty drives him back to the Bar for a livelihood."* Towards Washington, however, Madison's tone of veneration and respect never changed, although the inevitable course of political events finally drifted them far apart.

Their acquaintance began when Madison was in the Continental Congress, and their correspondence opened in the spring of 1783 with a friendly request from Washington that Madison should try to find, if he could, some place in the peace establishment for Dr. James McHenry, formerly Washington's military secretary, and afterwards Secretary of War. They became intimate friends and Washington depended much upon Madison's advice.† They were coadjutors in the Potomac Company; it was Madison who helped Washington to see his way clear to accepting service in the Constitutional Convention; they fought valiantly together to secure the ratification of the Constitution by Virginia. During the first four years of his service as President, Washington consulted Madison on public questions more than he did any other man outside of the Cabinet circle. He had extraordinary confidence in him, and before he accepted the Presidency confided his fear that an acceptance might be attributed to motives of personal ambition. Madison assured him that he was necessary to the safe inauguration of the Government, and suggested that he might manifest his disinterested motives later on by his retirement as soon as the Government had been successfully put in operation.‡

* "Works" (Cong. Ed.) II, 36.·
† Id., I, 64.
‡ Id., I, 556.

After three years of service Washington weighed the question of announcing his determination not to accept a re-election. In his official family he took Jefferson, Hamilton, Knox and Randolph into his confidence and they advised him not to retire. The only other person he consulted was Madison, who, of course, advised him as the others had done; but Washington wanted his opinion on another point. If he should conclude to retire, how should he announce his intention? Madison replied that a direct address to the people would be the most fitting way, and at Washington's request he handed him on June 21, 1792, a draft of a farewell address. Washington put it with his papers, and, concluding to accept a second term, had no occasion to use it, until five years later when he made it the basis of a part of his first draft of the immortal Farewell Address.* He sent his draft to Hamilton, and Hamilton sent him another draft which he used finally as the framework of the address. The first paragraph, announcing his purpose to retire, was substantially as Madison had written it; so was the second in which he promised continued zeal for the welfare of the country. The fifth, regretting his shortcomings, and the sixth, expressing gratitude for the honours bestowed upon him, and hope for the perpetuity of the Constitution were similar to the Madison draft. The draft also contained expressions in favor of the Union and the Government which appeared in the address in a different form. Everything, therefore, said in Madison's draft was incorporated in the address, but his draft contained only nine paragraphs and the address has fifty; nor can it be claimed that its striking features are the portion which Madison suggested.

The reason why Washington did not consult him in preparing the final address was that, at the time he was drawing it up, Madison no longer enjoyed his confidence or favour. He retained both, however, for some time after he prepared the first draft; for when Jefferson

* "Works" (Cong. Ed.) I, 554, *et seq.*

announced, July 31, 1793, his intention of retiring from the Cabinet, Washington said his first choice for Jefferson's successor was Madison, but he knew he would not serve in an executive office.* At this time, although Madison's political views and affiliations were well established, Washington still avoided taking sides with either of the political parties. He was naturally, however, a Federalist, for he had no sympathy with the idealism of the party which sympathized with the French revolutionists, and as a practical man of military training who believed in accomplishing results he thought a Government ought to be clothed with real authority and power. After Jefferson's separation from his administration there was no Republican element left, and consequently no influence to restrain the attacks upon the measures of Government which increased in severity. These attacks Washington took as meant to apply partly to him, and he broke with the leaders of the opposition. "With Madison," says Paul Ford,† "the break does not seem to have come from any positive ill feeling, but rather an abandonment of intercourse as the differences of opinion became more pronounced."

October 24, 1793, at Washington's request, Madison submitted an opinion on the President's power under the Constitution to call a meeting of Congress at some place other than Philadelphia where the yellow fever was raging;‡ and this was the last opinion he ever offered to Washington. Two years later, (August 10, 1795,) when the bitter struggle over the Jay treaty was in progress, he told Chancellor Livingston that unsolicited opinions were no longer desired from him by the executive.¶ He had either received an intimation to that effect or inferred it as a natural consequence of his opposition to administration measures. Their personal inter-

* Rives, III, 382, *n.*
† "The True George Washington," 258.
‡ "Works" (Cong. Ed.) II, 602.
¶ Id., II, 46.

course did not wholly cease, but there was an end, apparently, to its cordiality which was never resumed, because Washington died when party conflict was still raging and when his own feelings on the subject were embittered.

In speaking of him many years after his death Madison said: "If any erroneous changes took place in his views of persons and public affairs near the close of his life, as has been insinuated, they may probablv be accounted for by circumstances which threw him into an exclusive communication with men of one party, who took advantage of his retired situation to make impressions unfavourable to their opponents."* Regard for the truth compels the statement that Madison probably referred to an unfavourable impression of himself entertained by Washington; for, as fortune willed it, the last words spoken by Washington before he took to his bed with the ailment from which he died were words of condemnation of Madison uttered with asperity. He was alone with Tobias Lear, when as Mr. Lear records: "He requested me to read to him the Debates of the Virginia Assembly, on the election of a Senator and Governor, and, on hearing Mr. Madison's observations respecting Mr. Monroe, he appeared much affected, and spoke with some degree of asperity on the subject, which I endeavoured to moderate, as I always did on such occasions."

And yet among the men of this period who have stamped themselves upon our history the two least associated in the popular mind with extreme partisanship are Washington and Madison. It was inevitable, however, that as Washington's Administration progressed and his policy shaped itself it should arouse opposition, for the most part sincere and perfectly justifiable.

*Rives, III, 595.

CHAPTER XXIII

THE party feeling during Washington's Administration attained its highest point when the Jay treaty came before the country, and the denunciation hurled against the treaty party was not intended to leave the President untouched. That the public mind should be deeply stirred on the subject of the treaty was only natural, for the treatment which the feeblest and most contemptible States now receive from the strongest and most unscrupulous is honourable fairness itself when compared with the indignities and injuries which Great Britain inflicted upon the United States from the time of the treaty of peace until the close of the war of 1812. Our feebleness compelled us to endure an almost complete deprivation of international rights, and as long as the Confederation existed England had as a good reason for her contemptuous attitude the knowledge that our flimsy union could not long endure under our system of Government. When the break up should come she had every reason to hope that some, if not all, the States would return to the allegiance which they had held for a hundred years. When the Constitution was put into operation we were indeed a nation, but one tottering from very infancy, and safe to be insulted by a Power old, relentless and powerful.

Accordingly Great Britain continued to hold the frontier posts, which, under the terms of the treaty of peace, she had promised to surrender. In consequence, the neighbouring Indian tribes were under her jurisdiction and in a state of hostility to American settlers. The settlement of the frontier territory was retarded, some of the pioneers were killed, and the lives of the others were in constant jeopardy, while the sovereignty of the United States was insulted on its own territory. American ships under the American flag on the high seas were searched by British ships. Our sailors were impressed into the British service, cargoes and ships were seized and treated as prizes taken from an enemy. Great Britain closed her West Indian ports to our ships, and kept the carrying trade of those islands to herself, although their principal imports came from the United States.

In the face of these conditions three things could be done. We could continue to endure what was practically a state of commercial vassalage to Great Britain; we could go to war, but the outcome would probably be a failure of the objects of the war, and possibly the loss of our independence itself; we could retaliate by withdrawing from England every privilege which she denied us; we could discriminate against her ships and products and injure her as she injured us. Retaliation was not a strong weapon, because it could not touch an important part of the American grievances. It was objectionable, too, because to stop trading with your enemy is to stop your profits as well as his; but it was better than war, or continued submission. It was the policy which Madison had advocated at the first session of the first Congress.

He revived it in a set of resolutions submitted to Congress, January 3, 1794, when the report from Jefferson on the privileges and restrictions of American commerce came up,* and his action was greeted with hearty commendations. A number of masters of American vessels detained at Jamaica wrote to thank him and commend his plan as soon as they heard of it. General Gates called him the coming man of America, and the Republican Society of Charleston, S. C., passed resolutions in praise of "citizen Representative Madison."†

* Rives, III, 383, *et seq.*
† Dept. of State MSS.

In Congress the chief argument against the resolutions came from Smith of South Carolina, but it was commonly believed that Hamilton inspired the speech. The strength of the argument was that retaliation, if carried out, would cause England to go to war with us, or invoke even harder commercial measures against us. There was, therefore, nothing for us to do, but wait until we were more powerful and could resist. In his reply Madison said we consumed double as much of GreatBritain's goods as she did of ours, and to make reprisals would injure her more than it would ourselves. Her manufactures would not be sold to us, nor our raw material to her. The idea of war resulting from the policy of retaliation was ridiculous. It was the same system of reciprocity which Great Britain practised herself. He reminded Congress that after the treaty of peace had been made Pitt had introduced a bill in Parliament putting trade with America upon a reciprocal basis, supposing the United States would follow a like course; but when Lord Sheffield showed that there was no central authority in America to regulate commerce, Pitt had withdrawn his bill. The necessary authority had now been established by the Constitution and should be put to use.

Some members thought Madison's plan too spiritless, and proposed further negotiations with Great Britain, and, if they failed, a resort to arms. Madison replied that negotiations had already failed and that war would be most imprudent at present. Why not, he asked, try "commercial weapons"? Great Britain was more vulnerable in her commerce than she was in her army and navy. She valued our markets very much more than she feared our frigates and militia.

A test vote in Committee of the Whole showed that the House favoured the use of the "commercial weapons"; but before the question came up in the House the situation was changed by rumours of fresh outrages on American commerce by British cruisers. They were soon con-

firmed by the publication of the British instructions
dated Nov. 6, 1793, and by accounts of seizures and condemnations under them in the West Indies. Madison
wrote Jefferson on March 12, 1794, that a hundred vessels
had been thus seized, but he underestimated, for the
Annual Register for 1794 reported the number a
few months later at six hundred. The opportunity
was favourable for introducing bold measures, and
Sedgwick proposed that a provisional army of 15,000
men be raised to serve three years from the commencement of war, if war should be declared, and that the
President be impowered, "to lay an embargo generally,
or particularly, upon ships in the ports of the United
States, for a term not exceeding, at any one time, forty
days." The measure was identified by Madison as
coming from Hamilton, and he said was intended to
strengthen the power of the central Government. When,
however, its military features were dropped he consented
to withdraw his milder proposition, in favour of the more
vigorous retaliation. The House then eliminated the
President's agency in the embargo and declared for one
immediately for thirty days. Even more drastic measures of retaliaition were introduced and were pending,
when Washington announced his intention of sending
a special mission to England. He had a short time
before informed Congress of a slight mitigation of the
British instructions, which offered some hopes of further
relaxations,—"so that," Madison said, "Great Britain
seems to have derived from the very excess of her aggressions a title to commit them in a less degree with im-
punity."

On April 16 Jay, then Chief Justice of the Supreme
Court, was nominated as Minister to England, and the
plans of retaliation were all dropped by the House in
favour of a substitute offered by Madison, to the effect
that the injuries suffered made it expedient that the
commercial intercourse with Great Britain should be
less extensive than it then was, and, therefore, that after

November 1 following, the importation of British merchandise should be suspended. The House agreed to this by a vote of 58 to 34, but it was defeated in the Senate by the casting vote of the President. Nothing more was attempted and the country waited for the result of the mission.

Jay carried with him instructions of a positive character. He was to demand compensation for British spoliations of American commerce and that provisions should not be considered as contraband of war, except when an attempt was made to introduce them into a place actually besieged. He was to insist upon an immediate surrender of the frontier posts and compensation for the negroes carried off in violation of the treaty. If these matters could be satisfactorily arranged he might negotiate a commercial treaty on a basis of reciprocity in navigation and trade regulations. If they could not be arranged he was to sign no treaty, but to report to his Government for further instructions.

While the country waited for news of the result of Jay's mission the British outrages continued, and Governor Simcoe of Upper Canada, invading the United States with three British regiments, built a fort on American soil at the rapids of the Miami, and ordered an American settler away. Then a part of the correspondence between Lord Grenville, the British Minister, and Jay found its way into the newspapers and Jay's tone was so mild that it caused disgust among the French party, especially in the South, where he was already unpopular because of his willingness in 1786 to abandon the American right of navigating the Mississippi. Madison said Jay's memorial was humiliating, but thought his mission might succeed, because the military successes of the French would be apt to make England more conciliatory than she had been.

Congress adjourned March 7, and three days later the treaty arrived, having been signed November 19. The Senate was convened for June 8 to consider it. Strict secrecy was enjoined, but, of course, the terms of the treaty leaked out. Madison had an accurate knowledge of them by a very simple means. Pierce Butler, the Senator from South Carolina, wrote to him June 12,* that he would send him by each post a sheet of the treaty till he should have the whole. Having read it he was to forward it to Jefferson, who was not to communicate it to any óne. Madison was asked to give Butler the benefit of his free opinion of the treaty. By a bare two-thirds the Senate ratified it. The injunction of secrecy was not removed, but the public was to be permitted to know the substance of the treaty, although no copy of any part of it was to be given out. Stevens Thomson Mason, a Senator from Virginia, violated the injunction and gave the text of the treaty to a Philadelphia newspaper, which printed it June 30, only a day before Washington had determined it should be made public property. A combination of circumstances condemned it from the start, but, as we have seen, the leaders of the opposition knew its provisions before the public did and had time to plan a campaign.

Nevertheless, the treaty was a bad one, and the utmost that can be said in its favour is that it was probably the best obtainable and that it was better than war, and Jay probably did as well as any one else could have done under the circumstances. Concerning the frontier posts it provided that they must be evacuated by June 1, 1796, but in the treaty of peace their immediate evacuation was promised. The American contention that free ships should make free goods was disappointed by a provision that French goods in American bottoms might be seized by Great Britain. The list of contraband goods instead of being restricted was enlarged to include whatever served to equip a vessel, and provisions might be confiscated, subject to a claim by the owner for their value to be adjudicated in a British port by a British court. An equality of France and England in bellig-

*Dept. of State MSS.

erent rights was rendered impossible, because under our treaty with France British goods in an American vessel could not be seized. Not a word did the treaty say about the impressment of American seamen or the surrender of those already impressed. The West Indian trade was to be opened only to small American vessels of not more than seventy tons burden, carrying cargoes from the United States alone. Provision was made for a commission to determine the amount of indemnity due the United States for British spoliations, and in return for this one act of simple justice the United States was to assume the payment of British debts in America. The effect of the treaty Madison declared in a letter to Chancellor Livingston, August 10, 1795, would be to "monopolize us to Great Britain," and prevent our making treaties that would be of advantage to us. The treaty was evidence that Jay's party was a "British party, systematically aiming at an exclusive connection with the British Government, and ready to sacrifice to that object as well the dearest interests of our commerce as the most sacred dictates of national honour." Livingston replied: "Our disgrace and humiliation have in this instance, greatly exceeded my expectations." He thought the treaty abandoned the rights of the United States and that it was the duty of every well-wisher of his country to prevent its ratifications.*

Certainly the people of the country left no doubt that they did not wish its ratification. Samuel Adams and other prominent Bostonians united in a town meeting to denounce it. In New York Hamilton and his friends were roughly handled at a public meeting where condemnatory resolutions were passed. At Philadelphia a mob burned a copy of the treaty before the British Legation. Public meetings in almost every town North and South denounced the treaty, while from the New York Chamber of Commerce and a few other commercial bodies came the only words in its favour.

* Dept. of State MSS.

It was evident that Washington did not relish the treaty. After he received it he waited three months before he gave it to the Senate. After its ratification he held it a long time, in doubt, apparently, whether to proclaim it or destroy it. The people, it was said, stood three to one against it, but the Cabinet was three to one in its favour. It was an Administration measure and the President shared in the odium it excited. John Beckley wrote to Madison from Philadelphia, September 10, 1795: "You can have no idea how deeply the public confidence is withdrawing itself from the President, and with what avidity strictures on his conduct are received; sensible of this, his friends are redoubling their efforts to exalt his name and exaggerate his past services—But all in vain, the vital blow aimed at the Independence & best Interests of his country by the impending treaty, mark him in indelible characters as the head of a British faction, and gratitude no longer blinds the public mind."

When the new Congress met, December 7, 1795, the Republicans were still in a majority, and Madison was as usual made chairman of the committee to prepare an answer to the President's speech. His colleagues were Sedgwick and Sitgreaves, both Federalists, and they proposed a clause in the answer expressing the "undiminished confidence of his fellow-citizens in the President." Madison objected to this clause in committee, not only because he considered it too strong under the circumstances, but because he foresaw that it would be bitterly opposed if it were presented in the House. He prepared an adroit substitute, which was adopted: "In contemplating that spectacle of national happiness which our country exhibits, and of which you, sir, have been pleased to make an interesting summary, permit us to acknowledge and declare the very great share which your zealous and faithful services have contributed to it, and to express the affectionate attachment which we feel for your character." There was no mention in Washington's speech of the treaty, because it had not yet been proclaimed; but it was a sharp commentary upon the changed condition of affairs brought about by party feeling, that the House of Representatives was not willing to declare its "undiminished confidence" in George Washington.

The latter part of February he received word of the ratification of the treaty by Parliament and on the last day of the month he proclaimed it. It had been negotiated by an envoy clothed with full powers; it had been ratified, with an amendment by the United States Senate, and the amendment had been agreed to by the British Government; the ratifications had been exchanged and the proclamation now made the treaty law. On March 1 the President sent a copy of it to each House of Congress. In the House it was referred to the Committee of the Whole and taken up for consideration March 7. The fight against it was led by a new light in national politics. Edward Livingston had just taken his seat in Congress for the first time, and at once sprang into the front rank among the Republicans of the North. With ready and forceful argumentative ability, of radical and fearless political thought, accomplished as scholar and jurist, he seemed destined to play a conspicuous part upon the stage for years to come. His first act called up the only serious conflict of authority between the Executive and the Legislative that occurred during Washington's administration. He moved that the President be requested to send to the House copies of the instructions given Jay when he went to England as Minister and of the correspondence had with him during the progress of the negotiations of the treaty, except such papers as any pending negotiations might render it improper to disclose. Madison offered an amendment asking only for "so much of the said papers as, in the judgment of the President, it may be consistent with the interests of the United States at this time to disclose," but this peaceful modification was rejected, the Federalists voting against it, because they did not approve of any request for papers, and a few Republicans joining them, because they wanted the resolution to be as objectionable to the Administration as possible. The arguments for and against Livingston's resolution were interesting because the question involved has not yet been definitely settled beyond dispute.

The Federalists said a bold attempt was being made to encroach upon the prerogatives of the President and the Senate who were the treaty-making power. Treaties made by them were "the supreme law of the land," and the House had nothing to do with the question of how they were made. It was the duty of Congress to obey the law and pass such legislation as a treaty required to carry it into execution.

The Republicans replied that the Constitution vested in Congress certain prerogatives, among them being the right to regulate commerce, raise revenue and appropriate it. The general power of the Executive and Senate to make treaties could not supersede this particular authority. Whenever, therefore, a treaty required Congressional action to make it effective, Congress was bound to deliberate before enacting and to ask for information to assist its deliberations. The power to make treaties was not claimed, but the power to carry them out was insisted upon. The leading advocates of this view were Livingston, Gallatin, who had recently taken his seat as a member from Pennsylvania, Samuel Smith of Maryland, and the Virginia members, Nicholas, Page and Brent, with Madison to lead them. The other side had Sedgwick of Massachusetts, Vans Murray of Maryland, Smith and Harper of South Carolina. After three weeks' debate the call for the papers was agreed to March 24 by a vote of 62 to 37. On the 30th the President's reply was received, refusing categorically to comply with the request, because it was an interference with the rights of the treaty-making power, which did not include the House of Representatives,

"The absolute refusal," wrote Madison, "was as

unexpected as the tone and tenor of the message are improper and indelicate."* He attributed its author- ship, of course, to Hamilton.

When the message came before the Committee of the Whole, Blount of North Carolina offered resolutions, composed by Madison, briefly reaffirming as the sense of the House the arguments already made by the Repub- licans. Madison made a long speech in favour of the resolutions, supposing that they would be debated; but when the House met the day after his speech, to his surprise no arguments were made on the other side and the resolutions were passed by a vote of 57 to 35. Six members came in after the vote was taken and asked that they be added to the majority, but under the rules this could not be done. April 15, the treaty came up again, Madison making the chief speech against it and Ames replying. April 29, the necessary provision for the execution of the treaty was passed in Committee of the Whole by the casting vote of Muhlenberg, the Speaker. One Republican member was absent, another sick, but Madison noted with dismay that the ranks of his party were breaking.† The next day, April 30, the House confirmed the action of the committee by a vote of 51 to 48. Ten members who had voted for Madison's resolutions now voted to put the treaty in operation. The defeat was a most serious one and marked a turn of the tide against the Republicans. The people were back of the majority, for the impression had got abroad that the House wished to bring about war, and they rallied to the cry "to follow where Washington leads." Strangely enough it was in New England that this cry was the strongest and in the South where it was weakest. The only Southern members who changed their votes were three from Maryland. The Virginia members stood in solid array against the Virginia Pres-

* To Jefferson, April 4, 1796, "Works" (Cong. Ed.) II, 90.
† "Works," (Cong. Ed.) II, 94.

ident.   The result was a peculiar one.   The House had
reaffirmed its position and then receded from its action.
A situation exceedingly awkward not to say dangerous
had been relieved, and no principle had been settled.

CHAPTER XXIV

THE NATIONAL GAZETTE

THE principal newspaper organ of the Anti-Federalists until Jefferson left the Cabinet was *The National Gazette* edited by Philip Freneau and established largely at Madison's instigation. The chief Federalist organ was *The United States Gazette* with John Fenno for editor. Fenno's prospectus when he moved his paper from New York to Philadelphia in the autumn of 1790 said:

"At this important crisis, the ideas that fill the mind, are pregnant with events of the greatest magnitude—to strengthen and complete the *union* of the States—to extend and protect their *commerce*—to explore and arrange the *national funds*—to restore and establish the *public credit*—will require the *energies* of the patriots and sages of our country."*

Freneau announced his purpose:

"In this paper the Editor engages to support, as far as a newspaper can with propriety be supposed to support, the great principles upon which the American Revolution was founded, a faithful adherence to which can alone preserve the blessings of liberty to this extensive empire —an empire, in which the grand experiment is now making, whether or not the assertion of certain European philosophers be true, *that a pure republic can never subsist for any length of time, except in a very limited extent of territory.*"

Hamilton himself sometimes attacked the Anti-Federalists over a pseudonym through Fenno's columns, and Madison wrote a number of unsigned articles for Freneau, but they were all short philosophical or political dis-

* *The National Gazette*, November 3, 1790.

quisitions dealing in no personal abuse. Freneau's tone was really taken from Jefferson and the object of the paper was to counteract the effect of *The United States Gazette*, which it soon outstripped in abuse and vituperation of those with whom it differed.

Philip Freneau, a New Yorker of Huguenot descent, was at Princeton with Madison, and was one of the most popular youths of his class. He had in an extraordinary degree the qualities to make him a success among undergraduates, for he was quick, bright, versatile and witty. He could speak easily, he was full of enthusiasms, and he wrote poetry by the yard. As he entered college in 1771, the same year in which Madison graduated, there was no opportunity for prolonged college intimacy between them, but Madison liked the warm-hearted ornamental poetaster, probably because he possessed the very qualities which Madison himself did not have, or at any rate did not cultivate. Freneau on his side admired the great scholar and esteemed it a privilege to form one of his circle, and so the two became devoted friends for life. From Princeton Freneau went into a Maryland family at Havre de Grace as private tutor and opened a correspondence with Madison. He described himself as teaching all day and writing poetry all night and his first letters were enlivened by many impromptu rhymes.* He had just published a volume of poems, one being, as he expressed it, "to the Nymph I never saw," and another entitled "The American Village," which was "damned by all good and judicious judges." "It is now late at night," he went on, "not an hour ago I finished a little poem of about 400 lines, entitled a Journey to Maryland. I intend to write a terrible Satir upon certain vicious persons of quality in N. Y.—who have also used me ill—and print it next fall—it shall contain 5 or 600 Lines—Sometimes I write pastorals to show my wit." He was then five weeks less than twenty-one years of age and said he was already "stiff with age."

* Dept. of State MSS.

He was a charming fellow, doomed, like others of his kind, to literature, journalism and material failure. He took to a seafaring life, lost his privateer *The Aurora* in the Revolution, was captured by the British and confined on one of the prison ships in New York harbour till July, 1780.* He afterwards published numerous editions of his poems, which posterity now reads with more curiosity than admiration, but his contemporaries liked them and called him "The Poet of the Revolution."

In the summer of 1791 Freneau announced to his friends his purpose of starting a newspaper in New Jersey, and Madison and Henry Lee, also a Princeton man and friend of Freneau's, had little difficulty in inducing him to bring his paper to Philadelphia, and both of them acted for him in securing subscribers.† Madison had before this recommended him for employment in the Government service and now proposed to Jefferson to appoint him a translator of French in the State Department.‡ It was not supposed that his duties would require more than a part of his time, for his salary was fixed at $250 a year, which was half of the amount paid the regular clerks in the department. This pittance was, however, a desirable certainty to accompany the uncertainty of editing a newspaper, but it cannot justly be called a subsidy for the editor. The first number of *The Gazette* appeared October 31, 1791. It had a four-column page, and did not differ in make-up from Fenno's paper, except that it was even worse printed. It came out Monday and Thursday mornings, while Fenno's *Gazette* appeared on Wednesdays and Saturdays. There was a summary of the proceedings of Congress, several extracts from private letters from different parts of the country and abroad, translations from *The Leyden Gazette*, official announcements, a few advertisements, and usually an

---

* See " Philip Freneau, the Poet of the American Revolution."
† Dept. of State MSS.
‡ Madison to Edmund Pendleton, September 13, 1792, " Madison's Works" (Cong. Ed.) I, 569.

essay. One appeared in the first number by C. W. Peale, the painter, entitled "An Account of a Person Born a Negro, or a Very Dark Mulatto Who Afterwards Became White;" November 17 Thomas Paine had an article on the mint, and three days later Madison had one on "Population and Emigration." Thus far the paper was mild mannered, although it gave unusual prominence to all reports emanating from the State Department. On December 8, however, it printed a piece signed "Americanus," which attacked some of the Administration's acts, and this was followed by other communications of the same tenor, levelled especially against the funding, assumption and bank laws, and the Secretary of the Treasury. Side by side with the long articles which were generally able and well prepared were brief paragraphs by Freneau which were scurrilous without being clever. Much of this literature of vituperation was, however, in reply to articles of like characteristics on the other side, and it is only fair to say that Freneau disclosed no official secrets in his paper and displayed no facilities for information greater than were at the command of any one not connected with the Government. Of course, when the proper time came Fenno accused him of being subsidized by Jefferson. "Quere," he said, "whether this salary is paid him for *translations;* or for publications, the design of which is to vilify' those to whom the voice of the people has submitted the administration of our public affairs," etc; to which, in the issue of July 28, 1792, Freneau replied that the "vile sycophant" who thus unjustly accused him received greater public emoluments than he from the Government printing which was given him in order that he might "poison the minds of the people:" and so on in the style since rendered classic by the two editors of Eatonswill.

In September, 1792, Fenno attacked Madison for patronizing Freneau, but Madison regarded the charge with indifference, and never concealed his agency in bringing Freneau to Philadelphia. Freneau was appointed trans-

lator, August 16, 1791, a few months before *The Gazette*
appeared; he resigned October, 1793, soon after Jefferson's
retirement, and *The Gazette* stopped publication at the
end of that month. While it lasted Washington disliked its attacks upon his administration extremely, and
plainly hinted to Jefferson that he ought to dismiss
Freneau from the service, but he was useful to Jefferson
and was retained. Jefferson declared to Washington in
writing and with great solemnity that beyond furnishing
Freneau with copies of *The Leyden Gazette*, so that
the public might have good European news, he neither
wrote himself nor prompted others to write a line for *The
Gazette*,* but Jefferson had the talent of inspiring
others to do what he wished done without making a
direct request. But the articles in *The Gazette* always
spared Washington himself, and there is every reason to
believe that Jefferson and Madison were in the main
satisfied with the result of their effort to establish an
Anti-Federal paper.

When *The National Gazette* ceased publication its
place was soon filled by a number of party sheets which
far outstripped it in foulness, and the press became
furiously, recklessly violent in tone. "Peter Porcupine"
(Corbett) led for the Federalists. On September 27, 1797,
he thus wrote of a Republican Congressman: "This
is one of the most infamous wretches that ever existed.
He now stands charged with purloining the property of
children, whose father he visited on his death-bed; yet
this man is a member of Congress." Benjamin Franklin,
the grandfather of Corbett's editorial enemy, Benjamin
Franklin Bache, he alluded to pleasantly as "a crafty
and lecherous old hypocrite." Bache in *The Aurora*
spoke thus of Corbett: "He has not only condescended
to publish in his own paper, that he is a *liar* and a *scoundrel*, but has contrived to get himself flogged for being
actually both." Editors frequently engaged in personal
encounters, and certainly they deserved their floggings.

* " Jefferson's Writings " II, 106.

Most of them were foreigners newly arrived in America. "Peter Porcupine" had recently come from England, about the same time with Thomas Cooper of *The Reading (Pa.) Advertiser;* Callendar of *The Richmond Recorder* was a Scotchman; Bache of *The Aurora* was, it is true, an American, but upon his death in 1798 his place was taken by William Duane, born as it happened in America, but spending his life, until he came to Philadelphia to take part in public affairs, in Ireland, his parents' country.*

These newspapers were a cause and an effect of partisan bitterness. Their lurid tones were not too strong for their readers, and at the same time fanned the flames of the readers' hate. To quench or subdue a fire so obnoxious and dangerous was undoubtedly a thing to be desired. The chief offenders were in Philadelphia, because it was the capital. The Republicans were strong in the Middle States and the Federalists were strong in South Carolina and Maryland. The stronghold for Federalism was, however, New England, and the stronghold for Republicanism was, broadly speaking, the South.

* Wharton's " State Trials " gives a number of extracts from their newspapers, 24, *n.*

CHAPTER XXV

DOLLY PAYNE

IT IS not strange that the East and South should have so frequently found themselves in opposition on public questions, for their industries, products, climate and traditions were different. Moreover, the leaders of thought in either section had little personal knowledge of the other section, and more of them had been to Europe than had travelled extensively in their own country. The prejudice of the East against the South and of the South against the East was thus based partly upon ignorance.

"A human life, I think," says George Eliot, "should be well rooted in some spot of a native land, where it may get the love of tender kinship for the face of earth." Such a kinship existed for Americans of the time of which we are writing to an extraordinary degree, for they were nearly all countrymen. It existed especially for the Virginians, whose family associations tied them to their plantations. There their fathers had lived, and there they expected their sons to live. They constituted a landed aristocracy, a privileged order which governed the State.

Fine types of the class were Jefferson, Madison and Monroe, the two former with splendid inherited farms of baronial extent, and Monroe bending his energies to the establishment of a similar estate. It was after the parties formed in Congress and Jefferson became the leader of the Republicans, that the three Virginians made a league and became the three musqueteers of American public life. Henceforth they acted together on all questions and guarded each other's interests with perfect watchfulness and faithfulness. Madison and Monroe put Jefferson's interests as paramount to their own; Monroe was not the equal of the other two in knowledge or influence and he was disturbed by jealousy of Madison when the question of Jefferson's successor in the Presidential chair was under consideration, but the regular co-operation of the three went on, although, of course, they had never agreed to form an alliance.

It does not appear that Monroe ever went to New England until he was President and made his famous tour, and Jefferson and Madison were mature men with well-settled political convictions, when they took a glimpse of New England for the first time in a three-weeks' journey, from May 20 to June 16, 1791, during a recess of Congress.*

While Congress sat in New York they lived near one another in Maiden Lane, Jefferson having a house and Madison boarding with Mrs. Dorothy Ellsworth, the wife of Mr. Verdine Ellsworth. Most of the members of Congress were obliged to put up with narrow accommodations, but Mrs. Ellsworth's appears to have been a pleasant place, and her table was popular with members of Congress. Madison was on good terms with her, and was permitted to owe her part of his board when it was inconvenient for him to pay it all, and even to borrow from her and use her as a sort of banker. He kept a servant and a horse and there is no reason to believe he fared badly.†

It was different when the Government moved back to Philadelphia. Yellow fever had ravaged the city and people were afraid to live in it, the officers of the Government and members of Congress preferring to live in Germantown. There Jefferson and Monroe succeeded in getting one room with two beds in it, and when Madison came they took him in. They breakfasted at their lodgings and dined at a tavern across the street. They were

* " Jefferson's Writings " (Ford) V, 340.
† Dept. of State MSS.

better accommodated than many others, who found difficulty in getting even half beds. When the yellow fever
subsided there was a general movement back to Philadelphia and a dispersion among the taverns and boarding
houses of that city. A deep gloom hung over the city,
and there were many more vacant rooms to let than there
had been the year before.

Among the boarding houses was one presided over
by a Quakeress widow, Mrs. John Payne, and her daughter, Dolly Payne, whom the yellow fever had also left a
widow, her husband, John Todd, having died October 24,
and her infant son a few weeks before. Into Mrs. Payne's
lodgings was received the Senator from New York, Aaron
Burr. He and Madison had been at Princeton together,
but not of the same set, for Burr was prominent in the
Cliosophic Society, and Madison a founder of the American
Whig Society, and about these two rival organizations
clustered the social life of the college. When they met
in public service membership in the same political party
drew them together, but there is nothing to indicate that
they were ever on terms of friendship. Their natures
were antipathetic to each other. Madison was a genuine
man, of deep learning acquired because he loved it.
There was no false note, no evil tendency, no cynicism or
flippancy in him. His mind was fearless, and he neither
lied to others, nor deceived himself, nor fibbed, nor told
white lies, nor drew the long bow. It is inexplicable that
so intelligent and straightforward a man should not have
correctly read Aaron Burr, whose character was not very
complicated. He was simply a scoundrel, who held
nothing in respect, because he found nothing to respect
in himself. He hated Washington, hounded Hamilton
to his death and sneered at Madison. He studied only
for show and was all tinsel. He gambled with life, re-
garding it as a game, and, as it happened, he was the
agent who introduced Madison to life's greatest lottery,
in which Madison drew a prize.

Although a hard-working man, Madison was not a

recluse. He was a chess player at this time,* and he
liked to mingle in the social life of Philadelphia. He
saw and admired Burr's landlady's daughter, the widow
Todd, and requested an introduction. In arranging for
it Burr's agency in the matter appears to have begun
and ended. Mrs. Todd had already heard of Madison
as "the great little Madison," and she prepared for his
visit with fluttering expectancy. Her husband had
died only a few months before, but, being a Quakeress,
she wore no mourning, and being young in years and
naturally sunny-hearted she took life as she saw it about
her and did not brood over that part of it which lay behind her. When she was an old woman she described
herself to her friend Mrs. Samuel Harrison Smith of Washington as follows: "My family are all Virginians except
myself, who was born in N. Carolina, whilst my parents
were there on a visit of one year, to an Uncle. Their
families on both sides were among the most respectable,
and they, becoming members of the Society of Friends
soon after their marriage, manumitted their slaves, and
left this State for that of Pennsylvania, bearing with them
their children to be educated in their religion—I believe
my age at that time was 11 or 12 years—I was educated
in Philadelphia where I was married to Mr. Todd in 1790
and to Mr. Madison in '94, when I returned with him
to the soil of my Father, and to Washington, where you
have already traced me with the kindness of a sister.
In the year '91, and after the death of my Father, my
Mother received into her house some Gentlemen as
boarders—and in '93 she left Philadelphia to reside with
her daughter Washington—afterwards with my sister
Jackson—and occasionally with me."†

"Her daughter Washington" was the wife of General
Washington's nephew, George Steptoe Washington, of
Harewood, near Charlestown, West Virginia, and at her
house, September 15, 1794, by Rev. Dr. Balmaine, an

* Dept. of State MSS.
† Family papers of J. Henry Smith, Esq., of Washington.

Episcopal clergyman of Winchester, a connection of Madison's, Dolly Payne Todd and James Madison were married after an engagement of about six months. She was only twenty-six years old and he was forty-three.* They made the long journey from Harewood to Montpelier, and set up their establishment in the old house at Montpelier, which Madison had enlarged and which was henceforth their home as well as the home of Madison's father and mother.

She participated completely in her husband's life and contributed to the success of his career, for she was troubled with no doubts about its being the one best suited to him. She liked Philadelphia and Montpelier, and afterwards Washington. She was fond of the gaiety of the capital, but she created gaiety in the country. Her disposition was warm, ardent and impressionable. Her personality was sympathetic and charming. Although she was Quaker bred she was the opposite of a Quaker in nature, and her bright complexion, healthy plumpness and ready laughter were Celtic rather than Philadelphian. She expanded in the congenial social atmosphere of Virginia and her husband enjoyed an extraordinary domestic felicity from the hour of his marriage to the hour of his death. His own temper was genial and serene; he was never irritated and he did not worry about trifles. He took a keen interest in all the household arrangements and gave his wife perfect devotion. He owed her a great deal and she owed him everything.

Coming into the country of her husband, where a large number of the people were his relatives or connections, and where she was herself an entire stranger, she was in a family atmosphere which was highly critical, and the country criticism did not decrease when it was observed that her establishment was oftener of benefit to her relations than her husband's, and hers were numerous and

* See Mrs. Wilder's "Dolly Madison" for an interesting account of her life.

made frequent and long visits to Montpelier, and to the house in town. But no fault could be found by the Madisons with Mrs. Madison when they came in contact with her, for she treated them with a kindness which compelled their liking, and even when the querulousness of great age came upon her husband's old mother she had nothing but commendation and affection for her son's wife. *

Being now a married man and graduated from the army of boarding-house and tavern victims Madison carried his wife back to Philadelphia for the session of Congress in the winter of 1794-95, and occupied the house in which Monroe had lived the year before. The next session he took a house on Spruce Street, between Fourth and Fifth Streets, belonging to James Gamble. It was of brick, three stories high, with two rooms on each floor, beside the kitchen, and there was a good yard and stable. He paid a rent of £200 a year, and here he remained until he retired from Congressional service.†

He had earned a rest and wanted to live the life which he craved above all others, and which he now regarded as completely satisfying his earthly wants. Dreams of bucolic felicity with his wife for a companion floated before him. He would improve Montpelier, indulge his taste for architecture, and become a scientific farmer. There would be ample opportunity for reading and pursuing the non-political investigations which interested him so much. Visitors would come and go and he would not suffer from dulness. He would throw off the heavy burden of public care which he had borne for twenty years. During fourteen years of this time he had striven mightily to save the country from wreck, and being a man who looked the facts in the face and did not allow his desires to govern his beliefs, there had been many times when he thought his efforts would come to naught.

* In Orange County, Va., the recollection of Mrs. Madison is still vivid among members of the county families.

† Dept. of State MSS.

He had lived to see those efforts crowned with a success the glory of which he fully recognized. And, the Constitution having been adopted, the Union having been saved, a nation having been created, the results of the Revolution having been made splendid beyond his hopes, he found himself now one of a faction, engaged in partisan bickering, the victim of injustice and himself unjust, harbouring the bitterness which party strife engenders. He was fighting against men who had formerly fought with him and over issues which were petty beside those of the days before the Constitution. He did not care for victory for victory's sake, nor for the applause which it brings. He was really weary of the fight. As he left Congressional service March 4, 1797, his friend Jefferson took it up as Vice-President and President of the Senate.

More than a year before (in February, 1796) as soon as it became known that Washington would not serve for a third term, Madison announced to Monroe, who was in Paris, that the Republicans knew Jefferson was the only candidate whom they could hope to elect. He was afraid Jefferson would mar his candidacy by announcing an unwillingness to serve,* but no such announcement came, and when it became doubtful whether Jefferson would be the President or Vice-President, he wrote to him: "You *must* reconcile yourself to the secondary, as well as the primary station."† When Madison first broached the subject to Jefferson, the latter replied that he thought Madison himself ought to be chosen for the Presidency, but Madison did not deem the subject worth considering, Jefferson being, as a matter of course, the choice of the Republicans.

Adams was elected by a majority of two votes only. One elector from Pennsylvania, one from North Carolina, and one from Virginia voted for him. If the electoral votes of those States had been cast solidly Jefferson would have been the President, and there is no doubt that all

* "Works" (Cong. Ed.) II, 83.
† Id., II, 107.

three of the States, on a direct vote, would have voted for him.

During the last session of Congress before his retirement Madison took little part in the proceedings. His party was in the minority, and the House was in control of extremists, who paid small regard to the minority's feelings or rights. When the session began, December, 1796, Washington addressed to it his last speech, but the committee appointed to draft a reply had Fisher Ames as chairman instead of Madison, who during his entire Congressional service had always heretofore occupied this post of honour. He was placed on the committee, however, and agreed to the address submitted. It was his colleague Giles who made the motion to strike out the portions of the address which spoke of the wisdom of the Administration and expressed regret at Washington's retirement and moved its recommitment for alteration; and eight of the Virginia members moved to strike out the clause expressing the hope that Washington's example might be a guide to his successors, Madison, Nicholas, Page and Claiborne being the only ones who voted to retain the clause.

CHAPTER XXVI

FROM his retirement Madison watched the course of events at Philadelphia with intense and increasing solicitude. His own party was in the minority. The proceedings of Genet, the hideous excesses of the French Revolutionists, and finally the contemptuous treatment by Talleyrand of the American envoys, Marshall, Pinckney and Gerry, and his efforts to extract from them a bribe, combined to force many men out of the Republican into the Federalist party more from lack of sympathy with the former than from real sympathy with the latter. But the Federalists were in power; they had the President, the Senate and the House. In the Cabinet the Secretary of State was the most uncompromising Federalist of all. John Adams said of Timothy Pickering, after he had found him out: "Under the simple appearance of a bald head and straight hair, and under professions of profound republicanism, he concealed an ardent ambition, envious of any superior and impatient of obscurity." He was devoted heart and soul to Alexander Hamilton's interests and indifferent to the interests and opinions of his chief. He did not, therefore, share Adams's desire to avail himself of the "fine talents and amiable qualities and manners of Mr. Madison." Adams told Jefferson he would like to appoint Madison one of the envoys to adjust differences with France, but Jefferson said Madison would not go, as he had already refused foreign appointments on several previous occasions. Adams abandoned the idea for the additional reason that his Cabinet threatened to resign if Madison were nominated, and the Federalist leaders of the Senate said they would reject the nomination, if it came before them. Alexander Hamilton, taking a broader view of public policy than his followers did, favoured Madison's selection, but no appointment was offered him, and he would have declined it if it had been made, for he was perfectly honest in his desire to remain at home for a time.

The Federalists now had control of the machinery with which to make laws and determined upon three radical measures to check the political activity of the aliens who were in the country and to curb the licentiousness of the press. The first of these laws was passed June 18, 1798, and related to the naturalization of aliens. It prescribed fourteen years as the probationary period of residence necessary before an alien could be admitted to become a citizen of the United States. In the debate on the bill Harper of South Carolina said he thought no foreigner ought to be admitted to citizenship, and Otis of Massachusetts said that none should ever be permitted to hold office. A few days later, June 25, the Alien act was passed. It gave the President power to expel from the United States any alien whose presence he might judge to be dangerous to the peace and safety of the United States, or whom he might suspect of treasonable or secret machinations against the Government. Masters of vessels were required to report to him all alien passengers brought by them into the country.

A month later, July 14, the sedition law was passed. It provided that the printing, writing, or publishing of anything false, scandalous or malicious against the Government, President or Congress, or the stirring up of sedition against them, or the doing of anything to bring them into contempt, should constitute a criminal offence punishable with fine and imprisonment. The desire for these acts originated with the leaders in Congress; there was no popular demand for them; they interpreted no popular movement; they underwent no test before the people before they were enacted. Timothy Pickering was sorry they did not go further; Fisher Ames refused

to trust John Marshall because he did not approve of
them; John Adams fully approved of them; so did nearly
all of the other Federalist leaders.

As for the reception which the laws met among
Republicans it need hardly be stated. All their prog-
nostications of evils sure to result from the ascendancy
of the Federalists seemed about to be fulfilled. Jefferson
believed, or fancied he believed, or at any rate tried to
make others believe, that the obnoxious laws were an
experiment to see how much the people would stand and
that if they were submitted to propositions for life tenure
of the Presidency and hereditary succession would follow.
He wrote in this sense "with unwonted excitement,"
as Randall says, to Senator Mason, of Virginia,
September 26, 1789. J. Dawson, a follower of Madison's,
wrote from the House of Representatives, July 5, 1798,
before the sedition law had been passed, that it exceeded
anything that had disgraced the history of any country
pretending to be free. "What is to become of us," he
added, "I cannot tell, but think we are certainly ruined,
if the people do not come forward & exercise their
rights."

Madison's own opinion was that a grave crisis in the
liberties of the country had come and that it demanded
concerted action on the part of the Republicans. Accordingly, under the lead of Jefferson there was a notable consultation between John Taylor of Carolina, the brothers
George and Wilson Cary Nicholas, John Breckinridge
and Madison, and it was determined to obtain from the
Legislatures of Kentucky and Virginia declaratory resolutions against the Federal party's Constitutional tenets
in general and against the Alien and Sedition laws in particular; and to invite the co-operation of the other States
in asking for a repeal of those laws and a declaration that
they were unconstitutional and consequently null and
void. It was intended, also, that the declaration should
be a warning to the dominant party that an attempt to
carry out the programme, of which the alien and sedition

laws were supposed to be only a part, would cause a revolt, peaceful if possible, but violent if necessary.

The resolutions for the Kentucky legislation were drafted by Jefferson and amended by John Breckinridge, who introduced them in the Kentucky House where they were adopted by an almost unanimous vote.* Kentucky was a border State, fond of fighting and used to it, and indisposed to submit to authority when it became irksome. The Alien and Sedition laws had created a ferment among the people and the resolutions were radical enough to suit them. They declared that the Constitution had been adopted by the States as States who must be the judges of when the Constitution had been broken; and that in case of the passage of an unconstitutional law the several States had a right to interpose and nullify such a law. The Alien and Sedition laws were denounced as unconstitutional.

Madison had no hand in preparing the Kentucky resolutions and never saw them until after his own resolutions had been introduced, but there was, of course, an agreement beforehand that both Virginia and Kentucky should say substantially the same thing. Kentucky, however, went farther than Virginia did, and the time came when it was harder to explain the Kentucky resolutions than it was to explain those Madison had written. As Madison was not in the Legislature at the time, he gave the draft of his resolutions to John Taylor of Caroline, who submitted it to the House without alteration. Madison was himself in doubt whether the State Legislatures were really the proper instruments for dealing with a Constitutional question, since they had not been permitted to ratify the Constitution, and he had insisted in the Constitutional Convention that it be not submitted to them; but they had had a part in it, inasmuch as they had called the Federal Convention which framed it, and the State conventions which ratified it, so he suppressed his scruples and used the Legislature of Virginia for his purpose.

* Warfield's "The Kentucky Resolutions of 1798."

The Republicans of the State were in the majority, but there was a vigorous and respectable minority of Federalists, and the resolutions were adopted in the face of an ably conducted opposition.   The vote was 100 to 63, and the temper of the Legislature was conservative as compared with the temper of the Kentucky Legislature. The draft prepared by Madison declared the Alien and Sedition laws "unconstitutional, null, void and of no effect," but by general agreement the words "null, void," etc., although really no more than strengthening repetition, were stricken out as liable to misinterpretation. This was the only alteration made in Madison's draft. The resolutions were eight in number.   The third said: "That this Assembly doth explicitly and peremptorily declare that it views the powers of the Federal Government as resulting from the compact to which the States are parties, as limited by the plain sense and intention of the instrument constituting that compact; as no further valid than they are authorized by the grants enumerated in that compact; and that, *in case of a deliberate, palpable, and dangerous exercise of other powers not granted by the said compact, the States, who are parties thereto, have the right and are in duty bound to interpose for arresting the progress of the evil, and for maintaining within their respective limits the authorities, rights, and liberties appertaining to them.*"   The fourth resolution expressed alarm at the spirit manifested in Congress of construing certain general phrases in the Constitution "so as to destroy the meaning and effect of the particular enumeration which necessarily explains and limits the general phrases; so as to consolidate the States by degrees, into one sovereignty, the obvious tendency, an inevitable result of which would be to transform the present republican system of the United States into an absolute, or, at best, mixed monarchy."   The fifth resolution declared the Alien and Sedition laws "palpable and alarming" infractions of the Constitution.   The Alien act exercised power in no place granted in the Constitution, the Sedition act exercised power expressly forbidden. The sixth resolution said that as Virginia [Madison himself] had proposed the amendment to the Constitution confirming the liberty of the press, it would be unbecoming if she should show indifference to a violation of the amendment. Resolution seven said: "That the good people of this Commonwealth, having ever felt and continuing to feel the most sincere affection for their brethren of the other States, the truest anxiety for establishing and perpetuating the union of all and the most scrupulous fidelity to that Constitution, which is the pledge of mutual friendship, and the instrument of mutual happiness, the General Assembly doth solemnly appeal to the like dispositions of the other States, in confidence that they will concur with this Commonwealth in declaring, as it does hereby declare, that the aforesaid acts are unconstitutional; and that the necessary and proper measures will be taken by each for co-operating with this State, in maintaining unimpaired the authorities, rights, and liberties reserved to the States respectively, or to the people." The eighth resolution provided for sending the resolutions to the executives of the States for the Legislatures and to the Senators and Representatives of Virginia in Congress.

On January 10, 1799, the Assembly resolved that the State would co-operate with the authorities of the general Government in maintaining the "independence, Union, and Constitution" against all foreign powers, and that it was a calumny to charge that any party in the State was under the influence of any foreign power; that they beheld "with indignation" depredations on the commerce of the country, impressments of seamen, and other insults by foreign nations; but that a standing army was unnecessary and the policy of the United States forbade a war of aggression; that they would repel invasion at every hazard, but deplored the evils of war from any other cause.

On January 23rd was adopted an address to the people of the State. It was a vigorous arraignment of the Alien and Sedition laws. Non-acquiescence in infractions of the Constitution was, it said, necessary, otherwise there would be a speedy consolidation, or upon repetition of the infractions a revolution by the people aroused "in the majesty of their strength."

Madison was elected a member of the Legislature in the fall of 1799. All the Republican members of the Virginia delegation in the National House of Representatives had united in begging him to return to public life. They wrote to him from Philadelphia, February 7, 1799: "While the sentiments we entertain of your Talents, your experience & your Probity, have made your absence from the public councils, a subject of our very serious regret, our Confidence in the justness of your Motives assures us, that you stand completely justified.

"At the same time the Growth & conduct of the executive Party, since your retirement, have continued more & more to render the Inaction of republican Principles & Talents deplorable & injurious.

"Our extreme Solicitude to give energy to those virtues, in every possible direction, has urged us jointly to address you. We hope that obstacles to your serving in the State legislature, may be less imperious, than those by which you were withdrawn from that of the Union—it is quite needless to point out *to you*, the powerful agency of *wise* and *firm* State measures in preserving the general government within the just Limits of the Constitution, which from the nature of things, it must be ever struggling to transcend: but our present position enables us to discover, perhaps more clearly, the perseverance & success of those struggles. . . .

"We should be wanting in the Social Duties we profess, if we declined to invite you with earnestness, to take part in the councils of your State.

"Pretensions founded as yours are, can scarcely fail of success—our utmost aid, if it shall be in any way applicable, and our ardent wishes will attend you in the experiment."

This was signed by Walter Jones, John Nicholas, Carter H. Harrison, Joseph Eggleston, Abraham B. Venable and Richard Brent.*

The only replies to the Kentucky and Virginia resolutions ever made were dissenting resolutions from the Legislatures of the five New England States and New York and Delaware, and Madison wrote as a defence a report explanatory of the Virginia resolutions, which the Legislature adopted. The Constitution, it said, was, at the time its adoption was under discussion, constantly defended by the argument that the powers it did not express had been withheld from it, and the Twelfth amendment specifically expressed this. It was a compact between the States, meaning the people composing the several States in their highest sovereign capacity. That they had a right to interpose "in case of a deliberate, palpable, and dangerous exercise of other powers, not granted by the said compact" seemed plain. "Where resort can be had to no tribunal superior to the authority of the parties, the parties themselves must be the rightful judges, in the last resort, whether the bargain made has been pursued or violated." The resolutions, he went on, proposed such interposition only when the breach of the Constitution was *deliberate*, *dangerous*, and plain to all men, and only for the purpose of arresting the evil of usurpation. It was objected that the judicial authority should be construed as the sole expositor of the Constitution in last resort, but there might be forms of usurpation that could never be drawn within the control of the judicial department, and furthermore "if the decision of the judiciary could be raised above the authority of the sovereign parties to the Constitution, the decisions of the other departments, not carried by the forms of the Constitution before the judiciary, must be equally authoritative and final with the decisions of that department." The resolutions related to "those great and extraordinary cases in which all the forms of the Constitution may prove

* Dept. of State MSS.

ineffectual against infractions dangerous to the essential rights of the parties to it." If the judiciary concurred in usurpation the subversion of the Government was complete.

The resolutions and the report were welcomed by Madison's friends: "Your Report upon the Resolutions of the last assembly," wrote Rev. James Madison, January 9, 1800, "cannot be too highly estimated by every real Friend to free & rational Government; & particularly by those who are most attached to a federal Gov't—You have really swept the Augean Stable; at least you have cleansed the Constitution from that Filth which ambition, avarice & Ignorance were heaping up around it. If the Doctrine respecting common Law; if the continued Extension of the Powers of the federal Legislature, & federal executive; if also judicial subserviency to executive measures; if, too, the mad ambition of forming navies and standing armies, should prevail; or rather be the constant end & aim of all federal measures, it would not require the Spirit of Prophesy to foretell the Result. One or other of these evils must ensue. The Union will suffer a convulsive Death; or, we shall enjoy a *quitum servitium*, than which I can safely say a thousand times *malo periculosam libertatem*."

The Virginia resolutions enunciated doctrines which Madison had always advocated. One feature of the Virginia plan which he had unsuccessfully advocated in the Constitutional Convention lodged in the Federal Congress a right of negative over State laws and in a council a similar revision power over national laws, to curb legislative power. In the *Federalist* (No. XLIV) he pointed out that the danger of republican governments was to aggrandize the legislature at the expense of the other departments of government, and that whenever any one department encroached upon another there should be an appeal to the people to declare the full meaning and enforce the observance of the charter of powers for "preventing and correcting infractions of the constitution." In the first Congress he was alarmed at the power assumed by Congress. "In truth," he wrote, "the legislative power is of such a nature that it scarcely can be restrained, either by the Constitution or by itself; and if the Federal Government should lose its proper equilibrium within itself, I am persuaded that the effect will proceed from the encroachments of the Legislative Department." In 1792 Washington vetoed the act of Congress apportioning the Representatives among the several States, because it violated the Constitutional requirement that the apportionment be by population and not more than one to every 30,000 of inhabitants; and in 1794 the Supreme Court declared the act of March 23, 1792, conferring upon United States courts jurisdiction over claims for invalid pensions to be unconstitutional, because it was an attempt to confer upon the court power which was not judicial. Both of these checks upon Congressional power Madison commended as encouraging signs.* The Supreme Court had not yet, however, asserted roundly the right to declare an act of Congress, not concerning the judiciary, unconstitutional, and did not do so until Marshall rendered his decision in the case of Marbury vs. Madison in 1803.

* "Works" (Cong. Ed.) I, 554.

CHAPTER XXVII

THE MADISON DOCTRINE AND NULLIFICATION

MADISON's explanatory report of the Virginia resolutions having been given to the world and a solemn protest against the Alien and Sedition laws having been recorded by the Kentucky Legislature, the incident passed into history. John Adams never put the Alien law into operation, and no trial under the Sedition law took place in Kentucky; but in Virginia the wretched James Thompson Callender was peacefully tried for printing a scurrilous article against the President and other Federalists. The judge was Samuel Chase, who had declared before the trial came off his determination to root up a reed so rank, and at another of the sedition trials this judge said he did not see on what authority the Supreme Court could declare an act of Congress unconstitutional.* When the contest for the Presidency was being waged in 1800 Chase absented himself from the bench to stump Maryland for the Federalists, thereby leaving the court without a quorum; for Ellsworth, the Chief Justice, was absent as Minister to France. William Patterson, another judge, tried Matthew Lyon for sedition and showed clearly enough his thorough sympathy with the obnoxious law.

The Supreme Court was not at this time the calm, independent body it subsequently became, nor was it completely aloof from political or administrative affairs. John Jay, the first Chief Justice, acted as Secretary of State for nearly six months after his elevation to the bench. He was still Chief Justice when he negotiated the treaty with England which excited such furious party

* Wharton's "State Trials," 42, *et seq.*

259

discussion, and his effigy was frequently burned by those who did not like his political views. John Rutledge's nomination as Chief Justice was rejected in 1795 by a Federalist Senate purely on political grounds. For half the time that Ellsworth was Chief Justice he was absent from the bench serving as Minister to France, and to fill this office meant certain entanglement with political parties; and John Marshall himself performed the duties of Secretary of State and Chief Justice at the same time. It was after Jefferson's election and Marshall's dominance of the Court began that its separate and superior functions operated and were recognized.

There is grim humour in the fact that the next time the Virginia resolutions were invoked was by an assemblage of New England Federalists. The Hartford Convention of 1814, called to protest against the measures of James Madison, President of the United States, used this language in the course of its report:

"That acts of Congress in violation of the Constitution are absolutely void is an undeniable position. But in cases of *deliberate, dangerous and palpable infractions of the Constitution, affecting the sovereignty of a State and liberties of the people, it is not only the right but the duty of such a State to interpose its authority for their protection* in the manner best calculated to secure that end. When emergencies occur which are either beyond the reach of the judicial tribunals or too pressing to admit of the delay incident to their forms, States which have no common umpire must be their own judges and execute their own decisions."

This adaptation of Madison's words passed with little notice at the time, the Hartford Convention being almost universally reprobated as a disloyal assemblage of malcontents; but if the malcontents merely threatened disunion they were no worse than others before and after them. The truth is that before the question of the right of secession was definitely settled by the Civil War there was hardly an important question before Congress that

did not arouse sectional jealousy and suggestions of disunion from one side or the other. This cloud was always
threatening in the sky and it assumed its stormiest aspect
in 1828-32 when the Nullification Party formed in South
Carolina. The doctrine advocated by that party, stripped
of its philosophy and compressed into a simple sentence,
was that each State had the right to judge of the constitutionality of acts of Congress, and whenever a State should
decide that a Federal law was unconstitutional it had a
right to interpose and nullify the law within its borders.
It is necessary to glance at the nullification movement to
understand what Madison really meant by his resolutions of 1798, for his last important writings, when he was
over eighty years of age but still in undisputed possession
of his mental faculties, were a vigourous explanation that
the nullification doctrine was an absurd deduction from
the Virginia declarations he had written.*

These declarations were intended, he said, to solve the
interesting question of what should be done in the event
of controversies involving the partition line between the
powers belonging to the Federal and State Governments.
Manifestly the Supreme Court was the *immediate* provision, but the ultimate resort was another thing, and
the parties to the compact were the judges *in last resort*
according to the Virginia resolutions. The South Caro-
linians, he explained, charged that the majority was
oppressing the minority through the forms of government,
while the charge against the Alien and Sedition laws was
that they were Government measures which violated the
will of the constituents. When the Virginia resolutions
were passed it was asserted by the dominant party that
a State Legislature had no right to interpose even a
legislative declaration against a national law, nor against
an opinion of the Supreme Court. The resolutions were
a protest against this theory. When bad laws were
passed there were three remedies. First, the checks provided in the constitution itself; second, the ballot; third,

* Works (Cong. Ed.) IV, 204, *et seq.*

an appeal to the power that made the Constitution, and consequently can explain, alter or unmake it. The resolutions invoked the third remedy. As the report adopted by the Legislature in explanation of the resolutions showed, they were at most declaratory and usurped none of the offices of the judiciary. They were an expression of opinion, and asked for concerted action by the States to secure repeal of the obnoxious laws or an explanatory amendment to the Constitution; for it was an undisputed fact that while the Constitution was made by the people it was made by them as embodied in several States. The Virginia resolutions assumed that the States could interpose, notwithstanding a decision of the Supreme Court, as they were the parties to the Constitution and paramount to it. But the resolutions always used the plural term *States*, and the interposition contemplated was not to be a single but a concurrent interposition. A concert of action against a usurpation of power was the keynote to the movement. There could be no tribunal above the States, and they must be the ones to decide when the compact was violated; otherwise there could be no remedy for tyranny. The resolutions were an enunciation of first prinicples—of the sovereignty of the people over their Constitution. A great deal had been made of the fact that the Virginia Legislature had passed laws relating to an armoury and the preservation for members of the Legislature of the right of habeas corpus proceedings, as though they expected to be attacked. The Armoury law was, however, passed before the Alien and Sedition laws, and the Habeas Corpus law was a general one applicable to other as well as Federal arrests. South Carolina nullification Madison characterized as nothing but "an anomalous conceit." That any State could remain a party to the Constitution and nullify a law of the United States was simply absurd. The Government was no mere power of attorney revocable at the will of one of the parties granting it. No State could *at will* secede from its constitutional compact with the other

States; the others must consent, or there must be "an abuse of the compact absolving the seceding party from the obligations imposed by it." No support for nullification, he said, could be extracted from Jefferson's writings. He spoke of it as a *natural* right, not a *constitutional* right. The Kentucky resolutions, Madison admitted, were less guarded than were those of Virginia. He defended them incidentally, however, and insisted that the term "nullification" as used in them was meant to apply "to extreme cases as alone justifying a resort to any forcible relief."

When the nullification doctrine appeared the Virginia Legislature resolved by a vote almost unanimous that the Virginia resolutions of 1798 did not support it, and Madison wrote to Edward Livingston: "The doctrine of nullification [is] as new to me as it was to you." The conclusion is inevitable that those public men who were personally concerned in the movement of 1798 and who saw the South Carolina doctrine appear in 1828 did not believe that the former furnished a fair foundation upon which to build the latter. Thomas Jefferson Randolph, Jefferson's grandson, wrote to Madison in 1833 to say that people were trying to connect Jefferson with the new creed. Randolph had indignantly denied the justice of this and asked Madison to corroborate him, which Madison promptly did.* Thomas H. Benton was in the Senate when Calhounism was first preached in that body. As a firm Democrat, having Jefferson for his patron saint and presumably familiar with Jefferson's tenets, he declared that, although the nullification party had taken its name from a word used in the Kentucky resolutions, and used these resolutions to support its arguments, the creed had really originated after the enactment of the tariff of 1828 and was not held by Jefferson.† In 1829, when Hayne of South Carolina, to support this position, quoted the Virginia resolutions, Daniel Webster denied

* New York Public Library (Lenox) MSS.
† Benton's "Thirty Years' View," I, 138.

that they furnished him an argument, and said they were merely an assertion of a right to dissent from Government measures and of the right of revolution.* Albert Gallatin was an old man and no longer in public life when the Nullification Party formed. Thirty years before he had defended Edward Livingston from censure for an inflammatory speech against the Alien and Sedition laws by saying he concurred in thinking the people had a right to resist unconstitutional laws, although an appeal should first be made to the judiciary. He now pronounced South Carolina's position to be "outrageous and unjustifiable."† Apparently, also, "nullification" was hitherto unheard of by him.

Edward Livingston, as Secretary of State under Andrew Jackson, wrote the great proclamation against the nullifiers. His authorship is proved, not by the fact that a draft of the proclamation in his hand was left by him among his papers,‡ for such a draft might have been made by him from Jackson's notes, but by the identity of the constitutional arguments in the proclamation with those employed by Livingston, first in his speeches in Congress in 1796, and afterward upon his return to public life in 1824. In the interval his views had become less radical, and he said he no longer feared as he had formerly the assumption of undelegated power by the general government, but that his republican sentiments had undergone no change. In 1796, in opposing the enactment of the Alien and Sedition laws, he said: "My opinions, Sir, on this [the constitutional] subject are explicit and I wish they may be known: they are that whenever our laws manifestly infringe the Constitution under which they are made, the people ought not to hesitate which they should obey. Thus, Sir, one of the first effects of measures such as this, if they be not

* Id, I, 140.

† Adams's "Gallatin," 648.

‡ The papers are in the possession of his kinsman, Carleton Hunt, LL. D., at Livingston's country seat, Montgomery on the Hudson.

acquiesced in, will be disaffection among the people to your Government—tumults, violations and recurrence to first revolutionary principles." Again, in another speech he said: "Nor could he see how acts made contrary to the Constitution could be binding upon the people; unless gentlemen said Congress may act in contravention to the Constitution," and in replying to a question by Otis of Massachusetts he said the judges of an infraction of the Constitution were to be the people of the United States. The proclamation of 1832 said: "The ordinance [of nullification] is founded, not on the indefeasible right of resisting acts which are plainly unconstitutional and too oppressive to be endured." . . . There are two appeals to an unconstitutional act passed by Congress —one to the judiciary and the other to the people of the States." He paraphrased in the proclamation part of a speech on international improvements made by him in 1824: "The State Governments, although they did not finally adopt, yet gave it [the Constitution] their previous assent, without which it would not have been submitted to the people." Another sentence of the proclamation must be quoted: "The discovery of this important feature [the right of nullification] in our Constitution was reserved for the present day. To the statesmen of South Carolina belongs the invention, and upon the citizens of that State will unfortunately fall the evils of reducing it to practice." There is really nothing in the Virginia resolutions that could not have been written by the same hand which wrote the proclamation.

Madison said that Livingston's speech on "The Foot Resolutions" delivered in the Senate, March 13, 1830, shortly before he became Secretary of State, expressed his views. Livingston said: "It was an attribute of the sovereignty of the States to watch over the operations of the General Government and protect its citizens from unconstitutional measures. An act in the opinion of a State palpably unconstitutional, but affirmed by the Supreme Court, could be met—

"By remonstrating against it to Congress.

"By an address to the People in their elective functions to change or instruct their representatives;

"By a similar address to the other States, in which they will have a right to declare that they consider the act as unconstitutional and therefore void;

"By proposing amendments to the Constitution in the manner pointed out by that instrument;

"And, finally, if the act be tolerably oppressive, and they find the General Government persevere in enforcing it, by a resort to the natural right which every people have to resist extreme oppression."

Nullification by a single State was, he said, not implied by any right of sovereignty "not warranted by practice or contemporaneous exposition, nor implied by the true construction of the Virginia resolutions of 1898."*

Madison wrote to Henry Clay to say he fully approved of Clay's speech at Cincinnati, August 3, 1832, in which Clay said the doctrine of nullification was as new as it would be alarming, if it were sustained by numbers in proportion to the zeal and fervid eloquence of its friends. "I call it a novel doctrine. I am not unaware that attempts have been made to support it on the authority of certain acts of my native and adopted States [Virginia and Kentucky]. . . . At the epoch of 1798-9, I had just attained my majority, and although I was too young to share in the public councils of my country, I was acquainted with many of the actors of that memorable period; I knew their views, and formed and freely expressed my own opinions on passing events. The then administration of the General Government was believed to entertain views . . . hostile to the existence of the liberties of this country. The Alien and Sedition laws, particularly, and other measures, were thought to be the consequences and proofs of these views. If the administration had such a purpose, it was feared that the extreme case, justifying forcible resistance, might arise, but no one

*Hunt's "Life of Edward Livingston," 345.

believed that, in point of fact, it had arrived.   No one
contended that a single State possessed the power to
annul the deliberate acts of the whole.   .   .   .   The doctrines of that day, and they are as true at this, were, that
the Federal Government is a limited government; that
it has no powers but the granted powers.   Virginia contended that in case of a palpable, deliberate and dangerous exercise of other powers not-granted by said compact,
the States, who are parties thereto, have the right to interpose for arresting the evil, and for maintaining, within
their respective limits, the authorities, rights and liberties appertaining to them.   Kentucky declared that the
'several States that framed that instrument, the Federal
Constitution, being sovereign and independent, have the
unquestionable right to judge of its infractions, and a
nullification by those sovereigns of all unauthorized acts,
done under colour of that instrument, is the rightful
remedy.'   .   .   .   The power of a single State to annul
an act of the whole has been reserved for the discovery
of some politicians in South Carolina."*

But the politicians of South Carolina had in reality been
discussing for some years academically the question of
whether this right existed, and some of them thought
Virginia had said it existed.   The State was Federalist
in 1798, and even approved the Alien and Sedition laws,
and it continued to have a large body of Federalist or Whig
voters for many years afterwards.   In 1821 the publication of Yates's "Minutes of Debates in the Constitutional
Convention" drew forth this comment from *The Southern
Patriot and Commercial Advertiser*, one of the chief newspapers of Charleston: "Let us be assured of the ground
on which we stand; and whether any member of the
States constituting less than a majority of the people of
the Union have a right to declare the Constitution violated whenever they may conceive their rights infringed.
.   .   .   Let the people resume the power granted whenever it be abused, but let no single State assume the ex-

* Works of Henry Clay, V, 401.

travagant pretension of judging of such abuse under the plea of defending the sovereignty of the States. . . .

A single State, therefore, or any number, comprising less than a majority of the people of the United States, can have no right in good faith to release themselves from the compact by which the whole are bound to submit in certain cases to the decisions of that tribunal [the Supreme Court].

"If a majority of the people of the Union conceive this Court tyrannical, let them say so. . . . But until this manifestation of popular feeling takes place, we hold it to be the duty of the minority, whether consisting of one or more States, to submit in silence, because there can be no case of flagrant tyranny or wrong."*

John C. Calhoun was then the very man who did not follow a narrow constitutional construction. "He has," said a newspaper defender in 1822, "invariably deprecated refined [constitutional] subleties and far-fetched constructions, contending that as the Constitution was intended for the *people*, it ought to be construed by the plain and obvious maxims of common sense. It is to politicians of a different character that we are indebted for those technical and lawyer-like refinements which will carry the Constitution in either direction to any extent, even to the confines of anarchy and rebellion." This writer drew a contrast between the views of the public men of South Carolina and Virginia. "The former look upon the General Government as the guardian of the rights of the whole Union, and maintain that whatever powers it has under the Constitution are essentially supreme, and that the State Governments cannot interfere with the exercise of those powers; the latter conceive that the General Government can exercise no power that *they* may please to think a violation of the sovereignty of the States. The former believe that when all the departments of the General Government have affirmed the constitu-

* Files of South Carolina newspapers in the Charleston Library Society, Charleston, S. C.

tionality of an act of Congress, no State has a right to oppose it by penal laws any more than certain other States had a right to oppose, positively or negatively, the late war with Great Britain—whereas, the latter contend that a State, being sovereign, has a right to decide for herself whether the General Government has exceeded its power or not, and to refuse to yield obedience to its laws accordingly."

It was the threat of the tariff of 1828 that changed the tone of public opinion in the State. During the summer of 1827 the people of the various districts held meetings and resolved that a tariff having in view the encouragement of domestic manufactures was contrary to their free and chartered rights. "Our national pact is broken," they cried, and a large and growing sentiment in favour of the separation of South Carolina from the Union was manifested. The Union party of the State sounded the warning that the project of disunion was not the fantasy that Northern optimists believed it to be. On July 4, at a public dinner of the American Revolutionary Society, one of the toasts was: "The Union of the States—to be preserved only by mutual concession, not by unequal taxation." A public meeting in the Colleton District of South Carolina resolved: "That the adhesion of the State of South Carolina to the Union should depend upon the unconditional repeal by the present or next Congress of the tariff laws of 1816, 1824 and 1828, so far as they conflict with the constitutional rights of our citizens." "We may charge New England," said the *City Gazette* of Charleston, the organ of the Union party, "with having produced the Hartford Convention, an assemblage of traitors to their country ! But if we look at home we may find kindred spirits to the Hartford Conventionists, who have been and are now both secretly sowing the seeds of disunion throughout the State, and who are only waiting a favourable opportunity to sap the foundation of the Constitution and apply the torch of the incendiary to the sacred temple of our liberties."

The two parties in the State were the Union party and the Nullifiers, and the former, which until 1832 was probably numerically the stronger, regarded the latter as composed simply of disunionists. "But this everlasting cant," said the Camden, S. C., *Gazette*, "of devotion to the Union, accompanied by a recommendation to do those acts that must necessarily destroy it, is beyond patient endurance from a people not absolutely confined in their own madhouses." Many of the so-called Nullifiers, including some of the leaders of the party, were careless about their complicated creed and preferred the simplicity of rebellion*. Harriet Martineau, who visited Charleston when the excitement was at its height, said: "If not a single import duty had ever been imposed there would still have been the contrasts which they cannot endure to perceive between the thriving States of the North and their own. Now, when they see the flourishing villages of New England, they cry 'we pay for all this.'"† The contemporaneous literature of South Carolina at this time teems with this idea. Why was the State so poor? Why were so many of the people in debt? Why was there no emigration to the State? A tariff law unequal in its benefits was a fact visible to them in their suffering, and they set their teeth in it and worried it, as a dog does a stick which by itself cannot harm him. They would do away with it peaceably or forcibly, with or without separation from the Union, and the Kentucky and Virginia resolutions they took as a basis upon which to construct a constitutional argument, but there would have been the same resistance to the law, and in effect the same rebellion, if the resolutions had never been written and if Calhoun had never wrought from them his wonderful doctrine.

* This fact was vouched for to the author in Charleston some years ago by a distinguished survivor of the Nullification period, United States Judge George S. Bryan, whose source of information was personal knowledge.

† Society in America.

CHAPTER XXVIII

THE SECRETARY OF STATE

IF Jefferson was strong with the people when he came so near being elected President in 1796, he was stronger in 1800, when four years of Federal rule had filled them with disgust and fear.

That the Republicans should be successful in obtaining the Government was Madison's ardent wish. He did not, therefore, object to trials under the Sedition law, for he knew that its vigourous enforcement would strengthen his party. Prudence on the part of the Republicans coöperating with the recklessness of the Federalists would drive the latter from power. When it became evident that the selection of the President would devolve upon the House of Representatives he was alarmed lest Burr might be smuggled in, but he did not believe that Adams would lend himself to so contemptible a scheme. The possibility of the House making no choice, thus involving an interregnum in the office of President, was seriously considered, and he concluded that if it occurred the best course would be for the two candidates having a majority of the votes to call Congress together by joint proclamation. While the election was still pending Jefferson urged him to come to Washington, but he thought it would be impolitic to appear on the scene until the question of the Presidency was settled; and furthermore his father died February 27, 1801, and he was detained at home by private affairs. He had agreed before the election to accept the chief post in Jefferson's cabinet, and when it became known that Jefferson had been elected it was known at the same time who was to be the Secretary of State.

The two men were in striking contrast in many par-
ticulars. Jefferson was six feet two inches tall, sunny-
faced, loose-jointed, and careless in his apparel. He was a
talkative man and a man of speculative philosophy, and
he often pursued an idea to conclusions which were
apparently logical enough and yet plainly in violation of
common sense and the experience of mankind. This
characteristic opened to criticism and ridicule many of
the things he said and wrote, but whatever he did was
more carefully weighed. Being the most conspicuous
man in America, all that he said was repeated. Madison,
when he was present, used to adroitly moderate the extreme views he advanced, and after his death made the
plea that allowance ought to be made for his unthinking
verbal indiscretions; but his enemies found in them good
weapons to use against him. He was at the same time a
great political philosopher and the greatest party leader
our country has ever produced. He gave form and substance to a political philosophy which is imperishable,
and his party still appeals to his name whenever it makes
a new declaration of principles. Among the men of his
time no one had as large a following as he. The masses
of the people looked upon him as the great apostle of the
equal rights of man, and the educated class saw in him a
scholar and a man of refined breeding. As he was beloved, so was he hated, intensely, and against no other
of our public men has there survived so extensive a literature of hatred. His enemies accused him of a hundred
crimes. Because he fled when Tarleton captured Charlottesville during the Revolution, instead of remaining to
be captured or killed, he was called a coward. Because
he was latitudinarian in his religious views, he was denounced as an atheist, and the clergy of New England
shook the figure of anti-Christ at their congregations and
told them it was Thomas Jefferson. He was looked upon
as a man of grossly impure private life, but the charge
was a common one against Southern planters and was
false. He was believed to have paid or suborned the

most scurrilous scandal-breeders of the Republican press, and the charge had a basis of truth, the fact being that he encouraged them when he found them useful.

So strong was the light in which he stood that Madison was almost hidden in the shadow, for Madison had done nothing to startle the world and made no effort to obtrude himself upon its notice. Yet strangers were impressed favourably by Madison's simple, courteous manners and his dignified modesty, and they all admitted the charm of his conversation. Sir Augustus Foster, the British Minister, reported to his Government that he was a better informed man than Jefferson, "and moreover a social, jovial and good-humoured companion, full of anecdote, sometimes rather of a loose description, but oftener of a political and historical interest."* A sense of humour was not prominent in Jefferson, and if in Madison it sometimes took a broader tone than propriety now permits, it must be remembered that the jests of his day were not overdelicate; and the tradition is good that Washington himself was not averse to hearing and even making jokes which Smollett or Fielding might have chronicled. Madison was a more careful talker than Jefferson and less speculative in thought, and he wrote with rare purity and directness. This has been attributed by his biographer, Mr. Rives, to the fact of his having been a student of Addison, but a more reasonable explanation is that his style reflected his nature, which was not unlike Addison's in its purity, unaffectedness and scholarly and humourous bent. He never, however, wrote other than seriously, and nearly all his letters are narratives of events. Jefferson could not make a speech, and Madison was one of the best speakers of his time. His views of public policy were carefully formed and he had the constructive ability which Jefferson lacked. The qualities of leadership of Jefferson united with the more practical wisdom of Madison in forming a remarkable combination of talent at the head of the new administration.

* Henry Adams's "History of the United States," I, 190.

Into the ragged, unbuilt town, whose location on the banks of the Potomac his exertions had made possible, came Madison and his wife in the spring of 1801. That it was to be their place of residence for sixteen eventful years was a possibility which his mind may have entertained, for the people were better satisfied with the new Government than they had been with the old, and one reason for their satisfaction was that Madison, in whom all Republicans and many Federalists had confidence, was the Secretary of State. His party, if it managed its conduct skilfully, might retain power for a long time, and the mantle of his chief would naturally fall upon his shoulders.

The position accorded Madison in the official and social world of the little capital was second only to the President's. The President being a widower, the White House was presided over only occasionally by one of his daughters, so Mrs. Madison took her place at the head of Washington society. It was a small circle, composed of Government officials, a half-dozen diplomats and a few Georgetown and country families. An unwritten but generally observed law restricted it to people of polite breeding. Although the party of the common people was in power, the leaders were, generally speaking, gentlemen who selected their associates in private life carefully.

The scale of living of the Secretary of State was a lavish one. When he first came to Washington he took a small house, which in the course of a year he gave up for a more commodious one next door to his friend, Dr. William Thornton. It stood on the north side of Bridge Street (now M Street), west of High Street (now 32d Street), in Georgetown,* and belonged to one Nicholas Voss. He paid at first $600 a year rental, which was afterwards reduced to $500, and this was nearly twice as much as similar accommodations would have cost in Philadelphia. The house was modest enough, but Madison now branched

* The author is indebted to Hugh T. Taggart, Esq., of Washington, for this identification.

out into many extravagances, making considerable per-
chases of fine porcelain, plate and glass, and importing
large quantities of fine wines, Hermitage, White Virgin,
White Cotillon, etc., besides olives, olive oil, preserved
fruits and other delicacies. In 1802 he bought a fine
coach, second-hand, made in Philadelphia, paying for it
$510, and an expensive silver-plated harness. He
indulged his taste for good horses, and in partnership
with Thorton owned a race horse, although it does not
appear that they put him on the track. He lived like a
rich man, but his payments were not always made
promptly. Mr. Voss had occasionally to remind him
that his rent was overdue, and sometimes a creditor
politely dunned him, but a number of his friends owed
money to him, and he was never charged with avoiding
his pecuniary obligations. He had, in fact, a considerable
amount of property. He owned a house in Philadelphia
which he rented to Stephen Moylan for $200 a year,* and
by his father's will had absolute control of the Montpelier
tract of 1,800 acres of productive land, and a farm on the
Rapidan River in Culpepper County of 475 acres.† He
had half ownership in a farm of 219 acres in Louisa County,
and the whole of the farm adjoining Montpelier, which
his father had given him many years before, besides an
interest in enormous tracts of wild Ohio and Kentucky
lands, which his father had patented. He owned, partly
by purchase of his own and partly by inheritance, a
number of negroes. He had acquired several lots in
Washington and some stock in a few enterprises. His
salary as Secretary of State was $5,000 a year, and of
ready money he had not much in addition, for his
farms absorbed the income they yielded. But in spite
of the fact that he was often embarrassed in paying
for his open-handed hospitality, the social side of the
life in Washington must have been pleasant, and his wife
made it eminently successful by attaining a general

* Department of State MSS.

† Orange County, Va., MSS. records.

popularity, which she made contributory to her husband's success.

The political side of Washington life presented, especially in the beginning, a vexatious aspect, which must have sorely taxed the patience of a man unaccustomed as Madison was to deal with what is known as practical politics. The Republican party was composed of two schools—the radicals, who desired to keep the ranks of the party unbroken by dividing among them the spoils of office and driving the Federalists out, and the moderates, who wished to pursue a conciliatory course toward the Federalists in order to attract to themselves the milder Federalists. The Federalists had been in control of the executive branch of the Government during the greater part of the eight years of Washington's administration and during the whole of Adams's four years, and it naturally fell about, in the absence of any compulsory rule to prevent it, that the Federalist upper officials had generally surrounded themselves with Federalist under officials, and there were few Republicans in appointive offices. Jefferson's intention when he entered upon the Presidency was to fill vacancies as they occurred with Republicans and thus gradually secure to his party an even representation, but a clamour arose among the Republicans for quicker methods and he yielded to it. The pressure did not differ in character from that which greets a new President at the present day, and was met in the same accommodating spirit. As second in the administration and nearest friend to the President, Madison received many applications for office, but he did not receive as many as Gallatin, and he did not participate in the distribution of patronage, which was accomplished by the President himself with the aid of politicians having knowledge of local political conditions. What the radical Republicans expected was made plain to Madison. Just before he came to Washington, William Irvine, of Carlisle, Pennsylvania, wrote to him:

"Many of us, you and I amongst the first, have been

some years past vilely traduced, as men who were using every effort (insidiously, too) to destroy the Government. . . . They all now, at the present moment, affect great moderation, speak of conciliation as very desirable, extoll the President's speech, etc., etc.   But mark the end.   They expect and wish conciliation all on one side. So soon as they find that they and friends are to be dismissed from office, they will bounce and kick. . . . On general principles I am persuaded it will be highly injurious to the Republican interest if the changes are not pretty general. . . . If they are not turned out, in due time, it must and will discourage hereafter the exertions of the Republicans."

The views of the moderate wing of the party are shown in a letter from Ralph Bowie, York, Pennsylvania, March 24, 1807. He said the President's inaugural address had not only been received with general approbation by Republicans, but that Federalists were disposed to welcome it cordially, too.   The destruction of party spirit now lay in the President's power to his everlasting fame, but it could not be accomplished if there was a general removal of Federalists from office.

Noah Webster was a fair example of the moderate Federalists who might have been attracted to the Republicans if Federalists were not removed from office.   From New Haven, July 18, 1801, he wrote to Madison, that although he had been a supporter of Adams, he had determined when Jefferson came into the Presidency that he would sustain him, and had so instructed the three newspapers he owned.   Nothing of a light nature could have changed his intention.   "But the late removals from office in this & some other States have surprised & confounded us.   We all expected that the chief magistrate would gratify a number of his friends, & especially place about himself men in whom he has particular confidence, & be assured, Sir, that not a complaint was uttered, until the appointment of *foreigners* to the highest offices.   But when we found that the principle was adopted of *making vacancies*, especially when it was seen that the most meritorious officers were dismissed to make room for characters less meritorious as men & as citizens, & some of them ignorant, unprincipled & even contemptible: what do you imagine must have been our sensations !"*

The specific allusions were to the appointment of Gallatin, who was of Swiss nativity, as Secretary of the Treasury, and the removal of Elizur Goodrich, a man of high standing, as Collector of the Port of New Haven, to make way for Samuel Bishop, an old and inefficient man.

It fell to Madison to deal with the importunities of Callender, who conceived that he had claims upon the administration, not only for services performed for the Republicans, but for sufferings in the Republican cause. In the Spring of 1800 he had been sentenced to nine months' imprisonment and to pay a fine of $200 for his libel against John Adams. The prosecution being under a law which Jefferson considered to be unconstitutional, he was pardoned immediately upon Jefferson's becoming President. "I discharged," he explained in a letter to Mrs. Adams (July 22, 1804), "every person under punishment or prosecution under the Sedition law, because I considered, and now consider, that law to be a nullity as absolute and as palpable as if Congress had ordered us to fall down and worship a golden image." A part of the remission of punishment in this case included the return to Callender of the fine he had paid. Madison's acquaintance with Callender was contemporaneous with Jefferson's and began when Callender first came into prominence as a political writer, and when his productions were generally regarded with favour by the Republicans. Although Madison never held him in esteem nor pretended to do so, Callender had for Madison greater respect and confidence than he entertained for other public men who disguised their contempt for him. In 1796 (May 28) he wrote to Madison from Baltimore, saying he wanted to establish

* Dept. of State MSS. Applications for Office.

himself as a country schoolmaster. He envied the wages of a journeyman carpenter, he added, and had a wife and four children to support. He expressed a fear that Madison did not have a friendly feeling toward him.* It was about this time that Jefferson first relieved his distress by a pecuniary contribution, which with several subsequent donations from the same source Callender afterward represented to be a reward for his writings and purchase of his pen. Madison, however, neither found him employment nor sent him alms.

Four years after this incident Jefferson was President-elect, and Callender, who was nearing the end of his term of imprisonment, received from him assurances, or what he took to be assurances, that he would be pardoned and reimbursed the amount of his fine. When he was released he was in great pecuniary distress and became angry because there was delay in paying back his fine. He began to threaten at once, and wrote to Madison as "the one man in whom he reposed perfect confidence," to urge haste. "Does the President," he said, "reflect upon the *premunire* into which he may bring himself by the breach of an unqualified or even a volunteer promise? . . . I will not injure him by supposing that he cares a farthing for anything which I feel." Jefferson, he went on, should reflect that his services might be needed again, and he gave warning that he would not be sacrificed as a "scapegoat to political decorum." He admired Jefferson, he said, but had been stung to the quick because Jefferson had snubbed him. He confided this fact to Madison alone, and added that it was for Jefferson to say whether it would be safe to quarrel with him.†

The only thing that made Callender a man of importance was the fact that he had fallen a victim to the iniquitous Sedition law. He embodied the principle of opposition to that law, and the most distinguished lawyers in Virginia had defended him at his trial. It was easy,

---

* Dept. of State MSS.
† Dept. of State MSS.

therefore, for him to form an exaggerated notion of his personal importance, and the ill-advised attention paid to him by Jefferson's friends encouraged his belief. Monroe especially was overzealous, and seemed to fear the consequences to Jefferson if the man were cast off. He saw Callender soon after his threats to Madison, and Callender complained that no positive orders had been given to pay him the amount of his fine. Monroe wrote Madison that Callender wanted twenty-five dollars to enable him to go to Washington, but Monroe persuaded him to wait a few days, and in the meantime asked the United States Marshal whether the money to reimburse his fine could not be got from the State Department. Being answered in the negative, Monroe thought of raising the money by private subscription, but concluded that if he did Callender would use the fact to the discredit of the Executive. Monroe said there was nothing to do but order the money paid or positively decline to do so. If the latter course were finally determined upon, then "some person friendly to the Republican interests, sensible of Callender's service & misfortunes, might advance him the money and take his order on the Govt. for it when received. The amt. might be raised by subscription, tho' not easily here, and possibly if Callender knew nothing of the motive he might be quiet, especially if he believed the fine if reimbursed wod. never come to him. . . . Be assured that the President & yrself cannot be too circumspect in case he comes to Georgetown in yr conversations with him, for I think nothing more doubtful than his future political course. If from charitable motives either of you advance him money, it merits yr consideration whether he ought to know from whom it came . . . if he is not [an honest man] every act of that kind will be attributed to improper motives, and perverted hereafter to the injury of the benefactor."*

Callender came to Washington in June and confided everything to Madison. He would be placated only by

* New York Public Library (Lenox) MSS,

an office, and wanted to be postmaster at Richmond. The mother of his four children was dead, and he had fallen in love with a Richmond lady who was in a sphere above him. "He has flattered himself," Madison wrote to Monroe, "and probably has been flattered by others, into a persuasion that the emoluments and reputation of a post-office would obtain her in marriage." Madison met the man in no spirit of temporizing, and says he talked to him plainly. An arrangement was made with the Treasury Department to pay the fine, but he was sent back to Richmond without hope of obtaining anything more.* He at once put his threats into execution, formed a connection with *The Richmond Recorder*, and through its columns poured forth a flood of vituperation and abuse against Jefferson and the Republicans; and it is a fact discreditable to the Federalists that they hailed the slanders of the disappointed blackmailer with encouragement. In his mad career he appears to have spared Madison from any bespattering, although Madison was the agent chosen to withdraw from him all hope of attaining his ambition.

Callender was not the only Republican writer who thought himself entitled to recognition. William Duane, of *The Aurora*, had certainly done a great deal toward the election of Jefferson, and although the removal of the capital to Washington had deprived his paper of much of its prestige, Jefferson's administration owed more to Duane than it did to any other editor. He, too, had been tried under the Sedition law, but had escaped punishment. His party being now in power, he conceived that he was entitled to profit from the victory he had helped to win. As soon as Madison took charge of the State Department, Duane wrote to him (May 10, 1801) that while *The Aurora* had the largest circulation of any paper in the United States, he was hampered in securing advertisements by the hostility of the Custom House, and could not make a living. He had, therefore, determined to add

* Madison's Works (Cong. Ed.) II, 173.

to his business a book and stationery shop, and would like to supply books to the new Library of Congress and stationery to the State Department. He also suggested that the Acts passed by Congress, which the Secretary of State then paid the chief newspapers throughout the country to print, should be given only to Republican papers, in order that their emoluments and circulation might thereby be increased. Later, August 3, 1803, he complained that he often needed official information to enable him to refute charges against the administration made by the Federalist press, and thought it would be well if such information could be furnished to him and other Republican editors.* But Duane's theory of party Government was not Madison's and his request met with no favour. The influence of his paper was on the wane, and Madison was more interested in the new *National Intelligencer*, which Samuel Harrison Smith launched in Washington when the Jefferson administration came in. The unfriendly attitude of Duane toward Madison some years later may find a partial explanation in his disappointment at finding the State Department of so little use to him.

That Madison did not believe in allowing political considerations to play a part in the conduct of the business of his department was shown by the policy he pursued toward his subordinates. Among the letters received by Jefferson and turned over to Madison was one from William P. Gardner, dated November 20, 1807, making charges against Richard Wagner, the chief clerk of the State Department. Gardner himself had been dismissed from the Treasury Department by the Adams administration because he furnished official information to Republican newspapers, and Jefferson subsequently appointed him a Consul. "Mr. Wagner," Gardner wrote, "chief clerk in the office of Mr. Madison, has in my hearing frequently ridiculed Republicanism, declaring in the language of Mr. Adams that it

* Dept. of State MSS.

meant anything or nothing. He has said that he never knew a man among the Republicans trustworthy, of probity or principle. About two years since he made a Bet with Mr. Jeremiah Pearsal of this city that Mr. Gallatin in the course of one year from that date would either be hung or sent out of the country, observing at the same time that he considered himself perfectly justified in making the Bet from the well-known infamy of Mr. Gallatin's character."*

Nevertheless, Madison retained Wagner as chief clerk for five years, when he voluntarily left the Department, and John Graham, who had been Secretary of Legation and charge d'affaires at Madrid from 1801 to 1804, and who enjoyed Madison's friendship, was appointed in his place. As there were no assistant secretaries the chief clerk was the second man in the Department and was in charge of it whenever the Secretary was absent from Washington.

Only one personal appointment was made by Madison when he became Secretary of State, and this involved no disturbance of the existing force. The issuance of patents for inventions was until 1849 a part of the functions of the State Department, and to superintend this branch of the business Madison appointed his friend and neighbour, William Thornton, the first designer of the Capitol, a man of scientific education and of uncommon accomplishments. Thornton's salary was only $1,400 a year, but this was a little more than the annual fees from patents then amounted to.

When Madison took charge of the State Department on May 2, 1801, he found it in a condition of suspended animation. Adams had dismissed Timothy Pickering a year before, and John Marshall had filled an interregnum for ten months, when Levi Lincoln, the Attorney-General, took his place temporarily for two months. Except for his services from 1778 to 1780 as a member of the council of

---

* "Office-Seeking During Jefferson's Administration" (Hunt). American Historical Review, January, 1898.

the Governor of Virginia, Madison had never held an executive office before, but the business part of the State Department was not then extensive nor difficult to manage. The whole executive force consisted of nine men, one of whom was a messenger. The chief clerk received $1,500 a year and the under clerks from $500 to $900 each.*

The real task before the Secretary was, of course, the management of the foreign affairs of the country.

* "The Department of State: History and Functions" (Hunt).

CHAPTER XXIX

LOUISIANA

THE foreign relations of the United States involved important questions with three powers—Great Britain, France and Spain. With the two former there was the contention against their colonial system and consequent complaints and claims, and Spain held Louisiana and the mouth of the Mississippi River, and the trade of the whole Western country was at her mercy. The tone adopted by the administration toward England was, at first, the reverse of conciliatory. Rufus King, although a Federalist, was continued as minister, and full confidence was placed in him. On July 24, 1801, Madison instructed him that the two chief grievances which he was to endeavour to have redressed were "the spoliations of our trade, and the impressment of our seamen." The property, Madison said, unlawfully seized by Great Britain amounted to some millions of dollars. "The imperfect lists of impressed seamen which have been obtained by our agents and reported to this Department swell the number to near two thousand, more than four-fifths of whom are natives of the United States, not more than seventy are British subjects, and more than seventy aliens to both Great Britain and the United States, and consequently so distinguishable by their language and other signs as to take away all colour of apology for the outrage." Of those unjustly impressed, he said, only about a third had been set at liberty. "But it is proper to be known," he added, "that the wrongs have made a deep impression on the American mind, and that if no satisfactory change of conduct be soon apparent . . . the policy of this country can scarcely fail to take some shape more reme-

dial than that hitherto given to it." King was to press
for an adjustment of British duties to a real equality with
those of the United States and to lay stress upon the
ability of the United States to retaliate. In an instruction of December 22, 1801, Madison said: "Were the
Constitution not a barrier to duties on exports, it would
not be very difficult for Congress to provide a remedy of
themselves, by repealing the present discrimination on
imports, and imposing on our exports in British bottoms
precisely the same duty, which her countervailing clause
adds on the importation of them in American bottoms,
into Great Britain."*

The policy was thus a simple one—he would employ
against England those "commercial weapons" which he
had urged the first Congress to use, and which would have
been more effective if the right to levy export duties had
been included among them. The complaint against the
discriminating duties of England was, however, a complaint against a well-established system, which France
as well as England followed, and from which all nations
suffered. England's object was to make all the world
subservient to her maritime strength, and accordingly
she required her colonies to trade only with her and use
only her ships; but the system was relaxed in favour of
the United States so far as to permit the West Indies to
keep from starving by importing American foodstuffs
and send in return molasses and rum. The trading, however, was confined in effect to British bottoms. When
Jefferson's administration began England permitted neutrals to import the products of the French West Indies
and reship them to France. This carrying trade was
in American hands, and together with other American
shipping employed many seamen, a number of whom
were deserters from British ships who carried papers of
American citizenship fraudulently obtained. The embarrassment suffered by Great Britain in the loss of her
seamen she endeavoured to remedy by sending men-of-

* MSS. Instructions. Dept. of State.

war to overhaul American ships on the high seas, search
their crews for deserters, and take them off regardless of
their citizenship. As Madison showed in his instruction to King, many were taken off who were native
Americans and who were not deserters. But the tone in
which the outrages of Great Britain were resented soon
underwent a change in the face of complications with our
traditional ally of so grave a nature as to force the
Government to look for effective friendship to our traditional enemy.

As Minister to France Jefferson appointed Robert R.
Livingston of New York, one of the leaders of the
Republican party of that State and head of one of its
controlling families. He had seen service under the
Colonial Government and in the Continental Congress,
and was Secretary of Foreign Affairs from 1781 to 1783,
when he became Chancellor of New York. Jefferson
offered him a seat in his Cabinet as Secretary of the Navy,
but he declined. Later he expressed through Madison a
willingness to serve in a diplomatic capacity. He was in
full sympathy with the peaceful aspirations of the administration, and wrote to Madison, July 1, 1801, to say
that he thought the President's views of neutral rights
might be made to mark a new departure in international
law. "Pedantic compilers" had, he said, put down as
law what were merely the plundering practices of nations
at war, and had given little attention to the peaceful
rights of neutrals. The champion of those rights should
be America. "If a treaty is proposed," he went on,
"that is not to be supported by arms, but by commercial
exclusions, that shall not refer to the present war, and
that shall be open to all nations that chuse to adopt it, I
think it cannot fail to meet with sufficient support to establish a new law of nations, and that our administration
will have the glory of saying in the words of the gospel,
'a new Law I give unto you, that you love one another.'"*

Livingston seemed to think it feasible to propose treat-

* Dept. of State MSS.

ies of this kind and wanted a commission to negotiate them; but Madison knew that international intercourse was not governed by the Golden Rule, and Livingston himself after he got to Paris never thought of supporting the propositions he made to Talleyrand and Napoleon by quotations from the Scriptures. The attitude of Europe toward the United States he described in a letter to Madison from Paris, January 15, 1802. "We must calculate," he said, "upon every effort from every maritime power in Europe to diminish our commerce." France had excluded us from her African colonies; her bounties excluded our oil; her duty on tobacco in foreign bottoms compelled its transportation from the United States in French ships. Livingston proposed that Congress levy a duty on French articles imported in foreign ships in retaliation.* These questions were of the same character as those which distinguished our relations with England, but they were less important because our commerce with France was less and there was no inflaming question of human rights involved.

With Spain our relations turned on one great point— the free navigation of the Mississippi. For the sake of a shadowy alliance during the Revolution the South would have been willing at one time to permit the occlusion of the River, and after the Revolution the East narrowly missed accomplishing that result in return for unimportant commercial privileges. Madison, by opposing first his own section and then the East, had prevented action when it would have been unfavourable to American interests, and the occasion had come in a few years when a treaty highly satisfactory had peen negotiated. War was impending between Spain and England, and to gain the friendship of the United States Spain agreed that American products should be brought down the Mississippi and deposited free of duty at New Orleans, from which port they could be transshipped anywhere. If the right of deposit at New Orleans should ever be changed some

* Dept. of State MSS.

other point equally desirable was to be provided. This treaty was negotiated in 1795 by Thomas Pinckney of South Carolina, on the part of the United States, and the Prince of Peace on the part of Spain. It came up for action about the same time with the Jay treaty, and the unanimous approval it received from Congress and the people was in sharp contrast with the condemnations showered upon the treaty with Great Britain. When Madison became Secretary of State he supposed that negotiations with Spain would relate chiefly to the subject of this treaty, but secret negotiations were then in progress in Europe which soon changed the foreign policy of the American Government, and precipitated upon it a crisis which no one had thought of as remotely possible.

In August, 1800, it was agreed by Spain to cede Louisiana to France, its former owner, and a treaty of cession followed later. The whole affair was transacted in the dark and no inkling of it reached the ears of the American Government. September 30, 1800, France and America completed a treaty of friendship and commerce, and October 1 France and Spain completed the treaty by which Louisiana passed into French hands. The avowed purpose for which the negotiations for the retrocession were instituted was expressed by Talleyrand: "Let the Court of Madrid cede these districts to France, and from that moment the power of America is bounded by the limits which it may suit the interests and the tranquillity of France and Spain to assign her."* With France in possession the Mississippi would be closed—of that there could be little doubt.

But no one in America knew that the cession had been made. The rumour got about gradually, and in June, 1801, Madison instructed Pinckney at Madrid to find out if it was true. The reports from Livingston on the subject were inconclusive. He arrived in Paris December 3, and was able to write to Madison December 10, that while

* Adams's "History of the United States," I, 356.

he was disposed to believe the reported cession had taken place, Talleyrand had assured him nothing was settled. At this, his first interview with the French Minister, Livingston hinted that perhaps "both France and Spain might find a mutual interest in ceding the Floridas to the United States."* The suggestion, however, met with no favourable response. From the very beginning, therefore, it was the policy of the administration to settle the question by buying territory controlling the mouth of the river, and there were no vexing fears apparently of a constitutional question arising to prevent the purchase. As it became more certain that the cession to France had actually taken place a great fear fell upon the White House and State Department lest the cherished hope of continued peace should be rudely shattered.

Livingston was instructed April 30, 1802, that the reported cession caused painful apprehensions, and must have an instant effect in changing the relations between the United States and France. He was to make a friendly appeal to the French Government to "revise and abandon the project." Mere neighbourhood was dangerous, but a possession of the mouth of the Mississippi would be fatal to the friendly relations of the countries. May 11, 1802, Pinckney was ordered to press upon the court of Spain "the repugnance of the United States to it" (the cession). If it had not taken place Pinckney was to make every effort to buy New Orleans and the territory east of the Mississippi. If necessary he might offer as an inducement a guarantee to Spain of her territory west of the Mississippi. The idea of finding a way out of the difficulty by purchase had been formulated in the instruction of April 30 to Livingston. He was to find out the extent of the cession and whether it included the Floridas as well as New Orleans; and to "endeavour to ascertain the price at which these, if included in the cession, would be yielded to the United States." When the cession became a certainty the dread of French occupa-

* MSS. Instructions and Despatches. Department of State.

tion became almost frantic. Would France open the Mississippi to American trade by selling New Orleans and other territory on the east bank of the river, or must America league herself with England to obtain these necessities?

No consolation could be extracted from Livingston's reports. The taking possession of the new country was, he said, March 24, 1902, "a darling object with the First Consul, who sees in it a means to gratify his friends and to dispose of his enemies." The French people regarded Louisiana as a paradise, and thought New Orleans would command the commerce of the whole Western country. Next month (April 24) he reported that the Floridas were included in the cession, and that an armament was at that moment being fitted out to sail for New Orleans, unless Santo Domingo affairs should prevent it. May 28th he announced that the personnel of the expedition had been determined upon. Bernadotte was to command, Colot to be second in command, Adet the Prefect, and the expedition to sail in September.*

In the autumn of 1802 the Spanish Intendant at New Orleans suddenly withdrew the right of deposit to American commerce. A plain violation of the treaty, it was suspected at once that he had received his orders from the new master of Louisiana. D'Yrujo, the Spanish Minister, repudiated the Intendant's action and promised to have it withdrawn, but communication with New Orleans was so slow that when Madison sent an instruction to Pinckney, May 8, 1803, he said the last news from New Orleans was of January 20. The withdrawal of the right of deposit necessarily closed the river, and unless it were open before the Spring trade began a conflict seemed unavoidable—begun by the United States to compel Spain to open the navigation of the river, or by Spain because the Western people would be sure to attempt the navigation and resort to acts of violence if they found it closed. If Madison was right twenty years

* **MSS.** Instructions and Despatches. Dept. of State.

before in saying American trade down the river could no more be stopped than the current of the river itself, this was more true now when the trade was so large and had been permitted for so long. "This continuation of the obstruction to our trade," Madison wrote Pinckney, "and the approach of the season for carrying down the Mississippi the exports of the Western country, have had the natural effect of increasing the Western irritation, and embolding the advocates for an immediate redress by arms."

Not only were the Western people ready to fight Spain or France, if France was now the master, but the British Minister was able to report to his Government that public opinion had changed and was friendly to his country. So friendly was it, indeed, that an alliance was proposed. For the United States the question was whether there should be a war with France single-handed or in alliance with Great Britain, and on the whole it seemed better to form the alliance. Madison accepted it reluctantly. He told Monroe confidentially (April 20, 1803) that there was grave doubt in his mind whether a temporary abandonment of the right of deposit would not be better than a British alliance.*

To calm the heated temper of the West it was determined to appoint Monroe as coadjutor Minister to France and Spain. He was popular in the West, and the people would believe that under his care no effort would be spared to preserve their rights. In Livingston they did not have confidence, because he came from a part of the country which had voted in Congress to yield up the navigation of the Mississippi. From a domestic point of view, therefore, Monroe's appointment was a wise one, and it was openly avowed to be an alternative or precedent to war with France. The crisis, as Madison told Pinckney, January 18, 1803, "called for the experiment of an Extraordinary mission, carrying with it the weight attached to such a measure, as well as the advantage of a

* Madison's Works (Cong. Ed.), II, 180.

more thorough knowledge of the views of the Government and the sensibility of the public, than can be otherwise conveyed."

The instructions prepared for Livingston and Monroe jointly were elaborate and minute. Certain demands were to be made; the United States was prepared to go great lengths to obtain them; if they could not be got, England was to be asked to accept us as allies in a joint war, for it was evident that England would soon declare war on her own account. "The object in view," said Madison, "is to procure by just and satisfactory arrangements a cession to the United States of New Orleans, all of West and East Florida, or as much thereof as the actual proprietor can be prevailed on to part with." The time was ripe for the success of this object. "The instability of the peace of Europe, the attitude taken by Great Britain, the languishing state of the French finances, and the absolute necessity of either abandoning the West India Islands or of sending thither large armaments at great expense, all contributed at the present crisis to prepare in the French Government a disposition to listen to an arrangement which will at once dry up one source of foreign controversy and furnish some aid in struggling with internal embarrassments." In any arrangements which might be made it was to be stipulated that the Mississippi be kept free for the navigation of France and the United States. In buying the desired territory the President was prepared, if necessary, to pay 50,000,000 livres tournois. If France demanded that her remaining American territory be guaranteed to her, the demand was to be resisted, if possible, but acceded to if found to be necessary to obtain the object in view. If France would not cede New Orleans and the Floridas, the United States would accept less. If France would cede nothing, the Envoys were to negotiate for a continuance of the right of deposit. If the negotiations failed, an alliance with England was to be attempted.

April 18, 1803, Madison wrote Livingston, a month

after Monroe had sailed for France: "If the French Government instead of friendly arrangements or views should be found to mediate hostilities or to have formed projects which will constrain the United States to resort to hostilities, such communications are then to be held with the British Government as will sound its dispositions and invite its concurrence in the war." The terms of the alliance were sketched. The United States could not guarantee continued possession of such territory as might be conquered during the war, as this would involve us in England's future wars; nor would the United States give England the territory west of the Mississippi, as she would then have a hold on the river, which would be displeasing to the people of the West. To treat for the alliance two blank commissions were sent. Monroe's name was to be inserted as the Envoy, if the negotiations in France did not make it probable that he would be *persona non grata* to England; otherwise, Livingston was to have the commission.*

The appointment of Monroe was, of course, displeasing to Livingston, against whom no dereliction of duty or inaptitude in dealing with the French Court could be charged. His zeal had, in fact, been extraordinary, and he had succeeded in winning the personal good will of Napoleon. He endeavoured to convince the French that Louisiana would prove a useless possession to them. He obtained information by one means or another of the progress of the intended expeditions to take possession, although all movements in this direction were carefully hidden. August 31, 1802, Talleyrand told him France intended to take possession before listening to any offers to purchase. October 28 he reported that the expedition had met with a check. He entered into unofficial negotiations with Joseph Bonaparte, who asked him whether the United States would prefer the Floridas to Louisiana, and Livingston replied that "we had no wish to extend our boundary across the Mississippi. . . .

* MSS. Instructions. Dept. of State.

All we sought was security and not extension of territory."
He bore the suspense and alternate hopes and fears of
his position with calmness and made no blunders. One
day Talleyrand would snub him, and the next the First
Consul would treat him with unusual consideration. At
one time he confidently expected the armament to sail at
any moment, then it was so long delayed that he was encouraged to hope it would be abandoned. "Do not absolutely despair," he wrote, "tho' you may have no great
reason to hope." February, 1803, he wrote: "I have
proposed to them the relinquishment of New Orleans
and West Florida as far as the River Perdido, together
with all the Territory lying to the north of the Arcansas
under an idea that it was necessary to interpose us between them and Canada as the only means of preventing
an attack from that quarter. I did not speak of East
Florida, because I found they consider the navigation of
the Gulf as very important. For this I proposed an indefinite sum not wishing to mention any till I should receive your instruction." March 11, 1803, he reported
that he had hinted at the project of making the Island of
New Orleans an independent State under the Government
of Spain, France and the United States.

The next day (March 12) he gave an account of Napoleon's audience with the foreign ministers when he
accosted the British Minister with "I find, Milord, your
nation wants war again." This scene carried real hope
to Livingston, and a month later, April 11, Talleyrand
asked him whether he wished to have the whole of Louisiana. "I told him no," Livingston reports; "that our
wishes extended only to New Orleans and the Floridas."
Talleyrand said if they gave New Orleans the rest would
be of little value; and "he wished to know what we would
give for the whole." Livingston said he had not thought
of it, but supposed his Government would not object to
20,000,000 livres, providing the pending claims were paid.
Talleyrand said this was not enough.*

* MSS. Despatches. Dept. of State.

News had then arrived of Monroe's appointment as Special Envoy, but his coming was regarded with indifference by the French Court. The offer to sell Louisiana might easily have been delayed for his arrival, but was made to Livingston as a person with whom the French Government found it satisfactory to treat. When Livingston received Talleyrand's offer he knew that the game was over and that the United States had won, but he did not appreciate the magnitude of the value of the winnings.

"I would rather," he wrote Madison, "have confined our views to smaller objects & I think if we succeed it would be good policy to exchange the West bank of the district with Spain for the Floridas, reserving New Orleans."*

As Napoleon did not wait for Monroe, neither did Livingston, for events in France were moving with lightning rapidity. The day after Talleyrand asked Livingston if he would buy Louisiana orders were given to stop vessels from sailing from French ports and war with England was practically existent.

The following day Monroe arrived, and that evening he dined with Livingston. While they were at dinner Livingston happened to glance through the window and noticed Barbé de Marbois, the Minister of the Treasury, strolling in the garden. He sent a young relation, who was one of the company at dinner, to ask him to come in, but Marbois sent back word that he would return later and went away. While the gentlemen were over their coffee he joined them, and presently went with Livingston into an adjoining room, where he remarked that as the place was not appropriate for confidential conversation, he would be glad if Livingston would call upon him that night before eleven o'clock. Livingston's guests having departed, he kept the appointment, and in Marbois's house, close upon the hour of midnight, they discussed the terms of the sale of Louisiana. Marbois was a well-chosen agent, for he was familiar with America, having

* Id.

been Minister there during the Revolution, and was on good terms with Livingston and Madison, being a fellow-lodger with Madison when he had his love affair with Catherine Floyd. The subsequent negotiations were detail and in them Monroe assisted. That he had had nothing to do with the more important negotiations was not Livingston's fault. Talleyrand might have waited for him, but did not, and Marbois might have asked him to come to his house with Livingston, but failed to do so. Livingston could not safely delay his answer to Talleyrand or refuse singly a confidential conference with Marbois. Although Monroe participated in a final consummation which he had done nothing to produce, his mission had served no useful purpose in France. As it happened, he was able to give Livingston no essential assistance, all the more important steps having been taken before his arrival. The offer to sell the whole territory followed Livingston's repeated offers to buy a part of it, and would hardly have come if these offers had not been so pressingly made. Napoleon had a war with England on his hands, and if he occupied Louisiana would have the United States to fight too. He had failed to reduce Santo Domingo, and it had absorbed much treasure and many soldiers. He needed for his coming struggle with England every livre and every soldier he could get. In abandoning his original intentions with respect to Louisiana, he could boast that he had received "sixty millions [of livers] for an occupation that will not perhaps last a day." He should have added that he had given nothing for Louisiana, as he had not kept the bargain by which it passed over to him, and that in selling it to the United States he had violated his formal promise to Spain that he would never alienate it.

The stupendous purchase that Napoleon thrust upon Livingston and Monroe they accepted without authority, but the Government upheld them at once. "You were justified," Madison wrote to them, "by the solid reasons which you give for it, and I am charged by the President to express to you his entire approval of your so doing.

"This approbation is in no respect precluded by the silence of your commission and instructions. When these were made out, the object of the most sanguine was limited to the establishment of the Mississippi as our boundary." The commission, he said, had been created to meet an extraordinary crisis, which "consisted of the state of things produced by the breach of our deposit at New Orleans, the situation of the French Islands, particularly the important Island of St. Domingo; the distress of the French finances, the unsettled posture of Europe, the increasing jealousy between Great Britain and France, and the known aversion of the former to see the mouth of the Mississippi in the hands of the latter."*

Thus had come the end of the long struggle for the free navigation of the Mississippi begun by Madison in 1782. He thought Livingston had been precipitate in hurrying the negotiations without Monroe, but this was an opinion springing from the partiality of friendship.

The acquisition of Louisiana was the only completed act of Madison's term as Secretary of State. Other questions with foreign nations which fell to his management did not reach their most interesting stage until he himself became President.

* MSS, Instructions, Dept. of State.

CHAPTER XXX

On March 4, 1809, James Madison was inaugurated as President of the United States. Ten thousand strangers came to Washington to see the pageant. The retiring President and his successor rode in a carriage, escorted by the cavalry of Washington and Georgetown, from the White House to the Capitol, where in the newly completed hall of the House of Representatives Madison read his inaugural address in a voice so low that few could hear him. To pay a tribute to American manufactures, he was clothed in a suit of dark-brown cloth made from the wool of Merino sheep bred by Robert R. Livingston at his country seat, Clermont, on the Hudson River, the wool being carded, spun and woven in his house by his daughter, Elizabeth Stevens Livingston, the wife of her cousin, Edward P. Livingston.* The oath of office was administered by Chief Justice Marshall, and the new President returned to Taylor's Hotel, where he reviewed the military and held a reception.

In the evening, at Long's Hotel in Georgetown, occurred the first inauguration ball ever held. Foreign ministers, officials and citizens crowded the rooms to the number of four hundred. Mrs. Madison was dressed elaborately in yellow velvet, with pearls and a turban on her head. Her husband wore a black suit, as he nearly always did. The most conspicuous figure in the room was Jefferson, and the guests noticed the contrast between the glowing good humour of the retiring President's face and the dark clouds of care which hung over the new President, for Jefferson was in high spirits, laughing,

* Dept. of State MSS.

joking and telling anecdotes, and Madison was worn with fatigue and oppressed by a sense of heavy responsibility.* Washington Irving came to Washington to seek an office at this time and his humour played about the President and his wife, whom he described in a familiar letter: "Mrs. Madison is a fine, portly, buxom dame, who has a smile and a pleasant word for everybody. Her sisters, Mrs. Cutts and Mrs. Washington, are like two merry wives of Windsor; but as to Jemmy Madison—ah! poor Jemmy! he is but a withered little apple-John."

The White House was to have for the next eight years a career such as it had not known before, for Mrs. Adams had been there but little and Jefferson had no wife. It was newly and handsomely furnished under the supervision of Latrobe soon after the Madisons moved in; the doors were always open and it became the centre of Washington life. A bountiful table was spread and the importations of foreign wines were a large item of expense. Two fine coaches were bought, one for $928 and the other for $1,500, a stable of fine horses was kept, and the President rode a Kentucky thoroughbred, named "Speculator," with a long pedigree.

Long before Jefferson's administration closed it was known that Madison would be his successor. Jefferson had no visible agency in naming him, and repelled energetically a suggestion to the contrary. But he had written to Madison, December 28, 1795, before he became a candidate for the Presidency himself, that he must not retire from public life "unless to a more splendid and more efficacious post. There I should rejoice to see you; I hope, I may say, I shall rejoice to see you." Holding these views, and having Madison nearest to him for the eight years of his presidency, no word from him was necessary to make it plain whom he would wish for a successor. His correspondence reveals no desire that Monroe should be made President. He found it necessary, however, to assure Monroe that he was not interfering in the contest

* "Harper's Weekly," March 4, 1897.

between him and Madison for the presidency, as he regarded them both as the two principal pillars on which his happiness rested. Monroe, however, was not in good humour, and the three musketeers were not working together when the chief retired from public life.

When Monroe was Minister to England in 1806, William Pinkney, of Maryland, was named as joint envoy with him, and Monroe's pride was wounded, just as Livingston's had been when Monroe was made his associate at Paris. Monroe and Pinkney then negotiated and signed a treaty with Great Britain. Their instructions had required them to obtain: (1) the abandonment of the right and practice of impressing American seamen, (2) a restoration of the right to trade with enemies' colonies, (3) an indemnity for recent captures and confiscations by Great Britain. The treaty, however, abandoned each one of these requirements, and was less advantageous to the United States than even the Jay treaty had been. It was signed December 1, 1806, but before it arrived in the United States, Madison warned Monroe that it would be rejected if it excluded the essential points of the instructions. It was, accordingly, not even sent to the Senate to consider, but suppressed by the Executive. Madison tried to mitigate Monroe's mortification. "The President and all of us," he wrote March 20, 1807, "are fully impressed with the difficulties which your negotiation had to contend with, as well as with the faithfulness and ability with which it was supported." He added that they were ready to suppose that if they had been in his place they would have done as he did, and were certain that if he were in their place he would act as they were acting.* Monroe was pressed to stay and reopen negotiations, but he came home with a grievance. It was easy to charge that a trap had been laid for him; that he had been sent on a mission which was bound to fail, so that in failing he would cease to be a rival candidate for the presidency; but it was also charged on the opposite side that

* Works (Cong. Ed.) II, 404.

he had negotiated a treaty favouring England with the hope of winning Federalist votes.

At any rate, Monroe became a candidate for the presidency and attracted no Federalist votes. He was chosen as leader by John Randolph of Roanoke and a few disaffected Republicans who followed Randolph. Jefferson and Madison had not long been preserved from being quarrelled with by Randolph. He declared that Madison had told him he was willing to buy peace with Spain by paying tribute to France. Madison also favoured a compromise in the Yazoo claims, and Randolph's opposition to the claims was a passion. Therefore, Randolph called Madison a mere closet philosopher and a weak and timid statesman, and when the congressional caucus nominated Madison for the Presidency, Randolph and about sixteen others protested. The party of Tertium Quids was then organized, and in Virginia a convention was called which nominated Monroe against Madison, but when it became apparent that Monroe would receive few votes in Virginia and none in other States, Randolph's followers generally deserted him and voted for Madison.

General Charles Cotesworth Pinckney of South Carolina was nominated by the Federalists, but in the electoral college Madison received 122 votes to Pinckney's 47.

The position which he occupied when he came to the presidency was in many respects a fortunate one. He was acceptable to the Republicans because he belonged to the same school as Jefferson, and being a less radical partisan than Jefferson was not violently opposed by the anti-Jefferson party. Some optimists, like Henry Lee, held out to him the elusive prospect of uniting parties; but he had no hope of doing so, knowing that the Federalists could not be placated. He was fortunate, too, in that he inherited his office and owed no debts in consequence of having attained it. The offices were already filled with adherents of his own party, and only as vacancies occurred in the natural order of events would he be called upon to exercise his appointing power. Even a few Federalists were not afraid to write to him on this subject. "You are," wrote one from Georgia, August 24, 1809, "(as from a retrospect I would believe) in reality only what your predecessors only professed to be, a Federal-Republican. . . . It has, I believe, been granted on all sides, that so far as compatible with Gen'l W.'s engagements with or duty towards his compatriots in arms, he was impartial and just in his distribution of patronage, but not without a semblance of truth, has it been alleged, that his two successors were too much involved in the vortex of party spirit to follow his glorious example."* Madison did not, as a fact, appoint Federalists to office, but there was no office brokerage, no scramble for place, and a far higher tone prevailed in the executive departments than had characterized Jefferson's administration.

Madison intended to continue Jefferson's policy, which was indeed equally his own, but he was hampered from the beginning by a weak cabinet. To find some one who could take his place as Secretary of State and be to him what he had been to Jefferson was an impossibility, for Monroe, who would have come nearest to filling the requirements, was in bad humour and smarting under the preference shown for Madison over himself. Albert Gallatin, therefore, except Madison the only conspicuously efficient man in the old cabinet, was his choice for Secretary of State, but the President was warned by Wilson Cary Nicholas before the inauguration that the Senate would not confirm Gallatin's nomination.† The prejudice against him because of his foreign birth was never overcome and there was a faction of Republicans always working against him. Robert Smith had been appointed Secretary of the Navy by Jefferson in 1801. He was a member of a wealthy and influential Maryland family, and his brother Samuel Smith was a Senator from that State. He was of consequence only because of his friends, but Jefferson's policy had included the reduction of the

* "Early Office Seeking."—N. Y. Evening Post, Nov. 26, 1898.
† Henry Adams, V, 5.

naval establishment, and Smith had proved equal to the task of administering the affairs of a department of diminishing importance. It was suggested that Robert Smith's brother, the Senator, who was of the anti-Gallatin faction, could be induced to vote for the confirmation of Gallatin as Secretary of State, if Robert Smith were named for the Treasury Department, but Gallatin would not agree to this arrangement because he knew Smith would prove incompetent to perform the duties of the Treasury Department and that Gallatin himself would be obliged to perform them for him. Under these circumstances Smith was appointed Secretary of State, and Madison continued to do the work of that office in addition to his labours as President.

Thus, to start with, he had to manage foreign affairs an admittedly inefficient man, whom he had appointed for political considerations, and who consequently felt his allegiance due to the friends who had forced him on the President rather than to the President himself. For Secretary of the Navy Paul Hamilton, formerly Governor of South Carolina, a man without national reputation or following, was selected, and for Secretary of War, Dr. William Eustis, of Massachusetts, a respectable man who had seen service as a surgeon in the Revolutionary War. Cæsar A. Rodney was continued as Attorney General. The cabinet was factious as well as weak, for Smith and Gallatin were bitter enemies.

After the inauguration resolutions from public meetings in all sections of the country came to the President assuring him of loyal support and of willingness to accept further burdens from the government if they should be necessary. By many people it was believed that these burdens would soon include a war. General Henry Lee, who had long since parted company with Madison in politics but who remained steadfast in his friendship, told him in 1807 (July 19) that he considered war inevitable, and others declared that the time had come for calling

upon the States to furnish their quotas of troops.* But
at the outset of his term Madison enjoyed a diplomatic
triumph which for a time confirmed his faith in peaceable
commercial retaliation as an effective substitute for arms.

The war between France and England, begun in 1803,
which hastened a settlement of the Mississippi question
so advantageous to the United States, soon developed
measures of hostility between the belligerents which
affected the United States vitally, and precipitated it into
war with England, while straining to the breaking point
its amicable relations with France. The first of these
measures was taken by the British government, May 16,
1806, by an order in council declaring the whole coast of
Europe, from the Elbe in Germany to Brest in France, a
distace of 800 miles, in a state of blockade. In January,
1807, another order was issued forbidding neutrals from
engaging in the coasting trade between ports hostile to
Great Britain. November 17, 1807, another order prohibited all neutral trade with France or her allies except
through Great Britain. These were the famous "British
Orders in Council."

Following Great Britain's lead, on November 21, 1806,
from the "Imperial Camp at Berlin," Napoleon issued a
decree declaring the British Islands in a state of blockade,
forbidding all correspondence or trade with them, and
defining as contraband all English products or manufactures. December 17, 1807, from his "Palace at Milan,"
he decreed that every vessel which should submit to be
searched by British cruisers, or pay any tax or license to
the British Government, or be bound to or from any
British port, should be denationalized and sequestered.
These were the "Berlin and Milan Decrees," and about the
Orders in Council and the French decrees waged the battle
of the diplomats. So far as the Orders in Council were
concerned, Madison and a friendly British Minister determined to make them no longer a subject of contention.

David Montague Erskine, the British Minister when

* Dept. of State MSS.

Madison was inaugurated, was a protegé of Charles James Fox, was married to an American, and in his person represented everything that was conciliatory to America. He came to the new administration early in April with the proposition that if Madison would withdraw the demand for Admiral Berkeley's court martial for the attack on the Chesapeake he would agree to the other demands of the United States in satisfaction for the Chesapeake outrage. This was accepted; but the letter of withdrawal declared that, while the President forebore to insist on the punishment, he still thought its infliction would have been a just and useful example, "due from his Britannic majesty to his own honour." This question out of the way, Erskine next offered a repeal of the British Orders in Council in exchange for a proclamation by the President renewing intercourse with Great Britain. This was, of course, accepted, and simultaneously the proclamation and the promise of the British Minister that the Orders in Council would be repealed were given to the public. In making the arrangement, Erskine had exceeded his instructions, under which he could promise a repeal of the orders only if America withdrew all restrictions on British commerce, and at the same time renounced all pretensions to a colonial trade in time of war which she might not enjoy in time of peace. The United States must also recognize the right of Great Britain to capture American vessels attempting to trade with any foreign power acting under the French decrees. As such trade was forbidden by American law, this provision amounted to an agreement that Great Britain should execute American law. Although Erskine had been authorized to show his instructions to the American government, he had not done so, and Madison assumed he was acting within his instructions when he made his arrangement. It would have been an unheard of proceeding if Madison had refused an agreement fair to the United States on the ground that the envoy offering it was exceeding his authority.

The proclamation having been issued, the government and people of the United States lived in a fool's paradise for three months. A thousand ships sailed from American ports. The triumph of the policy illustrated in the embargo and non-intercourse acts was loudly proclaimed, and tribute was paid not only to Madison's success but to Jefferson's wisdom in inaugurating a policy which had resulted so satisfactorily. No one doubted that the Erskine agreement was a permanent fact.

When the rejoicing was still in full progress came a sudden dash to all hopes, and rage and despair were suddenly substituted. The whole Erskine agreement was repudiated by the British Government, Erskine was recalled and a new minister appointed in his place.* That the new minister could have any acceptable propositions to make was not to be expected. He was himself ill chosen if conciliation was intended, for Francis James Jackson was widely known and detested in Europe and America as the agent whom the British Government had chosen to demand the surrender of Denmark's fleet in 1807, and in default of the surrender to order the wanton bombardment of the city of Copenhagen; and in consequence of his fulfillment of his mission to the utmost extent of its horrors he became known as "Copenhagen Jackson." He came to Washington loaded with instructions which meant the failure of his mission or the degradation of the United States. The basis of these instructions involved a direct charge of bad faith against the administration, for he was not only to disavow Erskine's agreement, but to give as one reason for the disavowal that the American government had known when the agreement was made that Erskine had exceeded his instructions in making it, and that the President had issued his proclamation and published the terms of the agreement in the belief that the British Government would thus be forced to stand by the unauthorized acts of its agent. Jackson was instructed to enter complaint against the government

* Dept. of State MSS.

of the United States for having made the arrangement
under the circumstances. He might settle the Chesapeake affair only if the United States made a written
acknowledgment that the interdict against British ships
had been annulled.   The Orders in Council could be repealed only upon the express prohibition of all trade between the United States and France, or countries under
the French decrees as long as those decrees continued in
force.   But as if this was not enough, Jackson received
the final instruction that he was not to press for any
settlement of difficulties, as a settlement was not now as
important as it had been.   If the United States made
any proposals he was to refer them to his Government
and await further instructions, and it must be understood that Great Britain insisted upon her right to prohibit neutral trade with her enemy.   The United States
could make a treaty acknowledging it, or leave it to be
regulated by British orders in council.*

Madison was at Montpelier when the news of Erskine's
disavowal came, and Gallatin sent him the news and
urged him to return to Washington, which he did August
9, remaining only for a few days, during which the proclamation reviving the non-intercourse act against Great
Britain was prepared and signed. A month later (September 5) Jackson arrived, but Madison did not hasten
his return to Washington to meet him, feeling that the
disagreeable business before him need not be hurried.
The confident minister met the President October 1. He
found him "a plain and rather mean-looking little man,
of great simplicity of manners, and an inveterate enemy
to form and ceremony."   After the formal exchange of
greetings he was invited to take a seat, and was much
amused presently when a negro entered the room bearing
a tray with punch and cake. Jackson had been entertained in European palaces and sneeringly contrasted
their ceremony with his homely entertainment at the
White House. A short time afterwards he dined with

* Henry Adams, V, 99, *et seq.*

the President and was pleased at the deference shown him, for he was asked to hand Mrs. Madison in to dinner, and in this he saw a sign of concession because his predecessor, Merry, had been denied the distinction of precedence. He next had two important official interviews with the Secretary of State, at the second of which the fact was extracted from him that he had no propositions to offer in place of those of Erskine, which had been disavowed. ·The following day he received a formal note from Smith saying that further communications between them must take the form of writing. Upon objecting to this he was told that it was not meant to apply to minor official intercourse, but to important matters of which the record must be kept beyond the possibility of future misunderstanding. In reality, Madison could not trust Smith to conduct personal interviews skilfully, and as he expected to quarrel with Jackson he wished to control the contest. Jackson continued in bad humour and made the charge that Erskine's lack of power to make the concessions he had agreed to had been known to the American government. At first Madison did not reply to this imputation, but insisted that when a government disavows the acts of its agent it owes the other government affected an explanation; that the United States was bound to assume the adequacy of Erskine's powers, and that it still stood ready to accept any honourable settlement of the questions disturbing the relations of the two countries. In reply Jackson repeated that Madison had known the exact import of Erskine's instructions. Madison then demanded that before proceeding further Jackson should show precisely what his powers were, and closed with this sentence concerning knowledge of Erskine's instructions:

"After the explicit and peremptory asseveration that this government had no such knowledge, and that with such a knowledge no such arrangement would have been entered into, the view which you have again presented of the subject makes it my duty to apprize you that such insinuations are inadmissible in the intercourse of a foreign minister with a government that understands what it owes to itself."

Jackson's answer being mere reiteration, on November 8 he was informed that no further communications would be received from him. Thus terminated Jackson's encounter with the "plain and rather mean-looking little man." The defeated minister sought consolation among the Federalists, who generally upheld his course. In Baltimore he received much social attention, in New York still more, but in Boston he was given an ovation, and a public dinner was held in his honour, at which Senator Timothy Pickering offered this toast : "The world's lost hope—Britain's fast-anchored isle."

But if "Britain's fast-anchored isle" was determined to reduce the United States to the condition of a colony and leave it an independent nation only in name, France was equally determined to disregard its rights. There was, however, always this to be said: The original sin against neutrals, as Madison expressed it, lay with Great Britain, and her aggressions were far in excess of those of France. December 21, 1808, in response to a Senate resolution, Madison made a list of acts, decrees, orders and proclamations of foreign governments affecting neutral rights of commerce. From 1792 to 1808 there had been eighteen of such acts by France, three by Spain, and thirty-one by Great Britain. Moreover, the spoliations of Great Britain were harder to bear because our commerce with her was larger than that with all other countries combined.

When news of Erskine's agreement reached Paris it was proposed by Napoleon to modify the French decrees in a way favourable to American interests,* but as soon as Erskine's disavowal was known it became certain that unless America resisted British pretensions she must expect continued oppression from France. The only neutral in the world was then the United States—all the

* Henry Adams, V, 139, *et seq.*

other nations were involved in the convulsive struggle
between England and France, and the United States was
being ground between both nations.   March 23, 1810,
Napoleon issued the Rambouillet decree, providing for
the confiscation of American ships in France, Holland and
Italy.   Between April, 1809, and April, 1810, according
to the report of the American Consul at Paris, fifty-seven
American ships were seized in France, fifty-four in the
ports of Spain, twenty-eight in Naples, eleven in Holland,
making one hundred and thirty-four in all, valued at more
than a million dollars.   In point of fact, from now on
Napoleon regarded American ships as English ships and
subject to the same treatment.   He mitigated his decree,
however, so far as to treat as French ships those carrying
licenses issued by French Consuls, permitting them to
enter French ports and clear with French cargoes.   Of
Napoleon's policy Madison said: "The confiscations by
Bonaparte comprise robbery, theft and breach of trust,
and exceed in turpitude any of his enormities not wasting
human blood."   Confiscation of American property
and imprisonments of American seamen were the characteristics of Napoleon's policy.   The repeal May 1, 1810,
by Congress of the non-intercourse act left it to the President, in case either Great Britain or France should repeal
her measures against the United States, to prohibit by
proclamation all intercourse with the country not making such a repeal.   Upon information of this act France
held out the promise that if England would revoke her
orders or the United States would cause England to
respect her rights the French decrees would be repealed.
Madison had instructed Armstrong that in addition
France must agree to compensate the United States for
spoliations committed, but this condition was not
pressed, and in August Armstrong wrote to Pinkney at
London that the French decrees had been withdrawn.
The information had been officially conveyed to him in a
note from the Duc de Cadore, French Minister of Foreign
Affairs, August 5, 1810, and by way of England the news

reached Washington. The President believed it. It was authentic information conveyed through authentic channels; but no new French decree repealing the old decrees appeared to confirm it.

Under ordinary circumstances, in dealing with a nation of ordinary honesty an act stated as this repeal was stated would be accepted without doubt, but the times were not ordinary and Napoleon's definition of diplomacy was the art of lying. Nevertheless, the administration believed in the repeal and it wished to do so. Basing his action upon it, Madison began at once the last effort at peaceable coercion of Great Britain by issuing his proclamation reviving the law of non-intercourse with that power. He believed that the effect would be to so cripple her that she would have to make terms, or herself begin a war to compel the United States to renew commercial intercourse with her. The proclamation was issued November 2, and said: "It has been officially made known to this government that the said edicts of France have been so revoked as that they ceased, on the first day of the present month, to violate the neutral commerce of the United States." Simultaneously, a circular was issued by Gallatin to the various ports of the United States announcing that commercial intercourse with Great Britain would cease February 2, 1811.

Were the decrees actually repealed? A new Minister, Serurier, came from France, but he had nothing to say, except that the word of the French Minister of Foreign Affairs must not be doubted. He was instructed by Napoleon to say that the United States would receive every kind of aid and privilege from France if it decided to maintain the neutrality of its flag—that Napoleon would even not oppose the acquisition of the Floridas by the United States. In France Jonathan Russell, the American Chargé, was informed that ships really American would not be harmed—that the difficulty was to tell American and English ships apart. These fair words were taken to mean that the decrees had been repealed. It was expedient to accept them in that sense.

When Pinkney withdrew from London he demanded the repeal of the British orders on the theory that the French decrees had been repealed, but Great Britain replied that he was wrong in his facts. Simultaneously with his departure Augustus G. Foster was sent as British Minister to the United States. Nothing really was hoped from his mission, except to gain time by further negotiation, for he had no concessions to offer. But in the meantime (May 16, 1811) the long-standing Chesapeake affair was rendered unimportant in the controversy, not by exchange of notes, but by exchange of shots between the American frigate "The President," under John Rodgers, and the British ship "The Little Belt." War had not been declared, and there can be no doubt that the first shot was fired by the British ship, but it is also a fact that she was beaten by the American ship. Madison viewed the incident without alarm: "The occurrence between Rodgers and the British ship of war," he wrote to Jefferson, June 7, 1811,* "not unlikely to bring on repetitions, will probably end in an open rupture or a better understanding, as the calculations of the British Government may prompt or dissuade from war." It was when war was about to be declared that news came of fresh outrages by France and proof positive that France was acting under her decrees even if she had repealed them. Macon, of North Carolina, said "the devil himself could not tell which government, England or France, is the most wicked."†

By a law of August 26, 1794, "l'an 1ᵉʳ de la Republique Françoise," Danton signing the act, Madison had been made a citizen of France. The honour intended was somewhat marred by the ignorance of the French Assembly of small facts, for the act was for "N. Maddison" and included in it "Jean Hamilton," presumably Alex-

* Works (Cong. Ed.) II, 512.
† Henry Adams, VI, 196.

ander Hamilton, whose sympathy with the French Revolution was not apparent.* The French Republic had, however, intended to record an obligation to leading lights in American public life, but the sense of obligation did not descend to Napoleon, and he treated the United States and his fellow citizen Madison as though they were enemies instead of friends. Thus with both France and England the United States stood in a hostile attitude, and with Spain, too, our relations were soon inamicable, but as it happened through our own acts.

February 24, 1804, Congress passed a law extending customs regulations over the new territory bought from France, and authorized the President, whenever he should deem it expedient to do so, to make the bay and river Mobile to Pensacola a separate district and appoint the necessary customs officers. This was known as the Mobile act, and it excited such an indignant protest from Yrujo, the Spanish Minister, that Jefferson, in issuing his proclamation defining the new districts, did not extend authority over the territory claimed by Spain. Five years later the population, which had been increasing in parts of the new territory, became uneasy, held conventions, and part of them issued a declaration of independence and caused John Rhea, their newly elected president, to ask for annexation to the United States; but Madison refused to recognize the revolutionary government, because the territory in question belonged, as he contended, to the United States. The opportunity of rendering the claim impregnable could not be resisted, and October 27, 1810, Madison issued a proclamation ordering the governor of Orleans Territory to take possession of the district. The proclamation stated that failure to occupy it before had not been due to any distrust of the title, as the laws passed on the subject had shown, but in confidence that discussion and negotiation would give possession later. The confusion now exist-

---

* The original act is in the possession of F. D. Maguire, Esq., of Washington.

ent in the territory by the late uprising forced immediate action; but even now "in the hands of the United States it will not cease to be a subject of fair and friendly negotiations and adjustment." This was a bold stroke, but beneath the casuistry of the proclamation could be seen the determination of the President to take the territory, because he deemed its possession by the United States to be necessary for the protection of the Mississippi. Spain was powerless to retaliate, for she was beset on all sides— by her revolting colonies in America and by France and England in Europe.

CHAPTER XXXI

THE DECLARATION OF WAR

In March, 1829, when Henry Clay was the most conspicuous figure in American public life, he dined one Sunday with his political opponent, Samuel Harrison Smith, and the two fell to discussing the relative merits as statesmen of Madison and Jefferson. "Mr. Clay," says Mrs. Smith in an account of the dinner which she wrote to her son, "preferred Madison, and pronounced him after Washington our greatest Statesman & first political writer. He thought Jefferson had most genius—Madison, most judgment & common sense—Jefferson a visionary & theorist, often betrayed by his enthusiasm into rash & imprudent & impracticable measures—Madison, cool, dispassionate—practical, safe."*

It is not probable that Clay, who was an honourable man, would have used such language about Madison, if he himself had known that Madison was a man so ambitious and so weak that he was willing to buy a renomination to the presidency by plunging his country into an iniquitous war. Yet the Federalists charged that this was the very thing that Madison did, and that Clay sold the nomination for the war.

It was when news of more French outrages upon American commerce came, early in the summer of 1812, that, according to the story, Madison was visited by a committee of Republican leaders of the House of Representatives, with Henry Clay at the head, and informed that he must send a war message to Congress or the caucus of Republican members soon to be held would nominate some one

---

* Family papers of J. Henley Smith, Esq., of Washington.

else for the presidency. He sent the message and received the nomination.

Mr. Henry Adams, in his life of Albert Gallatin,* gives all the proof of this charge that the Federalists could produce, and pronounces it unfounded. It appears that James Fisk, a member of Congress from Vermont, declared he was himself a member of the committee which sold the nomination, but Henry Clay, who was the alleged head of the committee, pronounced the story untrue, and so did his friends. Timothy Pickering, to whom, of course, the charge, if true, would have been effective ammunition with which to damage his enemies, wrote to Abraham Shepherd, February 12, 1814: "At the last session, Mr. Hanson, noticing the manner in which the war was produced, in addressing Clay, the Speaker, spoke to this effect: '*You know, sir*, that the President was coerced into the measure; that a committee called upon him and told him that if he did not recommend a declaration of war he would lose his election. And then he sent his message recommending the declaration.'

"Now, my dear sir, I learn from Mr. Hanson that Colonel Thomas Worthington, Senator, on his way home to Ohio, gave you the above information, and mentioned the names of Henry Clay, Felix Grundy, and some other or others who composed the committee. This is a very important fact, and I pray you will do me the favour to recollect and state to me all the information you possess on the subject; at what time and from whom you received it."

Shepherd replied February 20. He said Senator Worthington had visited him for two days early in April, 1812, and had insisted in conversation that war was inevitable, but that Bayard would first be sent to England to make a last effort to prevent it; that Madison had consented to send Bayard; that he, Worthington, had had frequent conversations with Bayard and Madison on the subject, and that Shepherd could rely upon it that the measure

* P. 456, *et seq.*

would be adopted. After war had been declared, Worthington again stopped for a night with Shepherd and expressed his mortification that the mission had never been appointed. "He said," proceeds Shepherd, "as soon as he returned to the city (Washington) from my house he was informed of what had taken place by a set of hot-headed, violent men, and he immediately waited on Mr. Madison to know the cause. Mr. Madison told him that his friends had waited on him and said if he did send Mr. Bayard to England they would forsake him and be opposed to him, and he was compelled to comply, or bound to comply, with their wishes. I then asked General Worthington who were those hot-headed, violent men. He said Mr. Clay was the principal. I cannot positively. say, but think Grundy was mentioned with Clay . . . I did not ask him how he got the information. As I understood the business, a caucus was held and Mr. Clay and others appointed, and waited on the President in the absence of Worthington, which will ascertain when this business took place."

Pickering, if he pursued his investigation, found nothing further to support Hanson's charge, for he allowed the matter to drop. Shepherd's letter merely showed that the President had at one stage contemplated a final mission to England, although Worthington himself believed it would be useless, and that the President told him the leaders of the party would not support him in sending his mission.

George Bancroft, the historian, visited Madison in March, 1836, and at the time made this memorandum of a conversation with him:

"Madison was a friend of peace. But he told me 'that the British left no option; that war was made necessary; that under the circumstances of the negotiations with England war was unavoidable.' He further said, 'he knew the unprepared state of the country, but he esteemed it necessary to throw forward the flag of the country, sure that the people would press onward and defend it.' "

The truth is that a war message was the only kind that Madison could send, for his commercial weapons had failed and the resources of diplomacy were exhausted.

Any one who follows the intricacies of the diplomatic contest before the war message will find in the management of the case of the United States strength and capacity. Here the President was a master, and until Monroe succeeded Smith he worked without aid, writing all the papers which Smith signed as Secretary of State. Outside of the cabinet room Smith criticized these papers, and his brother in the Senate opposed and defeated the administration's bill for restricting commerce in 1810. As both members of the family were engaged in commerce, Madison believed their opposition was governed by their pecuniary interests. It became evident, therefore, that Smith must be dismissed, but Albert Gallatin hastened the cabinet crisis by writing Madison a letter in March, 1811, in which he resigned, pointing out the inharmonious condition of the cabinet and the injurious effect on the administration.* Madison refused to accept Gallatin's resignation, and caused Richard Brent, Senator from Virginia, to communicate with Monroe and find out if he would accept Smith's place. A favourable reply being received,† Madison dismissed Smith. The conversation in which he did so was a peculiar one. No hint of what was impending was conveyed to Smith, nor was anything done to soften the blow. With fatal good temper Madison told him he was aware of his opposition to measures which in cabinet council he appeared to approve, that he was incompetent, that Madison himself had been obliged to do his work, that the business of his department was conducted carelessly and grave blunders had resulted. Out of consideration for appearances,

* Adams's "Gallatin," 434.

† Monroe to Brent, March 18, 1811, Monroe's Writings (Hamilton), V, 178.

however, he was willing to appoint him Minister to Russia. Smith made a feeble denial of disloyalty and said he would prefer to be Minister to England or Judge of the Supreme Court, but Madison said he had other views as to those places, and that, besides, Smith could not be confirmed by the Senate for the Supreme bench, because he had not practised law for a long time and had lost his standing before the Senate. When Smith endeavoured again to deny the charge of disloyalty, Madison alluded specifically to the defeat of the non-intercourse bill, and added significantly that he could not find the motive for the opposition to that measure, unless he looked more deeply into human nature than he cared to do.* The president did not spare him, but he took the reproaches and insults heaped upon him tamely and at first intended to accept the mission offered him. Later, hearing it was said that it was only thrown as a sop to get rid of him, which was the truth, his pride revolted and he declined. He went into active opposition, printed an attack on Madison, and his family and friends became personal and political enemies of Madison's. One charge they made which Madison could not answer. He and Smith had been colleagues for nearly eight years in Jefferson's cabinet and Madison knew Smith's capacities as an official perfectly well. How did it happen, then, that he appointed to the most important office under him an incompetent man? He had, in fact, paid a costly price for the support of a faction and had not received the support.

On April 1, 1811, James Monroe took charge of the State Department, and any notion he may have had of changing the government's policy vanished before the Madison policy, which he found firmly entrenched and of which he himself became the instrument. Although that policy meant war, the government was not prepared. The army was disorganized, the navy was on a peace basis, the treasury was nearly empty, the non-intercourse act of 1809 having taken from it an important part of its

* Memorandum of Conversation; Works (Cong. Ed.) II, 495 *et seq.*

revenue. January 3, 1810, the President recommended the enlistment for a short term of twenty thousand men and that the subject of a navy be taken up by Congress. The non-intercourse act of 1809 was to expire by its terms with this session of Congress (1810), and a bill drawn up by Gallatin and approved by Madison was offered in its place. It provided that American ports should be closed to all British and French vessels, public and private, but British and French merchandise might be imported directly from the place of origin in American ships. This bill was introduced by Macon in the House and passed. It was the administration bill which Samuel Smith opposed and defeated in the Senate. The contest between the two houses terminated in a compromise by which the non-intercourse law was repealed, but the President was authorized, in case either Great Britain or France should repeal its measures against the United States, to revive by proclamation the non-intercourse law against the country not making the repeal. The avoidance of responsibility by relegating to the President functions which Congress should itself have performed was merely an evidence of the extraordinary inefficiency of that body.

Madison said that the restoration of commerce would create a revulsion of feeling in favour of commercial restrictions, and he still pinned his faith to them. To Pinkney in London he wrote May 23, 1810: "At the next meeting of Congress it will be found, according to present appearances, that instead of an adjustment with either of the belligerents, there is an increased obstinacy in both; and that the inconveniences of the embargo and non-intercourse have been exchanged for the greater sacrifices, as well as disgrace, resulting from a submission to the predatory systems in force. It will not be wonderful, therefore, if the passive spirit which marked the late session of Congress should at the next meeting be reversed to the opposite point; more especially as the tone of the nation has never been as low as that of its Representatives."*

* Works (Cong. Ed.) II, 476.

The tone of the Representatives was then deplorably low. There was not in the whole Congress a leader of power, and the President did not furnish the inspiration which the Congress lacked. His message of November 29, 1809, was a calm, unimpassioned presentation, in which he told Congress it must decide on the alternatives before it. But Congress was so torn by contending factions, each weak in itself, that it could decide on nothing. It proposed to decrease the expenditure for the army and navy. It rejected unanimously the motion for an increase of taxation made by Eppes of Virginia. The charter of the Bank of the United States was to expire by limitation March 11, 1811, and Congress failed to pass the bill for a new bank, although Madison was known to favour it, and the bank had been the mainstay of the treasury.

The new Congress was summoned to meet in November, a month earlier than the regular time. It comprised a new generation of men, just entering on the public stage to keep the public gaze for years to come. Henry Clay, John C. Calhoun, Langdon Cheves, Felix Grundy, Richard M. Johnson, and a few others, constituted the leaders of what were known as "the young war Republicans." They approached the impending crisis untrammelled by participation in the old controversies upon which the existing parties were formed, and for the time being stood together for a broad nationalism. One thing especially they stood for was action. War was practically existent. New York was blockaded; American ships were seized by British ships; American sailors were impressed.

The famous war message of June 1, 1812, was not the first suggestion of war made by the President to Congress. In his message of January 3, 1810, when he asked for a volunteer force of twenty thousand men, he said they were "to be enlisted for a short period and held in a state of organization and readiness for actual service at the shortest warning.

"I submit to the consideration of Congress, moreover, the expediency of such a classification and organization of the militia as will best insure prompt and successive aids from that source, adequate for emergencies which may call for them."*

In his third annual message (November 5, 1811) he said: "With this evidence of hostile inflexibility (of Great Britain) in trampling on rights which no independent nation can relinquish, Congress will feel the duty of putting the United States into an armour and an attitude demanded by the crisis, and corresponding with the national spirit and expectations.

"I recommend, accordingly, that adequate provision be made for filling the ranks and prolonging the enlistments of the regular troops; for an auxiliary force to be engaged for a more limited term; for the acceptance of a volunteer corps, whose patriotic ardour may court a participation in urgent services; for detachments as they may be wanted of other portions of the militia, and for such a preparation of the great body as will proportion its usefulness to its intrinsic capacities."†

This was not glowing language, but the President would not have used it if he had desired to restrain a Congress led by hot-headed men. He did not speak lightly, and he meant to go to war. As he explained in a letter to the South Carolina Legislature, December 20, 1813: "When finally and formally assured by the British government that its hostile measures would not be revoked, no alternative was left to the United States but irretrievable degradation, or the lesser calamity of a resort to arms."‡

Before this he wrote John Nicholas, April 2, 1813: "It had become impossible to avoid, or even delay, war at a moment when we were not prepared for it, and when it was certain that effective preparations would not take place whilst the question of war was undecided. . . . The calculations of the Executive were, that it would be best to open the war with a force of a kind and amount

* "Messages and Papers of the Presidents," I, 478.
† Id., 562.
‡ Works (Cong. Ed.) II, 579.

that would be soon procured, and that might strike an important blow before the enemy, who was known to disbelieve the approach of such an event, could be reinforced."*

On March 23, 1812, Serurier wrote to his government that Monroe had told him a few days before that within a week the President had intended to propose an embargo, to be followed by a declaration of war, but that their plans had been upset by news of the French outrages.† Nevertheless, when Foster called on Monroe he got no satisfaction, and April 1 the recommendation for the embargo went in. It was carried for sixty days by a vote of seventy to forty in the House; in the Senate, by a vote of twenty to thirteen, it was extended to ninety days, thus making it more a measure of negotiation than of war. The majority in Congress was obviously too small for the union necessary for war purposes.

In May, 1812, "The Hornet," sloop of war, arrived bearing news from England, and members of Congress thronged the State Department to hear if she had brought news of any concessions. On the contrary, Great Britain reasserted that her orders in council would not be rescinded against America even if France excepted America from her decrees.

On June 1 the expected war message went in. It was a paper of ability and strength. The question of impressment, which had for some time been in abeyance pending the discussion of other grievances, was now put first in the order of grievances against Great Britain, followed by a statement of the harassment of our coasts, the holding up of entering and returning commerce, the plundering of our commerce from "pretended blockades, without the practicability of applying one." The President said, also, illegal seizures had been made by France and outrages perpetrated on our vessels and citizens; but, he added, "I abstain at this time from

* *Id.*, 579.
† Henry Adams, VI, 194–195.

recommending to the consideration of Congress definite measures with respect to that nation."

Two days after the message was received Calhoun brought in his report in favour of war, and June 4 it was adopted in the House by a vote of seventy-nine to forty-nine. On June 18 it went through the Senate by a vote of nineteen to thirteen. The next day the President's proclamation was issued and he visited the War and Navy Departments, a thing he had never done before, "stimulating everything," as a private letter declared, "in a manner worthy of a little commander-in-chief, with his little round hat and huge cockade."*

In truth he was not an inspiring figure to lead in war. The hour had come but the man was wanting. Not a scholar in governments ancient and modern, not an unimpassioned writer of careful messages, but a robust leader to rally the people and unite them to fight was what the time needed, and what it did not find in Madison.

Nor was the emergency met by the Congress which declared war. The President had asked for an increase in the army, and he was given more troops than he asked for, but no increase of taxation was imposed, and the pay offered the soldiers was absurdly small. The War Department comprised beyond the Secretary not a dozen clerks and was impotent to meet the emergency. A request for two assistant secretaries of war was voted down, because Eustis was thought to be incompetent and his dismissal was desired. The militia force was increased, but authority to use it outside of the United States was not given. Of the preliminary military measures Madison sarcastically observed to Jefferson (February 7, 1812) "With a view to enable the Executive to step at once into Canada, they have provided, after two months' delay, for a regular force requiring twelve to raise it, and after three months' for a volunteer

---

* Richard Rush to Benjamin Rush, June 20, 1812, Qu. Henry Adams, VI, 229.

force, on terms not likely to raise it at all for that object."*

Before war was declared the President seriously thought of fighting both France and Great Britain. It might, he thought, hasten a peace with either power and a settlement of the question involved. On the other hand it would close all Europe to our ships and thus render them useless, and the belligerents might choose to prolong the war indefinitely in their own interests. He had no confidence that a war with both parties would attract the Federalists, as they were set in their determination to make capital out of all the difficulties of the administration. Monroe was not disposed to agree to this estimate of the opposition. "We have been so long dealing in the small way of embargoes, non-intercourse, and non-importation with menaces, etc., that the British Government had not believed us," he said. He thought we would have internal quiet if we opened our ports, and that we should "Trade and fight and fight and trade."

Madison's renomination for the presidency was effected May 18, a month before war was declared, by a unanimous vote and without visible opposition in the caucus, but De Witt Clinton was put in nomination by a convention in New York, and the Federalists supported him, his plan being to attract to himself all elements of opposition, however irreconcilable they might be the one to the other. He stood for nothing, therefore, except opposition. Of Clinton's ambition to be President Madison had been warned by Morgan Lewis, May 12, 1811, when he wrote that Clinton, who was then Mayor of the city of New York and Lieutenant-Governor of the State, intended to be Governor next and then go to Washington, if he could; that he was bitterly opposed to Madison, who had made a mistake in permitting Clintonians to hold the offices. Clinton had been actively stirring up strife and discontent over the distribution of patronage.† Nevertheless,

* Works (Cong. Ed.) II, 526.
† Dept. of State MSS.

Clinton, a Republican, received in the electoral college the votes of the Federalist States, all of New England, except Vermont, voting for him, together with New York, New Jersey and Delaware. Maryland gave him five votes and six to Madison. Madison received 128 votes and Clinton 89, but in the Congressional elections the Federalist gains were considerable, there being twice as many Federalists returned for the fourteenth Congress as there had been for the thirteenth.

CHAPTER XXXII

THE WAR PRESIDENT

FROM the very beginning the conduct of the war was a failure. August 15 Hull surrendered at Detroit and Fort Dearborn was also destroyed, thus giving Great Britain control of the lakes in the West. These disasters were attributed in part to the inefficiency of the War Department, but the President did not escape censure. The Secretary of the Navy was believed to be as incompetent as the Secretary of War, and Dearborn, the commanding general of the army, was an old man, who enjoyed no one's confidence save Madison's. Monroe said he was "advanced in years, infirm, and had given no proof of activity or military talent during the year" (1812). In the cabinet Monroe was the only one who enjoyed the confidence of the people and brought their force to the support of the administration. Gallatin was a far abler man than Monroe and was devoted to Madison's interests, but his enemies were implacable and in Congress opposed every measure he suggested. Monroe had seen service as a captain in the Revolution and had military aspirations. Seeing the sad plight into which the army had fallen, he volunteered to take the field, and a way was sought to put him in command of the army. Early in December, 1812, Eustis retired as Secretary of War, he himself recognizing that public opinion demanded his sacrifice. December 14 Monroe was made Secretary of War *pro tempore*. Such a concentration of power in the hands of the two Virginians caused general complaint, especially among Republicans in New York, so Monroe was put back in the State Department, and at the same time the project of his taking the field was definitely abandoned on account of the difficulties in the way.

General John Armstrong, of New York, lately Minister to France, was selected as Secretary of War, and entered upon his duties January 14, 1813. The objections to him were fatal to his usefulness. Long diplomatic service in which his ability was conspicuous had not fitted him for duty as an executive officer when quick decision and action were needed. He was an indolent man and energy was needed, and he was a member of the Clinton faction in New York and loyal co-operation in the cabinet was essential. He was unpopular in the West, and his nomination was confirmed by a majority of three votes only both Kentucky Senators voting against him; and Kentucky under Henry Clay's leadership was the most enthusiastic State in the Union in support of the war. Monroe, Gallatin and Jones, the new Secretary of the Navy, all distrusted Armstrong. Paul Hamilton resigned as Secretary of the Navy, probably on a hint from Madison, soon after Eustis left, and January 12, 1813, William Jones, of Pennsylvania, took his place. He had seen some sea service, was a merchant and had been a member of Congress. His ability was respectable but his career had been a negative one. Here were changes in the chief places in the cabinet at a critical time, and a reorganization of the executive departments. Of the original cabinet Gallatin alone remained.

When Congress met in November, 1812, the President put the state of the country before it and the picture was not a pleasing one. He recited as one of the "incidents to the measures of the war" "the refusal of the Governors of Massachusetts and Connecticut to furnish the required detachments of militia toward the defense of the maritime frontier. The refusal was founded on a novel and unfortunate exposition of the provisions of the Constitution relating to the militia . . . It is obvious that if the authority of the United States to call into service and command the militia for the public defense can be thus frustrated, even in a state of declared war and, of course, under apprehensions of invasion preceding war, they are not one nation for the purpose most of all requiring it, and that the public safety may have no other resource than in those large and permanent military establishments which are forbidden by the principles of our free government, and against the necessity of which the militia were meant to be a constitutional bulwark." But the President offered no suggestion for stopping so grave a defiance of federal authority. He told of his instructions to Jonathan Russell, who remained as chargé at London, to agree to an armistice on condition that impressments should stop, and of England's refusal. Opportunity for a reconsideration would, he said, be kept open, but "it would be unwise to relax our measures in any respect on a presumption of such a result."*

Officially the President put the best aspect possible on the state of affairs. Personally he did not deceive himself about the prevailing feeling of discontent. "I have not been unaware," he wrote to William Wirt, September 30, 1813, "of the disappointment and discontent gaining ground with respect to the war on Canada, or of the use to which they were turned against the administration. I have not been less aware that success alone would put an end to them. This is the test by which public opinion decides more or less in all cases, and most of all, perhaps, in that of military events where there is the least opportunity of judging by any other. No stimulus, therefore, has been wanting to the exertions necessary to render our arms successful in the quarter where they have failed.

"How far these exertions will prevail remains to be seen; and how far past failure is to be ascribed to the difficulties incident to the first stages of a war commenced as the present necessarily was; to the personal faults of those entrusted with command; to the course pursued by the National Legislature; or to mismanagements by the Executive Department, must be left to those who will

* "Messages and Papers of the Presidents," I, 514, *et seq.*

decide impartially, and on fuller information than may now exist."*

He explained what he had hoped to do. By taking advantage of the belief in Great Britain that the United States would not go to war, he had intended to open hostilities by quickly raising an army on short enlistments and reducing Canada from Montreal upwards before the enemy could make preparations to defend it. Congress had given him too big an army, had offered too little bounty and pay for its quick recruiting, had itself delayed too much, had refused to put the War Department on an effective basis, and the administration's plans had failed.

The blame for the most shameful instance of the failure of plans in the course of the war could not, however, be laid at the door of Congress, but fell upon his own immediate subordinates, acting and failing to act under his own eye. On the night of August 22, 1814, he received this hurried note from Monroe, who was busying himself in inspecting the military defenses of Washington:

"The enemy are advancing six miles on the road to the Wood-Yard and our troops retiring. Our troops were on the march to meet them, but too small a body to engage. General Winder proposes to retire until he can collect them in a body. The enemy are in full march for Washington. Have the materials prepared to destroy the bridges.   "JAMES MONROE.

"Tuesday, 9 o'clock."

At a cabinet meeting on July 1 the possibility of an attack on the capital was fully discussed and plans for its defense were drawn up and entrusted to the Secretary of War to be carried out, General William H. Winder, of Maryland, brother of Levin Winder, Governor of the State, being selected as the military commander. These plans would have proved adequate for their purpose, but they were never carried out, because Armstrong did not believe Washington would be attacked. About the middle of August it became known that Admiral Cock-

* Works (Cong. Ed.), II, 573, *et seq.*

burn had arrived in Chesapeake Bay and was proceeding up the Patuxent River, and the city of Washington fell into a panic.   The evening of August 22 the President, accompanied by his cabinet, rode out to see the troops under Winder, which were encamped ten miles from Bladensburg, and the next morning before nine o clock they passed him in review.   That day the records of the State and War Departments were taken first to an old mill on the Virginia side of the Potomac near Chain Bridge about six miles above Washington, and then to Leesburg.* The President remained with the troops the 23d, and in the evening went back to the White House, where, about nine o'clock, he received a discouraging report from General Winder in person.   Early the next morning, having read a note from Winder to Armstrong saying he needed counsel, he repaired to headquarters. Meeting Armstrong there he authorized him to go to the troops and give such assistance and counsel to General Winder as occasion required.†   He then intended to himself remain on the field, for he remarked to Campbell, the Secretary of the Treasury, that any conflict in orders could be settled by consulting him "as he would not himself be far distant."   Shortly before ten o'clock Winder started for Bladensburg, and a little while afterwards the President followed with the troops.   Before doing so Campbell had given him a pair of pistols, which he put in his holsters.   He and Attorney-General Rush were riding briskly towards Bladensburg, and had nearly gone into the British lines, when a volunteer scout told them of their danger, and they turned into an orchard, where they joined Monroe and Armstrong.   While there the troops about them were fired on and retreated.   The President then said to Monroe and Armstrong that "it would now be proper for us to retire to the rear, leaving the military movements to military men," and about two o'clock in

* Horatio King's Account, "Magazine of American History," Nov., 1885.

† Madison's "Memorandum," Works (Cong. Ed.), III, 423.

the afternoon he and Attorney-General Rush started for Washington. As he rode slowly back the stream of flying militiamen and civilians poured by him and around him, and about three o'clock in the afternoon he reached the White House. Before six o'clock he crossed the Potomac in a boat, and taking a carriage on the Virginia shore, along with Jones, Rush and one or two others, went westward about ten miles and passed the night at a house a few miles above the Little Falls. The next morning, August 25, he joined his wife at the inn six miles farther away, and about twenty miles distant from where the British actually were. He remained here all day and part of the night, and was insulted by some of the fugitives, who thought him responsible for their misfortunes. In the dead of the night a report came that the enemy was approaching, and the President and his wife parted, he going to a little hovel deeper in the woods, where he spent the rest of the night. The next day, August 26, he crossed the river and went to Montgomery Court House in Maryland, and hearing that Winder had gone to Baltimore, followed him for ten miles to Brookville, where he passed the night. August 27, receiving word from Monroe that the British had evacuated Washington, he sent notes to his cabinet officers to join him there, and he himself reached the city about five o'clock that evening. The enemy's squadron was still battering the forts below Alexandria, and his frigates could be seen off Alexandria until August 31. The President found lodging with his sister-in-law, Mrs. Anna Cutts, in her house on F Street, a block away from the Treasury Department, and after staying there about a month moved into Col. John Tayloe's Octagon House, a handsome residence which the ingenious Thornton had designed.

He had been absent from the city for three days. When he left he had instructed his cabinet to meet him at Fredericktown, Maryland, and had been unable to notify Armstrong of his change of plans, so Armstrong was not with him when he returned, and Winder was at

Baltimore. In the emergency he instructed Monroe to
assume charge of the War Department and the military
defenses. Throughout the catastrophe Monroe was the
only one who had been of practical use to him. He was
now the only one whom the military would obey, for they
mutinously announced they would take no orders from
Armstrong.

That illstarred official returned to Washington at one
o'clock August 29, and the same evening the President
called upon him and told him the military had rebelled
against him, and added that he himself was an object of
suspicion. He suggested, therefore, that Armstrong
permit some one else to remain in charge of the defenses
of the city. Armstrong replied with indignation that he
must have all his authority or none. Madison would
not then accept his resignation, saying he did not wish to
go so far, but it was agreed that Armstrong should leave
the city the following morning, which he did, and from
Baltimore resigned,* making public at the same time the
circumstances which prompted him to do so. On September 3, before his resignation had reached Washington,
the President gave Monroe a commission as Secretary of
War *pro tempore*, dating it August 31. September 25,
Monroe demanded a permanent commission† and received
it September 27. Madison made no pretense to military
knowledge and put himself in the hands of the only person
near him who had such knowledge. Armstrong contended that he had been forced out by intrigue in order
that Monroe might have his place. It was true that those
who complained most loudly of Armstrong wished Monroe
to succeed him, but after the fall of Washington no power
could have kept Armstrong at the head of the War Department, a fact which the President made clear to him at
their interview.

The President escaped with light censure for this
supreme disaster of the war. His own sin was in trusting

---

* Madison's Memorandum, Works (Cong. Ed.) III, 425.
† "Monroe's Writings" (Hamilton) V, 293.

others to attend to their duties. A great deal of ridicule was visited upon him for his flight from the city, but the circumstances did not warrant it. From the beginning to the end of this humiliating incident his conduct was dignified and showed no personal trepidation. He was not thinking of his safety, but of the disgrace which had come upon his country and his administration by the capture of the undefended capital.

One point in which the conduct of the war was weakest he could, however, charge primarily to Congress. In 1811 Gallatin's report showed an excess of receipts over expenditures for the year before, but the ensuing year he estimated that there would be a deficiency of over $1,000,000. He recommended that a loan of $1,200,000 be contracted and that taxes be increased. The latter alternative was refused, and at the end of October, 1812, Gallatin reported that a loan of $20,000,000 would be necessary to meet the expenses of the year 1813. The treasury was on the verge of collapse, but Congress left the tax bills untouched and authorized a loan of $16,000,-000 and an issue of $5,000,000 of treasury notes. April 1, 1813, the treasury was empty when John Jacob Astor came to its relief with the aid of Stephen Girard and David Parish. Although the $16,000,000 was to be borrowed at seven per cent. for the first thirteen years and six per cent. thereafter, only about $4,000,000 of popular subscriptions were offered. A national bank as an agency to assist the government in borrowing was earnestly desired by Gallatin, and in 1814 the Ways and Means Committee of the House reported a bill to incorporate one with a capital of $30,000,000, but it came to nothing, and a loan of $25,000,000 and an issue of $5,000,-000 interest-bearing treasury notes were ordered, and the President was given authority to issue $5,000,000 additional notes, if he could not borrow the full amount of the loan.

In the midst of these complications Gallatin went abroad and Jones took his place temporarily, but after a service of ten months Jones informed Madison that he could not continue his double service, the labour of the Treasury Department being too exacting. Gallatin's service abroad was then made definite. Alexander J. Dallas, of Pennsylvania, whom the President wished to nominate as his successor, would have been rejected by the Senate as Madison ascertained, so he offered the place to Richard Rush, then Comptroller of the Treasury, but Rush declined. Finally, February 8, 1814, he sent in the name of George W. Campbell, a Senator from Tennessee, and he was commissioned the following day. He had been a consistent supporter of the administration, but he was possessed of no conspicuous characteristics to inspire belief that he could overcome a desperate financial situation. In May, 1814, he attempted to float a loan, and received offers for $13,000,000 on hard terms, and an additional offer of Jacob Barker, a private banker in New York, to take $5,000,000 of the bonds was accepted, although Barker's ability to carry out his contract was doubted. Barker afterwards declared that there was an understanding between him and Campbell that $300,000 of the bonds were to be paid in London, the stock being sent by Campbell to the government bankers in that city to be sold, but that Campbell changed his mind and Barker's plans were embarrassed in consequence. Barker failed to keep his contract, and twenty-nine separate suits were afterwards brought against him by the United States.*

On May 22, 1814, Campbell reported to the President that the funds on hand would last two months longer. Astor, he said, proposed two methods for floating the loan, one being to negotiate in Europe through an agent, the other to make an arrangement with Astor and his friends, who, Campbell presumed, did the negotiating on their own account. He said then that he was apprehensive Barker would have difficulty in paying his installments. In July he attempted a second loan of $6,000,000, and

* Dept. of State MSS.

could sell only $2,500,000 of bonds at eighty. As the expenses of the government must be met he suggested the issue of treasury notes. A month later Washington was sacked and the banks of Philadelphia and Baltimore suspended specie payments, and were soon followed by all the banks throughout the country, except in New England. Campbell's statement of national bankruptcy was his last message. He resigned, and Alexander J. Dallas succeeded him October 6, 1814, the Senate having withdrawn its objection to him in view of the emergency. For 1815 the revenue was estimated at $18,200,000, not half enough for the running expenses of the Government, and there was $18,627,000 of outstanding treasury notes. March 3, 1815, a loan to absorb these was authorized, but Dallas rejected the bids made on the ground that they were too low. Soon after he came into office, October 17, 1814, he wrote to Eppes, Chairman of the House Committee on Ways and Means, recommending the establishment of a United States bank, and by a vote of sixty-six to forty the House resolved that such an assistance to the treasury ought to be created, but no agreement could be reached on any of the bills introduced, until at the last moment a bill drawn by Daniel Webster was carried. It authorized the creation of the bank, but without obligation to lend to the government, and Madison vetoed it, chiefly for that reason. More tax bills were passed at this session and $10,000,000 of treasury notes were issued. At the next session a new bank bill was under discussion when the treaty of Ghent arrived and postponed discussion, but a year later, on January 8, 1816, Calhoun reported a bill to incorporate the bank for twenty years with a capital of $35,000,000, and this bill became law April 10, 1816. Hardly any of the Federalists supported it and hardly any of the Republicans opposed it. Henry Clay, who had voted against a similar bill in 1811, completely changed front, and James Madison, who had opposed the bill creating the first bank of the United States in 1791, put his name

to the bill of 1816 and made it law. He had already
stated his attitude on the subject in his veto message of
January 30, 1815. "Waiving the question of the constitutional authority of the Legislature," he said, "to
establish an incorporated bank as being precluded in my
judgment by repeated recognitions under varied circumstances of the validity of such an institution in acts of the
legislative, executive and judicial branches of the government, accompanied by indications, in different modes,
of a concurrence of the general will of the nation," he was
now ready to approve a bank bill, as he regarded as
settled the question of its constitutionality.* John
Randolph attributed Madison's signing the bill to the
weakness of old age, but Madison always insisted it was
due to the necessities of the occasion. The chief opposition to the bill had not come from strict constructionists,
but from the state banks, which refused to coöperate with
the treasury or to assist it. After the bank was authorized Dallas wrote to Madison, August 31, 1816, to con-
gratulate him on the financial prospect.

"The national bank," he said, "grows in the public
confidence. I believe its immediate uses will be as great
as was anticipated by its most strenuous advocates.
Under a prudent and skilful director acting in concert
with the government, it will restore the national currency, and destroy the artificial differences of exchange.
But I look with peculiar pleasure to the establishment,
as furnishing a machinery to frustrate the usurpations
of the state banks, and to retrieve the constitutional
powers of the Government over the coin and currency
of the nation."†

When Dallas retired from the Treasury Department
three months later, Madison wrote to Gallatin, who was
serving as Minister to France, and offered him his old
post again, but Gallatin preferred to remain abroad, and
William H. Crawford was appointed.

* "Messages and Papers of the Presidents," I, 555.
† Dept. of State MSS.

The record of the cabinet was singular.   Robert Smith, the first Secretary of State, was a failure and was dismissed.   Eustis, the first Secretary of War, broke down in the face of emergency and was forced to resign, and his successor, John Armstrong, was sent precipitately away from Washington in 1814.   Paul Hamilton, the Secretary of the Navy, was forced out of office when Eustis was, and for the same reason.   George W. Campbell, Madison's third Secretary of the Treasury, resigned because he could not cope with the difficulties of his position.   Monroe's service at the head of the State Department was interrupted by four assignments to act as Secretary of War.   Walter Jones served as Secretary of the Navy and of the Treasury for nearly a year.   Dallas remained in the Treasury for only two years, during which time he also acted as Secretary of War for two weeks.   William H. Crawford, who was appointed Secretary of War August 1, 1815, served for a little more than a year when he was transferred to the Treasury Department.   Jefferson's Secretaries of State, War, the Treasury and the Navy went through practically the whole of his two terms with him; Adams changed the Secretaries of State, the Treasury and War once; Monroe completed his eight years of the Presidency with hardly a break in his cabinet.   Madison's administration fell in more critical times than the administration of Adams, Jefferson or Monroe, but his task would have been an easier one and the credit of his administration would have been greater, if he had surrounded himself with a compact body of able men, devoted to his interests and expert in their management of public affairs, instead of having strange faces about the cabinet table, and coadjutors who were inexperienced and even disloyal.   In his long public career he had never, until he became President, had the duty of selecting and commanding men.   His concern had been rather with public measures, and when he was called upon to choose the instruments for their execution he was too old to acquire the quality of choosing them well.

CHAPTER XXXIII

As the war progressed, that Madison was in secret alliance with Napoleon was extensively believed. In writing to Col. David Humphreys, March 23, 1813, Madison expressed surprise that any one should believe so absurd a story, and pointed to his own and Jefferson's messages, and his recent instructions to Barlow, limiting his negotiations in France to the subjects of indemnity and commerce. "With such strong presumptions and decisive proofs before the public it is impossible," he said, "that a purpose in this government of allying itself with that of France can be seriously believed by any intelligent individual not in a temper to reject a witness even from the dead."* Those who believed this charge had during the diplomatic contest preceding the war generally sided with England, and, according to Henry Lee, did not believe that Madison wished to accommodate matters with that country. The situation in Washington was so uncertain and had been so prolonged that not even the Republicans themselves thought war was really coming. Many of them wrote to Madison and implored him not to enter into it, giving as one reason that it would injure his political fortunes. Governor John S. Barbour, his neighbour, asked him in strict confidence, March 30, 1812, to tell him whether or not there was to be war. If it was really impending he wished to put Virginia in a state of defence; if not, he did not wish to alarm the people by unnecessary preparations. Elbridge Gerry, then completing his term as Republican Governor of Massachusetts, wrote two weeks later (April

* Works (Cong. Ed.) II, 560.

12), that he was doing his best to forestall the disloyal spirit in his State. He had appointed three division commanders and three brigadiers of State troops who were firm friends of the national government. Others appointed by him were of different politics, because he could not find competent Republicans, but they would do their duty, he thought, and their superior officers would control them. May 19, he wrote that the strength of the opposition was increasing with delay and that war would be a check. "By war we shall be purified as by fire," he said. When war came his hopes were not realized. July 13, he reported that Governor Strong, his successor, was removing Republican militia officers and filling their places with Federalists. If the British attacked there was grave danger. The Republicans would be to blame if they stood "with folded arms to leave it in the power of such a disaffected executive to deliver up our fortresses to the enemy; to enable those who may be disposed to rebel to unite with our foes; to aid them in making a diversion of our western army and to subject the State to be overawed by a fear of traitors."

St. George Tucker, Williamsburg, July 27, 1812, gave Madison the Southern opinion of Massachusetts Federalists: "I am mortified to observe," he said, "the probable predominance of a faction in Boston whose designs have long been suspected by me, and whose present determination seems to be either to rule or to dissolve the union." Mathew Carey, of Philadelphia, said that in his opinion (January, 1812), the Federalist newspapers were to blame for the Federalists' attitude. "The mass of Federalists," he said, "are as good citizens as ever existed. They are, however, made tools of by men who have the very worst views. They have been led on step by step, through fraud and misrepresentation, till they have arrived at the verge of civil war." The Federalist papers were, in fact, distributed free in parts of New England, the consequence being that the people saw no others, being unwilling to pay for them. But according to Carey there was yet another reason for a disunion spirit. It was fostered, he said, by men who hoped to attain higher offices in the prospective confederacies than they could attain under the union.* These men had, however, been busy with their schemes for many years. In 1804 Timothy Pickering deliberately proposed a Northern secession to his friends of the Essex Junto. They decided against it as impracticable, and not a good remedy for existing evils, but they made no pretense of attachment to the union.†

Pickering, Griswold and others plotted with Anthony Merry, the British minister, as early as January, 1804, for dismemberment, and, of course, Merry reported the facts to his government.‡ His successors had similar reports to make, and the French minister sent information of the spirit of disunion to Paris. These reports had their effect in the conduct observed towards the United States by England and France. Turreau, the predecessor of Serurier, reported to his government, March 19, 1809: "I had informed your Excellency of the disunion projects shown by some of the Northern States," and a month later (April 20) he said the separation of New England was openly talked of, and that it was to be carried out under British protection.¶

That such a scheme was in contemplation Madison believed and endeavoured to prove in 1811 by the purchase for $50,000 of the papers of John Henry, formerly secret agent in the United States of Sir James Craig, Governor of Canada. These papers did not, however, establish a conspiracy. They showed the discontent in New England and that the British government had maintained a secret agent there, but the names of those with whom he had had dealings were lacking and no overt acts against the government were proved. One object of the pur-

---

* Dept. of State MSS.
† Henry Adams, II, 160–161.
‡ *Id.* II, 391.
¶ Henry Adams, V, 34, 36.

chase, Monroe told the French minister, was to arouse the war spirit of the country, but the effect in this direction was insignificant, and the feeling against the Federalists needed no increasing.

When the war measures came before Congress the leading Federalists voted for them. Some of them told the British minister, with whom they were on friendly and confidential terms, that they hoped for a short war which would throw out of power the Madison administration. On February 1 two of them called on Foster and gave advice as to the best course for his country to follow. Under no circumstances, they said, should England accede to Madison's demands. A short war would be beneficial to England. "In short," reported Foster to his government, "they seemed to think that Great Britain could by management bring the United States into any connection with her that she pleased."*

Secretary Eustis reported in 1812 a conversation with one John Wait, "a gloomy Federalist from Boston."

" 'Then, Mr. Wait, they will separate from the union.'

" 'O no, sir, they cling to the union.'

" 'But they have said it and will do it.'

" 'No, unless they see commerce entirely destroyed and themselves ruined—unless the laws are unconstitutional.'

" 'And they, the minority, are to be the judges!' "

Here the conversation was interrupted. Eustis said Mr. Wait was a perfect representative of the Massachusetts Federalists.†

When Erskine's agreement was made the Federalists were reconciled, as peace with Great Britain seemed assured, and John Henry went home because there was nothing for him to do. When the short-lived supposed security terminated the Federalist determination to find an escape from Virginia supremacy revived with vigour. "Nearly all the New Englanders," says Henry Adams, "on

* Henry Adams, VI, 172, *et seq.*
† Dept. of State MSS.

the contrary, looked to ultimate disunion as a conservative necessity."

After the war began Madison was informed that in Vermont the success of American arms was necessary to save the State from passing over to the control of the Federalists and that a disaster to American arms would cause disaffection to the union.*

Governor Strong of Massachusetts, on June 26, proclaimed a public fast for a war declared "against the nation from which we are descended, and which for many generations has been the bulwark of the religion we profess." The Supreme Court of the State declared that the determination of the question whether the constitutional exigency existed for calling the State militia into the service of the United States belonged to the Governor and not to the President. When Congress authorized a loan of $11,000,000 from New England, where there was the greatest amount of capital, only $1,000,000 was subscribed. The agents for the loan in Boston were obliged to advertise that the names of subscribers would not be made public, and the Federalist papers advised all people against taking up the government's bonds.†

In Providence, when the news came that war had been declared, the bells of the meeting houses tolled as for a funeral. Many of the shops were closed and flags were flown at half mast. Christopher Ellery, who reported these facts to Madison, said that many Federalists hoped to hear of British success in the war.‡

In Connecticut, Republicans said the legislature was a treasonable body, but that *one-third* of the citizens would defend the government. March 13, 1809, the Republicans at Litchfield passed resolutions which show the opinion in which the Federalists were held:

"When, too," they said, "combining with these impending dangers from abroad, we find among our own citizens,

* *Id.*

† Randall's "Life of Jefferson," III, 388.

‡ Dept. of State MSS.

in our own councils, men so miserably misled and so unhappily forgetful of the rights and duties of Americans as to hail, in unison with the multiplied agents and incendiaries of a foreign court, who have found a resting place in the bosom of our country, that nation as a *protecting shield* which above all others has outraged the rights of mankind," etc.*

Before the war began the prospects in New England were painted in dark colours by a number of well-informed people. Benjamin Stoddart said, January 18, 1809: "To me it is and always has been as clear as noonday's sun that further perseverance in this embargo would produce open and effectual resistance to the laws of the union."†

Undoubtedly the embargo harmed the political fortunes of the Republicans. In New York it threw out of employment seamen, shipwrights, rope and sailmakers, riggers, calkers, draymen and 'longshoremen. It was computed by Morgan Lewis that of seamen there were in New York City nearly 4,000, and they were an active force in politics against the administration and proposed to elect De Witt Clinton to the presidency.

Robert R. Livingston said the reports of distress from the embargo were much exaggerated. The check to commerce had come at a most opportune moment. "We have," he wrote, "stopped full-handed; we have a capital [with] which we can long remain unemployed. It must then find that occupation in manufactures which it can no longer find in commerce, and when once invested in them it cannot be easily withdrawn, even on the return of peace . . .

"I hear with contempt the exaggerated accounts of the distress of the country. I have just traveled through that in which it was said chiefly to exist. I have been to Boston by the way of Hartford. I returned by another

---

* *Id.*

† Reported to Madison by Commodore Thomas Tingey, Dept. of State MSS.

route. I have also been to almost the northeastern town of Vermont, traveling thro Massachusetts and New Hampshire. Never have I, at any time, witnessed more ease and comfort than I have seen in the whole of this extensive journey."*

New England was more prosperous than any other part of the country. John Lowell said in 1814 that the banks were at their wits' end to lend their capital. A few made secret loans to the United States, but others bought British government bills at more than twenty per cent. discount rather than assist their own government.

Even when war was in progress officers in the army complained that military reverses were pointed to by Federalist officers as an evidence of Republican incapacity, and that they constantly criticized Madison and his whole administration. It became a question whether they ought not to be removed for disloyalty.

There were mass meetings, protests and pulpit oratory against the war, and some people thought it their duty to tell Madison how much they disapproved of it. A man eighty-nine years old wrote from Woodstock, Conn., November 23, 1814, that it was a "cruel, unnecessary, unjust war, esteemed so by thousands of the good people of the United States, and the expenses of it too heavy and grievous to be borne."†

Josiah Quincy was one of the most earnest of the opponents. It was he who in 1811, when the bill to admit Louisiana into the union of the States was pending in the House, said:

"If this bill passes, it is my deliberate opinion that it is virtually a dissolution of this Union; that it will free the States from their moral obligation; and, as it will be the right, so it will be the duty of some, definitely to prepare for a separation—amicably if they can, violently if they must."

When prospects of peace first appeared he wrote to

* Dept. of State MSS.
† Dept. of State MSS.

Senator Outerbridge Horsey of Delaware, June 18, 1813: "In relation to the Russian mediation, I have but little faith . . . However, I am of those who are willing to wait for the disclosures of time. And though I believe little in peace, yet should it come I am perfectly convinced that it is owing to other circumstances than anything contained in the authorities of our cabinet. Had I less belief that Mr. Bayard desired the appointment, I should have more confidence in his judgment concerning the event . . . And in the meanwhile French successes or French defeats will settle the vibrations of our policy, unless the refusal of supply or despair of loans should make a quicker result inevitable."*

Although the Federalists did not feel towards Madison the same degree of personal animosity which they had felt towards Jefferson, they said in effect, "as Mr. Madison has declared war, let Mr. Madison carry it on," and many of them indulged in robust abuse of him,† denouncing him as a "miscreant," etc. They professed to believe that he should resign. The Boston *Gazette* said: "Do the Democrats think that a Madison, whose highest ambition is to balance a sentence and round a period, that the rhetorician who once glimmered in harmless debate in times of peace, can now balance the conflicting parties of our country, or direct the energies of a powerful nation?" The Baltimore *Federal Gazette* published a letter from Washington dated January 15, 1815, saying Madison would be called on to resign, and the *Federal Republican* said there was no hope of preserving the Union unless he resigned or was removed from office. This was just before the battle of New Orleans, and before the news of the Treaty of Ghent had been received.‡ Naturally after those events no further suggestions of Madison's resignation were made.

---

* Family papers of the late Outerbridge Horsey, Esq., of Needwood, Md.

† Randall's "Life of Jefferson," III, 370, *n.*

‡ Randall's "Life of Jefferson," III, 416, *et seq.*

The discontent and disloyalty of the Federalists found their supreme culmination in the Hartford Convention of 1814. Randall, in his life of Jefferson, gives a fair estimate of those who attended and favoured it:

"They were rich men, indignant at the stoppage of their gains by commercial restrictions and war—colonists in spirit, who like Talmadge thought a war against England was a war against religion and order—aristocrats dreaming of the restoration of those palmy days when political wisdom and rights sprung from hair-powder and shoe-buckles—sectional fanatics, unwilling to have the 'moral and religious' people of New England form part of any political compact wh:ch they could not control—politicians who were keen consolidationists when they were the Ins at Washington, but who regarded their own banishment from the theatre of national politics as a procedure which demanded the formation of a 'confederacy' which would better appreciate their capacities for government. But even among the latter class, by.far the most dangerous one, ran the conservatism of personal character, of caste, and of the cautious New England mind. There was not among the members one hopeless enough to be desperate, depraved enough to delight in blood and disorder, or warm enough in temperament to become a dangerous enthusiast."*

The discontented leaders undoubtedly looked forward to the formation of a New England confederacy. Pickering wrote July 4, 1813: "On the contrary, I believe an immediate separation would be a blessing to the 'good old thirteen states,' as John Randolph once called them." John Lowell, who was the maker of literature to spread Pickering's plans, published a pamphlet this year entitled "Thoughts in Answer to a Question Respecting the Division of the States; by a Massachusetts Farmer." The year before, July 21, 1812, a public meeting in Essex County adopted resolutions proposed by Pickering, favouring a State convention to concert measures in

* Randall's "Jefferson," III, 418.

opposition to the administration, but it failed of acceptance in Boston because of the intrepid opposition of
Samuel Dexter, himself a Federalist, but one of a considerable number who refused to follow the popular tide
into the gulf of disloyalty.*

In the General Court of Massachusetts, the committee
having under consideration the resolutions of the county
meetings reported, February 18, 1814:

"Whenever the national compact is violated and the
citizens of this State are oppressed by cruel and unauthorized laws, the Legislature is bound to interpose its
power and wrest from the oppressor his victim.

"This is the spirit of our Union, and thus it has been
explained by the very man who now sets at defiance all
the principles of his early political life." Accordingly,
they proposed a convention of the States to amend the
Constitution. "This," they said, "was the mode proposed by Mr. Madison [in *The Federalist*, No. 46] in
answer to objections made as to the tendency of the
general government to usurp that of the States."

A convention of the States was, of course, not an
objectionable suggestion, but nothing that Madison had
ever said could be so twisted as to sanction the first sentence of the report. The Legislature did not adopt the
report, but referred the whole question to the next Legislature in order that the sense of the people might in the
meantime be taken on it. The action of the ensuing
Legislature must, therefore, be accepted as a correct index
of public opinion in Massachusetts. After Washington
had been sacked by the British, when the treasury was in
desperate straits for funds and New England believed
that the collapse of the national government was impending, the Massachusetts Legislature pronounced, October
8, 1814, in favour of seizing the Federal revenue collected
in the State and using it for the State's defense, and
sanctioned the holding of a convention of New England
States. The vote was three to one in favour of the con-

* Henry Adams, VIII, 4, *et seq.*

vention, and after protesting against the action taken the minority withdrew. October 19, twelve delegates to the convention were chosen. The Connecticut Legislature fell into line and named Hartford as the place and December 15 as the time for a meeting to devise "such measures for the safety and welfare of these States as may consist with our obligations as members of the National Union,"—this language being intended to draw a distinction between the Union and the Constitution. The Legislature of Rhode Island also appointed delegates, and these were the only three States giving official sanction to the convention. Vermont declined to name delegates, but when the meeting took place one county sent a member. New Hampshire had a Republican Executive Council which stood in the way of the Legislature's desire to name delegates, but two were sent by popular meetings. After the convention had been decided upon, but before it was held, the elections to the national House of Representatives took place, resulting in the return of thirty-nine Federalists and two Republicans from New England. Popular approval of Federalism had increased, for in the preceding Congress there had been thirty Federalists and eleven Republicans.

The Hartford convention was really composed of the less radical element of the Federalists, and could have gone much further than it did with the certainty of receiving popular support. It comprised only twenty-six members in all, and George Cabot of Massachusetts, who was chosen president, was determined to restrain it within temperate bounds. Harrison Gray Otis, it is presumed, drew up the report which it adopted, and which was the only result of its labours given to the public, the sessions and proceedings being guarded with inviolate secrecy. The report said that the time for a change was at hand; that a severance of the union of the States could not be justified, especially in time of war, except upon grounds of absolute necessity; but that it was the duty of the State to interpose its authority to protect its citizens from infractions of the Constitution by the general government. Therefore, State laws should be passed to protect the militia and citizens from conscription or drafts by the Federal government, and an arrangement should be made authorizing the States to assume their own defense and retain for the purpose a part of the Federal taxes collected in their borders. Until the result of an application for this purpose to the general government should be made known, it was recommended that there be no further proceedings, but if the application failed another convention was to be called. The report was approved by the Massachusetts and Connecticut Legislatures and delegates were appointed, with Harrison Gray Otis at their head, to proceed to Washington to ask the contemplated arrangements.

October 17 William Wirt called on Madison at the Octagon House before the Hartford convention had been determined upon. He described him as looking shattered and heartbroken, his mind and heart full of the New England sedition.* The fact that the capital had been wrecked by a foreign foe seemed not to concern him so much as the solicitude he felt for the integrity of the frame of government he had done so much to erect. A month later (November 25) he wrote to Wilson Cary Nicholas:

"You are not mistaken in viewing the conduct of the Eastern States as the source of our greatest difficulties in carrying on the war; as it certainly is the greatest if not the sole inducement to the enemy to persevere in it. The greater part of the people in that quarter have been brought by their leaders, aided by their priests, under a delusion scarcely exceeded by that recorded in the period of witchcraft; and the leaders themselves are becoming daily more desperate in the use they make of it. Their object is power. If they could obtain it by menaces, their efforts would stop there. These failing, they are ready to go every length for which they can train their followers. Without foreign coöperation, revolt and separation will

* Kennedy's "Life of Wirt," I, 339, Qu. Henry Adams, VIII, 231.

hardly be risked; and what the effect of so profligate an experiment would be, first, on misguided partisans, and next on those remaining faithful to the nation, who are respectable for their consistency and even for their numbers, is for conjecture only."*

After the convention had done its work, Monroe spoke the administration's views when he said:

"They cannot dismember the Union, or league with the enemy, as I trust and believe, & they cannot now retreat without disgrace. I hope that the leaders will soon take rank in society with Burr & others of that stamp."†

But no such serious ignominy was theirs. The commissioners regularly named by their States in accordance with the recommendation of the convention, started for Washington about the time the battle of New Orleans was fought, and the news of that battle and of the treaty of peace reached Washington in advance of their coming. In the universal rejoicing their existence was almost forgotten, and they did not invite public notice, but quietly went home without presenting themselves to the President. The New York *National Advocate* advertised for tidings of some unfortunate gentlemen who had started for Washington from the Hartford convention, but who had missed their way and it was feared had been drowned,‡ and other newspapers noticed them with similar raillery.

Thus terminated the only movement looking to a dismemberment of the Union made by a combination of States before the Southern secession movement. The President knew of its existence from the beginning, but he never believed it would result in disunion. He did nothing to stop it, feeling himself powerless, and being, moreover, unwilling to abandon the restrictions of trade for political purposes, which was a part of his system, and which brought the discontent in New England to a crisis.

* Works (Cong. Ed.) II, 593, 594.
† Writings of Monroe (Hamilton) V, 306.
‡ Randall's "Life of Jefferson," III, 417.

CHAPTER XXXIV

WHILE the charge of the Federalists that Madison was in league with France in making war against Great Britain was absurd, his relations to that power were nevertheless peculiar, and required at least an appearance of belief in her good faith towards the United States; and the consequence of this necessity soon put him in an extraordinary position.

The immediate basis for his demand for the repeal of the British orders in council was that the French decrees had been repealed. He was assured of their repeal again and again, yet there was evidence before his eyes that they were being enforced against American shipping. In 1811 Joel Barlow was sent as Minister to France. He had lived there for many years and his personal familiarity with French official life made him hope to unravel the entanglement into which the two countries had become involved; but no one could be said to meet Napoleon on even terms in a diplomatic contest, because his methods were without example and his moves could not be anticipated even by the imagination. When, in May, 1812, Barlow asked for the hundredth time for proof of the repeal of the decrees, the Duc de Bassano, Minister for Foreign Affairs, put into his hands an imperial decree dated April 28, 1811, declaring the Berlin decree non-existent against American vessels after November 1, 1810. No one had ever seen this paper before, for the very good reason that it had only been written and signed a few days before Barlow saw it. What could Madison do in the face of such methods? Simultaneously with the production of this bogus decree came reports of the

353

most reckless enforcement of the decree it purported to repeal, and Barlow was instructed again to demand indemnity. The reply of France was merely to invent tricks for delay. Bassano had followed Napoleon on his way into Russia as far as Wilna, and he requested Barlow to come to him for further negotiation. Being of an adventurous turn, Barlow left Paris at the end of October and arrived at Wilna November 18, when Napoleon was in full retreat from Moscow. He abandoned his army December 5, and started for Paris, and the court at Wilna disbanded. On the way back to Paris Barlow contracted inflammation of the lungs from exposure and died at the village of Zarnovitch, near Cracow, in Poland, December 24, 1812.

The false decree of April, 1811, purported to have been issued because of Madison's proclamation of non-intercourse with Great Britain, and the basis of the non-intercourse proclamation dated November 2, 1810, had been that the Berlin decree was repealed. The President was thus put in a false position, and his indignation was intense. The conduct of the French government would, he said, be "an everlasting reproach to it." If he could only get through his war with England he would be able to deal with France. Then, he said, "the full tide of indignation with which the public mind here is boiling will be directed against France, if not obviated by a due reparation of her wrongs. War will be called for by the nation *una voce*."* He instructed Barlow to be prepared to retire from his mission on sudden notice. Yet the victory of Russia and England over Napoleon was likely to affect America unfavourably, as England would be unlikely to listen to American demands. The situation resolved itself into this: Napoleon's supremacy was necessary to the American policy against England, while it steadily tended to a break between America and France.

Fortunately there was one country whose interest was on the American side in her war with Great Britain.

* To Barlow, August 11, 1814; Works (Cong. Ed.) II, 540, 541.

Russia herself feared England only less than she did France and foresaw in British triumph over America increasing difficulties for herself. The friendship of the Czar Alexander for America was partly a personal sentiment, but his offer of mediation between England and America, made in March, 1813, was, as Madison said, "with the collateral view, there is reason to believe, of deriving advantage from the *neutral* interference with British monopoly in the trade with her."* "We are encouraged," he said in another letter, April 2, 1813, "by the known friendship of the Emperor Alexander to this country; and by the probability that the greater affinity between the Baltic and American ideas of maritime law than between those of the former and of Great Britain, will render his interposition as favourable as will be consistent with the character assumed by him."†

Negotiations for the Russian mediation had begun as early as September, 1812, through the American Envoy, John Quincy Adams. The offer reached Washington March 8, and was accepted at once, although it was not known whether Great Britain would agree. It was decided to name two additional Envoys to be associated with Adams in the negotiations, and to help in uniting the country. James A. Bayard, a Federalist, was named as one of them. Gallatin, at his own request, was named as the other. There was precedent for the employment on a foreign mission of one in the domestic service, as Chief Justice Jay had served as Minister to England and Chief Justice Ellsworth as Minister to France.

Before Gallatin and Bayard arrived in St. Petersburg, July 21, 1813, it was known to the Russian government that Great Britain had declined to accept Russian mediation, but the refusal was not accepted as final and the Envoys were kept in idleness awaiting developments. The British government preferred direct negotiation to

* To Jefferson, March 10, 1813; Works (Cong. Ed.) II, 559.

† To John Nicholas; Works (Cong. Ed.) II, 563.

the association of a third party whose sympathies were not with her, and November 4, 1813, Lord Castlereagh wrote to Monroe proposing the reopening of negotiations. Gallatin and Bayard were accordingly authorized to go to London.

There the war was as unpopular in the beginning as it was in America. England had never supposed the United States would fight, and public opinion was unprepared to support the unexpected war. Spencer Percival, the Prime Minister, was assassinated May 11, 1812, after Madison's preliminary war message had gone in to Congress, and Percival's successor, Lord Liverpool, suspended the obnoxious orders in council June 17, the day before Congress declared war. This suspension had been brought about by the evident approach of war, and was the first success scored by the United States.

The letter of Lord Castlereagh to Monroe proposed Gothenburg as a proper place for negotiating, and on January 14 the President nominated as United States Commissioners Adams, Bayard, Henry Clay and Jonathan Russell. A few weeks later, February 8, he nominated Gallatin, simultaneously filling Gallatin's place as Secretary of the Treasury, and thus compelling the confirmation which had been refused before on the ground that Gallatin could not properly hold a foreign mission and be Secretary of the Treasury at the same time. The commission was so constituted as to give each section of the country a representative in hopes of having united acquiescence in their action.

But while commissioners had been appointed there was no armistice, and the war went on, Gallatin and Bayard remaining in London till June 21. In the spring Clay came over with the commissioners' instructions, he being the only member of the commission not already in Europe, and the place of meeting was changed from Gothenburg to Ghent, the latter being a more convenient place. The British commissioners chosen to meet those of the United States were Lord Gambier, Henry Goulburn and William Adams.

None of them enjoyed a wide reputation, and in ability none was in the same class with the Americans. Both commissions were armed with instructions to adhere to which meant the failure of the negotiations. The Americans were ordered to insist upon an abandonment by Great Britain of impressment. "If this encroachment of Great Britain is not provided against," said Monroe, "the United States have appealed to arms in vain. If your efforts to accomplish it should fail, all further negotiations will cease, and you will return home without delay."

The British commissioners, on the other hand, were to offer the state of possession as the basis of the territorial arrangement to revive peace. This would have meant the loss to the United States of half of Maine, the northern part of New York, Vermont and New Hampshire, and other points. The American instructions included a demand for "the upper parts and even the whole of Canada," and arrangements about rights of blockade, contraband of war, the maritime rights of neutrals, and fishery rights As early as February 14, 1814, William H. Crawford, whose knowledge of popular wishes in the United States was exceptionally good, told Madison that any peace which did not include the cession to the United States of Upper Canada would be unfavourably received by the administration's friends in the interior and western parts of the country, and even on the seaboard the people would not be satisfied with less.*

But the extravagant position assumed by each power underwent a change as the negotiations progressed. The most fundamental modification was that in the instruction of June 27 to the American commissioners, authorizing them to abandon the impressment question as a *sine qua non* of acceptance of a treaty. The reasons given were simple. Owing to the peace in Europe Great Britain might now throw her whole force against America, and according to Bayard and Gallatin's despatches from London the month before, "the popular exultation, in

* Dept. of State MSS.

consequence of the success against France," demanded strong prosecution of the war against the United States.* Moreover, as long as the peace in Europe lasted it was not probable that the right of impressment would be claimed. This reasoning applied equally to the question of blockade and neutral rights. While the negotiations were progressing news was received of the failure of the British expedition against Baltimore, of Drummond's defeat at Fort Erie, and of Prevost's retreat from Northern New York. The *uti posseditis* became in consequence a poor basis for claim of territory on the part of the British government, and was abandoned for the *status quo ante bellum.*

The meetings of the two commissions began August 8, at the Hotel des Pays Bas, and afterwards were held alternately at the British and American commissioners' residences, being finally signed, December 28, at the house of the American commissioners, at the corner of the Rue de Champs and Rue Toulons.†

The original antagonistic conditions upon which peace could be arranged having been withdrawn by the governments of both countries, there remained nothing for the commissioners to do but to draw up a treaty agreeing to the one thing that both countries insisted upon having, and peace was really the only thing arranged for in the treaty. It comprised eleven articles. They provided for restoration on either side of territory conquered during the war; return of all property, records and slaves taken; the mutual surrender of prisoners of war; joint commissions to be appointed to decide upon boundaries and disputed ownership of islands in Passamaquoddy Bay. Neither impressments, nor blockades, nor violations of neutral rights were even hinted at, but with peace in Europe none of these things existed. The misfortunes of the United States had arisen from the measures of France and England against one another. Now that these

* Monroe's Instructions, Monroe's Writings (Hamilton) V, 371.
† "Magazine of American History," November, 1888.

measures were withdrawn the United States was fighting for abstract principles, and not against actual oppressions. She could well afford to leave the former to a future settlement.   To continue the struggle with her own people disunited and dissatisfied and England free to hurl its undivided power on her shores, would have been an act of madness.

Peace having been declared, congratulatory addresses poured in upon the President and he was given credit for closing the war with honour.   So long had the people been distracted with contention and strife that from sheer exhaustion they became amiable.   A great wave of prosperity and general contentment swept over the land. The Federalists were deserted, dwindled to a little band of men who were out of joint with the times, and soon to be called a Federalist became an opprobrious epithet. And in the midst of this sunshine and good-humour, James Madison retired from public life.   His shortcomings as President were for the time forgotten, and in the calm of the closing months of his administration the people saw again the man of blameless life, the well-balanced scholar and the conservative statesman whom they had elected to the Presidency eight years before.

In his inaugural address he had laid down the principles which were to govern his administration:

"To cherish peace and friendly intercourse with all nations having correspondent dispositions; to maintain sincere neutrality towards belligerent nations; to prefer in all cases amicable discussion and reasonable accommodation of differences to a decision of them by an appeal to arms; to foster a spirit of independence too just to invade the rights of others, too proud to surrender our own."   No one could truthfully say he had not lived up to this declaration, for in spite of his persistence in the belief that commercial retaliation was a good instrument to use against unfriendly nations, he never pretended that by this or any other means yet discovered could war be eliminated as a last resort of a nation whose rights were persistently trampled upon.

"To support the Constitution, which is the cement of the Union, as well in its limitations as in its authorities; to respect the rights and authorities reserved to the States and to the people as equally incorporated with and essential to the success of the general system." The bank bill intrenched upon the limitations of the constitution, according to his doctrine, but he signed it, because he believed it to be a necessity, and because he regarded the constitutional question involved as having been settled against him by the action of the three branches of the government. His last message to Congress (March 3, 1817) was, however, a veto of the bill "for constructing roads and canals, and improving the navigation of watercourses, in order to facilitate, promote and give security to internal commerce among the several States." The powers of Congress were, he said, specified and enumerated in the constitution and did not include a right to appropriate money for internal improvements. The general defense and general welfare clause could not be stretched to cover such schemes, excellent as they were in themselves.*

"To avoid the slightest interference with the rights of conscience or the functions of religion, so wisely exempted from civil jurisdiction." On February 21, 1811, he vetoed an act of Congress "Incorporating the Protestant Episcopal Church in the town of Alexandria, in the District of Columbia," because it "exceeded the rightful authority to which governments are limited by the essential distinction between civil rights and religious functions," and violated the article of the Constitution which declares that "Congress shall make no law respecting a religious establishment." "The Bill," he said, "vests in the said incorporated church an authority to provide for the support of the poor and the education of poor children of the same, an authority which, being altogether

* "Messages and Papers of the Presidents," I, 584.

superfluous if the provision is to be made the result of pious charity, would be a precedent for giving to religious societies as such a legal agency in carrying into effect a public and civil duty." February 28, 1811, he vetoed a bill for the relief of certain individuals and the Baptist Church at Salem Meeting House in Mississippi Territory, "because the bill in reserving a certain parcel of land of the United States for the use of said Baptist Church comprises a principle and precedent for the appropriation of funds of the United States for the use and support of religious societies" contrary to the Constitution.*

"To liberate the public resources by an honourable discharge of the public debts; to keep within the requisite limits a standing military force, always remembering that an armed and trained militia is the firmest bulwark of republics—that without standing armies their liberty can never be in danger, nor with large ones safe." This expressed an aspiration which war had dashed, but in his last annual message he was able to announce that the receipts of the treasury exceeded the expenditures by about nine million dollars, and that there could be an early extinction of the debt.

"To promote by authorized means improvements friendly to agriculture, to manufactures, and to external as well as internal commerce; to favor in like manner the advancement of science and the diffusion of information as the best aliment to true liberty." He saw the manufactures of the country given an impulse by the non-intercourse laws which they could not have acquired in fifty years of natural development, and he approved in 1816 a more thoroughly protective tariff bill than had yet been enacted. But a national university so much desired by him and others no steps were taken to establish, although in his last message he renewed his recommendation for one.

"To carry on the benevolent plans which have been so meritoriously applied to the conversion of our aborig-

* "Messages and Papers of the Presidents," I, 490.

inal neighbours from the degradation and wretchedness of savage life to a participation of the improvements which the human mind and manners are susceptible in a civilized state." This was a creditable wish, but the civilization of the Indians was a task beyond his powers.

His purposes, as he announced them when he was inaugurated, were thus not fully accomplished, but as nearly realized as he could have reasonably expected they would be.

In his last annual message (March 3, 1816) he spoke his words of farewell with the same modesty and absence of vainglory which always distinguished him.

"The period of my retiring from the public service being at little distance," he said, "I shall find no occasion more proper than the present for expressing to my fellow-citizens my deep sense of the continued confidence and kind support which I have received from them. My grateful recollection of these distinguished marks of their favourable regard can never cease, and with the consciousness that if I have not served my country with greater ability I have served it with a sincere devotion, will accompany me as a source of unfailing gratification.

"Happily, I shall carry with me from the public theatre other sources which those who love their country most will best appreciate. I shall behold it blessed with tranquillity and prosperity at home and with peace and respect abroad. I can indulge the proud reflection that the American people have reached in safety and success their fortieth year as an independent nation; that for nearly an entire generation they have had experience of their present Constitution, the offspring of their undisturbed deliberations and of their free choice; that they have found it to bear the trials of adverse as well as prosperous circumstances; to contain in its combination of the federal and elective principles a reconcilement of public strength and individual liberty, of national power for the defense of national rights with a security against wars of injustice, of ambition, and of vainglory in the fundamental provision which subjects all questions of war to the will of the nation itself, which is to pay its costs and feel its calamities. Nor is it less a peculiar felicity of this Constitution, so dear to us all, that it is found to be so capable without losing its vital energies of expanding itself over a spacious territory with the increase and expansion of the community for whose benefit it was established.

"And may I not be allowed to add to this gratifying spectacle that I shall read in the character of the American people . . . sure presages that the destined career of my country will exhibit a government pursuing the public good as its sole object; . . . a government which avoids intrusions on the internal repose of other nations, and repels them from its own; . . . and which, while it refines its domestic code from every ingredient not congenial with the precepts of an enlightened age and the sentiments of a virtuous people, seeks by appeals to reason and by its liberal examples to infuse into the law which governs the civilized world a spirit which may diminish the frequency or circumscribe the calamities of war, and meliorate the social and beneficent relations of peace; a government, in a word, whose conduct within and without may bespeak the most noble of all ambitions —that of promoting peace on earth and good will to men.

"These contemplations, sweetening the remnant of my days, will animate my prayers for the happiness of my beloved country, and a perpetuity of the institutions under which it is enjoyed."

CHAPTER XXXV

THE RETIRED STATESMAN

HAVING seen Monroe take the oath of office, March 4, 1817, Madison departed for Montpelier, never again to hold Federal office. He continued the example set by his predecessors in the presidency, and preserved the dignity of his retirement carefully, keeping entirely aloof from participation in political affairs, and refusing to lend his influence in favour of any man's candidacy for office. Soon after he returned to Montpelier he had printed a form of letter, which he sent to office-seekers who solicited his recommendation.* It stated that his personal relations with the President were such that he would not embarrass him by asking favours, and that he had determined to refuse to recommend any appointments.

When the wave of Jackson enthusiasm was at its height he resisted a concerted effort to extract from him some assistance to the party opposed to Jackson. It was confidently believed that he was in sympathy with that party, and the anti-Jackson convention at Richmond determined to put him at the head of its list of nominations of presidential electors, Monroe being also named. James Barbour, formerly Governor of Virginia, and a number of others importuned him to accept, Barbour declaring that by doing so he would decide the election,† but he would not yield; and when he and Monroe were nominated in spite of their refusal, they declined positively to serve. With Jackson's conduct of the presidential office he had no sympathy, and he did not conceal the fact from his

* "Early Office Seeking,"—N. Y. Evening Post, Nov. 26, 1898.
† Dept. of State MSS.

friends, although he resolutely refused to put it in the form of a public statement. He was not troubled by fears that Jackson's methods would be an example for a successor to follow. "That a series of them [Presidents of the United States] should do so," he said, "with the support of the people, is a *possibility* opposed to a moral *certainty*."*

When it was arranged to hold a convention in 1829 to make a new constitution for Virginia, he felt obliged to accept an election as a delegate from his county. He had advocated such a convention when he was in the Legislature nearly fifty years before. His chief objections to the constitution of 1776 were that it was passed before the Declaration of Independence was made, and consequently when the power of forming a permanent State government did not exist, and that it had never been submitted to the people for their ratification. The proposition for a second convention could not then be carried, mainly because Patrick Henry was opposed to it, and the constitution continued in use for fifty years. Before going to the convention of 1829, Monroe, who was also elected a delegate, proposed that Madison be chosen for president, with a vice-president to perform the active duties of the position,† but Madison would not agree, and when the convention met himself put Monroe in nomination, and he was elected without opposition. Madison was seventy-eight years old and quite infirm in health, but his mental faculties were unimpaired. The Governor of the State, William B. Giles, sent him and Mrs. Madison a pressing invitation to be his guests while the convention was in session, but they refused to embarrass him, and stayed at a Mr. Duvall's.‡ Every deference was shown to Madison in the convention and he accepted a fair share of labour on the committees. He made a speech December 2. The official report says: "The members rushed

*To Edward Coles, October 15, 1834. Works (Cong. Ed.) IV, 366.
† Dept. of State MSS.
‡ *Id.*

from their seats and crowded about him."* Among them was John Randolph of Roanoke, who held his hand to his ear to catch what was said, but soon dropped it with a gesture of despair, for Madison spoke in so low a tone that none but those in close proximity could hear him. The question upon which the convention divided was that of the ratio of representation in the legislature and whether or not slaves should be counted in estimating population. If they were not counted the part of the State where they were most numerous would not be protected against burdensome taxation of slave property. Madison spoke in favour of reckoning slaves at three-fifths of their number, the proportion which he had introduced into the Federal Constitution. "It is due to justice," he said; "due to humanity; due to truth; to the sympathies of our nature; in fine, to our character as a people, both abroad and at home, that they should be considered, as much as possible, in the light of human beings, and not as mere property. As such they are acted upon by our laws, and have an interest in our laws, they may be considered as making a part, though a degraded part, of the families to which they belong." If they were white, he added, like European serfs, this position would not be denied them. "But the mere circumstance of complexion cannot deprive them of the character of men."

The proportion which he recommended was finally accepted by the convention, but in its proceedings Madison, mindful of the weight of years, did not attempt a dominant part, and the side he voted on was often in the minority. Indeed, on one occasion upon a minor motion he voted Aye when every other member of the convention voted No.†

In the years immediately preceding and following the convention came to him the deep rumble of the storm in South Carolina over the nullification question. He heard in it the most ominous warning against the safety

* Proceedings and Debates of the Va. State Convention, 537.
† Journal of the Convention, 118.

of the Constitution that had arisen since its ratification, and he threw himself into the breach, as we have seen in a former chapter of this book, to protest that there was no connection between this destructive doctrine and his protest against the alien and sedition laws in 1798. He gave such sympathy and assistance as he could to the Union party of South Carolina, and among his correspondents was one of the most valiant leaders of that party, Thomas S. Grimke, of Charleston. He realized the full import and effect of the nullification propaganda. To Edward Coles he said, August 29, 1834: "Nullification has the effect of putting powder under the Constitution and Union, and a match in the hand of every party to blow them up at pleasure; and for its progress, hearken to the tone in which it is now preached; cast your eye on its menacing increasing minorities in most of the Southern States without a decrease in any one of them. Look at Virginia herself, and read in the *Gazettes*, and in the proceedings of popular meetings, the figure which the anarchical principle now makes, in contrast with the scouting reception given to it but a short time ago.

"It is not probable that this offspring of the discontents of South Carolina will ever approach success in a majority of the States. But a susceptibility of the contagion in the Southern States is visible, and the danger is not to be concealed that the sympathies arising from known causes, and the inculcated impression of a permanent incompatibility of interests between the South and the North, may put it in the power of popular leaders aspiring to the highest stations, and despairing of success on the Federal theatre, to unite the South, on some critical occasion, in a course that will end in creating a new theatre of great though inferior extent. In pursuing this course, the first and most obvious course is nullification; the next secession; and the last, a farewell separation."*

Public labours of a non-political character Madison

* Works (Cong. Ed.) IV, 357, 358.

accepted to a limited extent. The year before his death he was elected president of the Washington National Monument Society to succeed Chief Justice Marshall and accepted the post as a purely honourary one. His connection with the University of Virginia was, however, his chief active employment after his retirement. In the founding of that institution he was the devoted assistant of Jefferson. November 14, 1794, Bishop James Madison wrote to tell him that two years before Jefferson had broached the scheme of establishing a State university in some central position "upon a liberal & extensive plan." When Jefferson retired temporarily from public life he suggested that Madison might come into the Legislature and further the scheme. "Will you give us your aid," said the Bishop, "in perfecting the plan?" Madison replied that the plan was Jefferson's, and he thought ought to wait on Jefferson, so it was agreed to permit it to sleep.* It was evident from Bishop Madison's letters that he hoped himself to become the head of the faculty of the new university, but he died in 1812 before anything tangible towards establishing it had been accomplished.

The Albemarle Academy was chartered, but got no further, and from the project came in 1816 Central College, with Jefferson at the head of the board of visitors and Madison a member. Two years later both were of the commission that formed from Central College the University of Virginia, and Madison was elected on the first board of visitors, continuing on every subsequent board, until on Jefferson's death in 1826 he succeeded him as Rector. This office, concerned directly with the management of the University even in minute details, he filled actively until his feebleness became so great that he could not go out.† In his will he bequeathed to the university his library, and it remained a noble monument to his in-

* William and Mary College Quarterly, July, 1902.

† "Thomas Jefferson and the University of Virginia," **Bureau of** Education Circular, 1888.

terest in the University until it was swept away by the fatal fire of 1895.

Upon Charles Carroll's death in 1833, Madison was elected President of the Colonization Society, and although he did not accept he had hopes that it might succeed in its object. In 1831 (December 28) he wrote: "Many circumstances of the present moment seem to concur in brightening the prospects of the Society, and cherishing the hope that the time will come when the *dreadful calamity* which has so long afflicted our country, and filled so many with despair, will be gradually removed, and by means consistent with justice, peace, and the general satisfaction; thus giving to our country the full enjoyment of the blessings of liberty, and to the world the full benefit of its great example."*

In an old age rendered bright by optimism slavery was the one dark shadow that hung over him. Harriet Martineau visited him about the time of his election to the Presidency of the Colonization Society. "I will only mention," she says, "that the finest of his characteristics appeared to me to be his inexhaustible faith; faith that a well-founded commonwealth may, as our motto declares, be immortal; not only because the people, its constituency, never die, but because the principles of justice in which such a commonwealth originates never die out of the people's heart and mind. This faith shone brightly through the whole of Mr. Madison's conversation except on one subject. With regard to slavery he owned himself almost in despair. He had been quite so till the institution of the Colonization Society."†

Harriet Martineau wrote a full account of her visit to Montpelier for the gratification of "the strong interest felt in England about this virtuous statesman." When she saw him he was eighty-three years old, and so disabled by rheumatism that he lived in one room. He rose before nine o'clock and sat in his easy chair till ten at night. He

---

* To R. R. Gurley. Works (Cong. Ed.) IV, 213.
† "Retrospect of Western Travel," I, 191, *et seq.*

complained of one ear being deaf and that his eyesight was not good. He could, however, hear ordinary conversation, and could read perfectly well. He sat in his chair with a pillow behind him, dressed in a black silk dressing-gown, with gray worsted gloves on his hands to keep them warm; and a gray and white cap on his head, because he was bald. His voice was clear and his manner lively and playful. His teeth were still good, and Miss Martineau says he had "an uncommonly pleasant countenance." His energy is illustrated from the fact that he maintained through Miss Martineau's ear-trumpet an animated conversation almost continuously for the three days of her visit. "He talked more on the subject of slavery than on any other," she says, "acknowledging without limitation or hesitation all the evils with which it had ever been charged." He "admitted the great and various difficulties attending the scheme [of colonization] and recurred to the expression that he was only 'less in despair than formerly about slavery.'" The conversation ranged over a wide field. He spoke of Malthus, and said Franklin and two others had anticipated him in comparing the rates of increase of population and food, but that Malthus had been the first to draw out the doctrine. As we have seen, Madison himself had touched upon it some years before Malthus wrote. He spoke in favour of international copyright, "and wished that English authors should be protected from piracy in the United States without delay." He recurred to the subject of religious liberty in the United States, and "declared himself perfectly satisfied that there is in the United States a far more ample and equal provision for pastors, and of religious instruction for the people, than could have been secured by a religious establishment of any kind; and that one of the greatest services which his country will be hereafter perceived to have rendered to the world, will be the having proved that religion is the more cared for the more unreservedly it is committed to the affections of the people."

Miss Martineau was introduced to the Madisons in a friendly letter from Josiah Quincy, then President of Harvard College. One of the most pleasing features of the Montpelier life was the revival of old friendships and the mellowed tone cast by time over past political enmities. Charles Pinckney wrote from Charlestown, September 2, 1820: "Within a few days it will be 33 years the day we dined together on signing the Constitution— what changes have taken place since & in my opinion one of the worst to us is that we are so much older than we were then, for in spite of all that the divines and philosophers may tell us I am honest enough to confess that I think old age is not the most comfortable state in the world." He had, he said, often said this to Franklin, who had agreed with him and remarked "'that it had been a good world to him & his life a successful one & that he should like to live it over again.'"*

In 1824 there was a resumption of the friendly relations with Edward Livingston which had been interrupted for many years. "Mr. Livingston," Monroe wrote, "intimated to me some time since, his desire to hold with you and Mr. Jefferson, the same relation which he held in 1798, & that I could communicate that sentiment to you on his part, & apprize him of the result." Livingston's overtures were willingly accepted, and Madison encouraged him thereafter in his political and scientific career.†

The old contemporaries were dying off and the great triumvirate was broken by Jefferson's death in 1826. February 17 he wrote a long letter to Madison about the University and his private affairs, which were in a distressing condition: "But why afflict you with these details?" he said. "Indeed, I cannot tell, unless pains are lessened by communication with a friend. The friendship which has subsisted between us, now half a century, and the harmony of our political principles and pursuits, have been sources of constant happiness to me through that

* Dept. of State MSS.
† *Id.*

long period. And if I remove beyond the reach of atten-
tions to the University, or beyond the bourne of life itself,
as I soon must, it is a comfort to have that institution
under your care, and an assurance that it will not be
wanting. It has also been a great solace to me, to believe
that you are engaged in vindicating to posterity the course
we have pursued for preserving to them, in all their purity,
the blessings of self-government, which we had assisted
too in acquiring for them. If ever the earth has beheld
a system of administration conducted with a single and
steadfast eye to the general interest and happiness of those
committed to it, one which, protected by truth, can never
know reproach, it is that to which our lives have been
devoted. To myself you have been a pillar of support
through life. Take care of me when dead, and be assured
that I shall leave with you my last affections."

On July 2 Jefferson conversed for the last time. The
welfare of the University was in his thoughts, and he expressed confidence that Madison would carry on the work.*
The next day he was unconscious, and he died on July 4.

Five years later, on the same great anniversary, Monroe
died. His last letter to Madison was dated April 11,
1831. He described his plans, which compelled his leaving Virginia and going to live in New York, where his
daughters were settled. "I deeply regret," he said, "that
there is no prospect of our ever meeting again, since so
long have we been connected and in the most friendly
intercourse, in public & private life, that a final separation is among the most distressing incidents which could
occur. . . I beg you to assure Mrs. Madison that I
never can forget the friendly relation which has existed
between her & my family. It often reminds me of
incidents of the most interesting character. My daughter,
Mrs. Hay, will live with me, who with the whole family
here unite in affectionate regards to both of you."

On June 30 came a letter from Alexander Hamilton,
Jr., saying that Monroe was dying, and July 7 Tench

---

* Tucker's "Life of Jefferson," II, 495.

Ringgold wrote that in his last illness he had often spoken of Madison and their friendship of forty years and his great regret "that he should leave this world without beholding you."* From the friendly offices of Alexander Hamilton's son on this occasion it would seem that his father left no legacy of bitterness towards Madison, but this had been shown some years before by a cordial letter from Mrs. Hamilton asking a favour of Madison.

During his retirement there was no abatement in the reading or writing, and he was regarded by literary men as their patron. From them he received many books, some of which he read and all of which he politely acknowledged. His literary taste was versatile, but the variety of productions offered to it was excessive. F. R. Hassler sent his popular exposition of the system of the universe and his elements of geometry; Richard Emmon's "Fredonaid," a long poem, reached him through the poet's brother; John Finch sent his essay on "The Boundaries of Empires"; John A. Graham, "Graham's Junius"; Weems, whose "Life of Washington" was then (1819) in its twenty-first edition, begged his acceptance of his "Life of Marion"; Mary Randolph sent him a copy of the second edition of her cookery book and asked his opinion of it. From George Ticknor came the "Memoir of Lafayette" which the Marquis had himself corrected; Matthew Carey rained economic pamphlets upon him; and George Tucker, as a neighbour and friend, consulted him freely in his literary work. In 1831, he was invited by the American Peace Society to serve on a committee in conjunction with John Marshall, John C. Calhoun, William Wirt and Joseph Story to award a prize for the best essay on "A Congress of Nations for the Amicable Adjustment of National Disputes and for the Promotion of Universal Peace without Recourse to Arms," but he declined the labour. He received countless reports and proceedings of political, educational, charitable, scientific, agricultural and learned societies; he took a real interest

* Dept. of State MSS.

in the literary work of some of his correspondents—in
Edward Livingston's Criminal Code; in R. H. Lee's life
of his grandfather of the same name, Madison's old opponent; in Wheaton's "Life of William Pinkney," and
Saunderson's "Lives of the 'Signers.'" Noah Webster
begged his patronage of his new dictionary in 1826, and
explained to him the extent and nature of his researches
in preparing it. Gales and Seaton of the *National
Intelligencer* occasionally wrote to him in confidence, asking him to settle some controversy involving the politics
of the past, but he was disposed to avoid everything
tending to involve him in disputation, although he
freely gave such information as he had to those who were
engaged in legitimate historical work. One of these was
Jonathan Elliot, to whom he loaned the printed accounts he had collected of the proceedings of the conventions in the various States called to consider the
question of ratifying the Constitution. So far as his own
speeches were concerned in the Virginia Convention of
1788, while he was not thoroughly satisfied with Robertson's report, he was willing to let it pass as in the main
substantially correct. Jared Sparks came to him in
1827, fresh from his examination of the Washington
papers at Mount Vernon, and he loaned him such of
Washington's letters as he desired to use. He assisted
Sparks also in preparing the "Diplomatic Correspondence of the American Revolution" and the "Life and
Letters of Gouverneur Morris." He wrote many letters
himself, some of them long ones, several sketches
on the theory of the government of the United States,
and in the last year of his life a long refutation of the
doctrine of nullification. The most important literary
labour of his declining years was the arrangement of his
notes of the Constitutional Convention of 1787, which he
designed for posthumous publication, making, however,
few alterations in the report as he had taken it down.

CHAPTER XXXVI

ALTHOUGH Madison was a man of public affairs and of books, he was a careful and progressive farmer and took a practical interest in agriculture. Through Robert R. Livingston, who first introduced them in America and regarded them with much favour, he was induced to raise those Merino sheep from the wool of which his inaugural coat had been made, and he sold their wool and exchanged them with his neighbours in order that the breed might be tested. He sold hams, bacon, tongues, barrels of beef and pork. He took great interest in his garden, and through Latrobe procured a great variety of cabbage and other garden seeds. He was fond of experimenting and assisted the experiments of others. To Isaac Coffin, a Virginian who had moved to England, he sent a pair of wild turkeys, receiving as a return some English pheasants, which he liberated in the woods of Montpelier. He was a horse breeder on a moderate scale, kept a stallion, and paid part of the bill for medical attendance of his family physician with the horse's services. He experimented with mules for a time, receiving ten from Kentucky through his cousin, James Taylor.

The main source of income from his farms was from tobacco. This for many years he shipped to his agent at Liverpool, James Maury, but the last ten years of his life he found it more advantageous to sell it in Richmond, John A. Lay being his agent and the Farmers' Bank his depository. In May, 1825, Lay deposited to his credit

* In the latter part of his life Madison spelled Montpelier with two "l's," the more correct way, as the name was derived from Montpellier in France; but he did not so spell it during his earlier years, and the spelling with one "l" has always maintained in Virginia.

for tobacco sold, $787.56; in June, $597.80; in July, $548.11; and in August, $213.90. These figures would indicate a considerable sum in gross receipts from the crop, but the actual profit was probably not half as much. In the last ten years of his life he was unable to himself actively superintend his estate on account of his failing health, and decreased his farming activity. He realized also that this industry, like all others, was cursed by slavery. Francis Corbin wrote to him October 10, 1819: "I think slavery is working its own cure. Under the best management, with daily vexation and never-ending violence to our feelings, it does not afford us two per ct. upon our capital, and often brings us into debt. . . . You have now had experience enough, my dear sir, as a *practical* Farmer, to be convinced, I suspect, that my opinion, namely, that farming and slavery are incompatible" [is correct].*

The social duties of his position in the country he performed with enjoyment. Of his visitors he said that some were bounties and others taxes, but there were enough of the former to counteract the disagreeableness of the latter. His house was well adapted for receiving guests, having become by successive improvements more than merely a comfortable residence. The chief enlargements were made in 1809, upon designs drawn by William Thornton, who made the first accepted plans of the Capitol at Washington, and Latrobe lent his assistance in further improvements, which included the addition of the wings. The result was simplicity, but symmetry of proportion and faultlessness of taste. In the basement there were two kitchens, one being for his mother's establishment, which during her life was entirely separate from the rest of the household, several large wine cellars, and rooms for a few household servants. On the first floor were the rooms his mother occupied—parlour, dining-room, and two bedrooms,—the large drawing-room, his own study, a small room adjoining, where his secretary had his desk, the

* Dept. of State MSS.

dining-room, and library. On the second floor were eight large bedrooms. After his mother's death in 1820 the rooms which she had occupied became four additional bedrooms, making in regular use twenty-two rooms, besides the servants' quarters, which were entirely separate from the house. The principal living rooms of the house were profusely ornamented with pictures and busts, one being commonly known as "the statuary room." Only a few of the ornaments need be enumerated. In the vestibule from which opened the drawing-room was an engraving of the Descent from the Cross, a print of Charles II of England, a group of Venus and Psyche, a pastoral piece, and a landscape by Teniers; in the drawing-room was a portrait and bust of Washington, a portrait of Jefferson, bust of Paul Jones, busts of Homer and Socrates, engravings of the Falls of Niagara, Raphael's La Belle Jardiniere, Love Chained, the Death of Montgomery, the Battle of Bunker Hill, a marble bust of Joel Barlow, a portrait on ivory of the Empress Josephine, and a miniature wax profile of Madison's mother by Valaperto, beside several portraits of Madison and his wife. In the dining-room was a portrait of Louis XVIII after the drawing by Isabey, and a Chinese drawing of Confucius.

In addition to these he bought in 1819 from the artist, G. Cardelli, busts of Jefferson, Monroe and Adams, and in that year Cardelli made busts of himself and his wife. John H. Browere made their busts in 1827, James B. Longacre made his sketch of Madison in 1833, and in the same year A. P. Durand painted him for George P. Morris, of the *Mirror*. He had already been painted by Gilbert Stewart and his friend Charles Wilson Peale. The greatest work of art in the house was the life-sized marble medallion bust of Madison which hung in the vestibule. It had been made in 1792 by Giuseppe Ceracchi, the illstarred Italian sculptor, who was guillotined in 1801 for complicity in the plot to murder Napoleon. Being a born revolutionist, he came to Philadelphia when Madison was

in the Continental Congress, and made busts of Hamilton,
Washington and others. He contemplated creating an
elaborate monument commemorative of the Revolution,
and under Madison's encouragement issued a circular
asking for subscriptions to defray the expense, but suddenly conceiving that his patrons wanted to get rid of
him, he went back to Italy, leaving behind him drafts
upon Washington and others for payment for the busts
he had given them.*

The taste shown by Madison in the architecture of his
house and the ornamentation of the rooms had a further
illustration in the planning of the grounds. About a
hundred yards west of the house he laid out before his
retirement a large terraced garden in the form of a horse-
shoe, intended, according to local tradition, to have a
general resemblance to the Hall of the House of Representatives. North of the house he planted an avenue of
pines leading to a circular collonade above an ice-house.
This was built in 1809, and was the first ice-house constructed in that part of Virginia. The country people
would not believe that ice could be kept all summer, and
to convince his incredulous overseer, Edward Brockman,
Madison promised him ice for a mint julep on July 4
in return for a Christmas turkey. In front of the house
lay a stretch of meadow fringed by the deep forest, and
about twelve miles distant the main range of the Blue
Ridge Mountains rises in the heavens. Surrounding the
sides and back of the house was a sweep of lawn dotted
with large forest trees and a few smaller trees of rarer
variety which Madison set out.

Those who had the privilege of resorting to Montpelier
were charmed with the beauty of the park, the elegance
of the house and the grandeur of the mountain view,
but better than all of these, they found in the master of
the place a perfect host. The serenity of his temper was
never disturbed, and only two instances have been dis-

* Madison to George Tucker, April 30, 1830. Works (Cong. Ed.)
IV, 71.

covered of guests who were displeased with the treatment they received. One of these was his cousin, Zachary Taylor, afterward President of the United States, who dined at Montpelier when Madison was President, and being then a junior officer in the army, seized the occasion to ask a favour. He was told that public favours were not granted for private or family reasons, and being offended at the rebuff, left the house ahead of his party without bidding his host good-bye. The other instance was that of a brother-in-law who took offense at some fancied slight one evening and sent a challenge to mortal combat by a small coloured boy early in the morning; but Madison burned the note and made no answer.

In the current of domestic life which ran so smoothly there was one element which caused uneasiness. John Payne Todd, Mrs. Madison's son by her first marriage, was a mere infant when she married Madison, and was treated by him as a son. Never severe with any one, the step-father probably erred on the side of too great indulgence towards his wife's child. The boy was sent to a French seminary in Baltimore, went abroad with Clay when the Treaty of Ghent was negotiated, and basked in the favours of society, which came to him easily because of his mother's position and of his own adaptability to a life of pleasure. He ran up bills for fine clothes and drifted into the gambling habits prevalent among a class of the population in Washington. He took to the bottle, and from a graceful youth of wild tendencies developed into a graceless man of confirmed dissipation, whose misconduct caused grief and mortification to the fond mother and her husband.

The burden of meeting the indebtedness incurred by Todd fell entirely upon Madison, and was a considerable financial strain. In addition he contributed to the support of his nephews, paying for the education of one at Hampden Sidney and another at William and Mary. They wrote to him in a filial spirit and did not hesitate to ask him for money when they needed it. These family obligations were not, however, the main cause of the pecuniary embarrassments which harassed the last years of his life. To support such an establishment as that of Montpelier was an attempt sure to end in disaster except to a man of well-assured income. The household was large, the flow of guests incessant, the hospitality lavish; there was the cost of clothing and feeding a hundred negroes, and the returns from planting were distressingly small. Retrenchments became necessary a few years after the permanent return to Montpelier from Washington. The French gardener, whose wages of $400 a year were considered enormous in Virginia, was dismissed and his place filled by one of his black assistants. The stable of driving and riding horses was decreased year by year, until at the end there was but a single pair of driving horses. In 1825 Madison asked Nicholas Biddle, President of the Bank of the United States, for a long loan of $6,000 on his farms and was refused. The bank, Biddle said, already had an embarrassing amount of real estate and had adopted a rule against long loans on such property.* Madison was obliged, accordingly, to sell some of his land, and even to part with some of the shares of stock he owned. He was repeating in a less degree the experience of Jefferson, who, if he had lived much longer, would have been obliged to abandon Monticello, and of Monroe, who was finally obliged to give up Oak Hill.

One asset Madison had which was an embarrassment and expense rather than a useful possession. His slaves had been acquired from time to time, partly by inheritance, and most of them had been with him for many years and could not be sold. The kindness of his nature extended to them and was rewarded by faithful attachment on their part. They knew him in distinction to his brothers as "Mas'r Jimmy." A survivor among them, Nancy Barbour, still living at a great age in the village of Orange, declares that he never got angry with any of

* Dept. of State MSS.

them, and that they preferred going to him with requests to going to his wife. She recalls one instance of his personal castigation of a slave, when Reuben, a worthless scamp, returned from some unlawful errand with a palpably false excuse and was punished by three light taps on the shoulder from his master's walking stick.

The personal impressions of Madison taken down from the lips of his cousin, Miss Sarah Conway, of Smithfield, Va., when eighty-nine years of age and still in the full possession of her faculties, may be put down here. She often visited Montpelier as a girl from twelve to fifteen years of age, and Madison and his wife were both fond of young people and made them feel at home. He was always neat in his dress and was assisted in his toilet by Paul (Jennings), his body-servant, and Paul always accompanied him when he travelled. He wore shorts with long silk stockings, and silver buckles that almost covered the tops of his shoes. His hair was in a queue, tied with a bow of black ribbon. The pitch of his voice was moderate and he spoke clearly and distinctly. He did not gesticulate in ordinary conversation, but did when telling an amusing story. At his dinner table there was always wine, which he drank, but he was temperate and sober in all things. He was a very liberal man, and after his retirement from public life on one occasion invited every family in Orange County to an entertainment, and the grounds were covered with tables to accommodate the people, the more distinguished guests and elderly people being entertained in the house. He was without ostentation, and moved about among his neighbours as any private gentleman would have done. He and his wife lived together without straining their prerogatives, and everybody admired and loved Mrs. Madison. She was an excellent manager and had everything about her in abundance without waste. His temper was even and placid and not easily ruffled. He never laughed boisterously, but was cheerful and playful in temperament, fond of a pleasant joke, but always dignified.

In the daily routine breakfast was eaten at about nine o'clock and dinner at three, the table being set with a liberal display of silver and fine china. In the evening the family gathered in the drawing-room, and the young ladies, of whom there were usually several in the house, played the piano and sang. Madison spent much of his time in his study, but was the life of the evening circle. When his ailments increased so that he could not get up and down stairs without discomfort, he had a bed put in his study, the door of which opened into the dining-room, and when he was too ill to sit at the dinner table he would have his chair pushed to the door, where he could join in the conversation. Miss Conway says that he did not laugh boisterously, but there is good evidence that in circles of intimate friends he sometimes gave way to unrestrained facetiousness and set his hearers into roars of laughter. "A gentleman," says Randall in his Life of Jefferson, "who was intimate at Montpelier, long after its owner's retirement, mentioned to us visiting him on one occasion when he was severely indisposed and confined to his bed. When the family and friends sat down to dinner, the invalid desired the door of his apartment to be left open 'so that he could hear what was going on.' Every few moments he was heard to cry out in a feeble but most humourous voice, 'Doctor, are you pushing about the bottle? Do your duty, Doctor, or I must cashier you.'"

Of the jokes with which the merry old man amused his friends none have been preserved, but one of his favourite subjects was the adventures of the Baroness Reidesel, the wife of General Reidesel, a prisoner of war during the Revolution. They lived at Collé, Mazzei's plantation, and the Baroness, who was big, handsome and a great gossip, rode her horse astride like a man, and was well known to all the country people. She wrestled bravely with the English tongue and made many remarkable mistakes in using it.

CHAPTER XXXVII

THE END

"My dear Husband is still confined to his bed. In addition to a disabling Rheumatism throughout the winter, he has had a bilious fever, which has reduced him so much that he can only walk from one bed to another. I never leave him more than a few minutes at a time, and have not left the enclosure around our house for the last eight months on account of his continued indisposition, concerning which friends at a distance have recd but too favourable reports. Our Physicians have advised the Warm Springs for Mr. Madison, and we hoped to have taken him there, but as he could not travel unless conveyed on his bed, we dare not think of it at present." This was the report of Mrs. Madison to her friend Mrs. Tobias Lear, in Washington, in a letter which is undated, but was doubtless written early in the spring of 1836.*

The last struggle of the old man against the disease which had held him captive for so many years was beginning. In a postscript to one of his wife's letters to Mrs. Samuel Harrison Smith he wrote in trembling characters (January 17, 1835):

"I am very thankful, my kind friend, for the interest you take in my health. It is not good, and at my age nature can afford little of the medical aid she exerts on younger patients. I have indeed got through the most painful stages of my principal malady, a diffusive & obstinate rheumatism; but I feel its crippling effects on my limbs, particularly my hands and fingers, as this little effort of the pen will show."†

* Family papers of J. Henley Smith, Esq., of Washington.
† *Id.*

The crippled condition of his fingers was almost constant for the last four years of his life. February 19, 1832, he wrote a note to Robert Treat Paine, labouriously printing each letter.

There was no continuous period after his retirement when his health was good. In the Autumn of 1821, he had the prevailing bilious fever, but he recovered quickly. He had at this time and occasionally afterwards the benefit of the advice of an eminent physician, Robley Dunglison, who held the chair of medicine at the University and was at the head of the faculty until he went to Baltimore in 1833. It was on one of Dunglison's half friendly, half professional visits that he found his patient reclining on a sofa and talking to the ladies of the household. He remonstrated with him for not lying still. "Oh," said Madison, "you know I talk most easily when I lie."*

He was quite ill in 1827 and in 1829 before he went to the State convention. The intermissions in his rheumatic seizures became less frequent and in the summer of 1831 he was taken violently. The following June Dunglison came to him hurriedly, having heard alarming reports, but he rallied. For the last twenty years of his life his regular family physician was his cousin, Dr. Charles Taylor, and associated with him towards the last were Drs. Thomas Slaughter and Peyton Grymes, both of Orange.

Early in the summer of 1836 the report went forth that he was sinking. Nevertheless, he was moved each day from his bed to his chair, and his mind continued active, for he would be read to by his wife and would dictate. His mind was clear, although he expressed a few days before his death some concern that he was unable to connect the memory of events readily. On the evening of June 27, his physicians were with him for the last time. He had become extremely emaciated, was mere skin and bones, and was growing gradually weaker. On the morning of June 28 he was moved from his bed to his chair as

* Randall's "Jefferson."

usual, and his niece brought him his breakfast and left it with him, urging him to eat. When she returned to the room a few minutes later he was dead. No one was with him at the time; he made no parting speeches and took no sorrowful farewells; but among his papers was found this, his last message to his fellow-countrymen:

"ADVICE TO MY COUNTRY.

"As this advice, if it ever see the light, will not do so till I am no more, it may be considered as issuing from the tomb, where truth alone can be respected, and the happiness of man alone consulted. It will be entitled, therefore, to whatever weight can be derived from good intentions, and from the experience of one who has served his country in various stations through a period of forty years; who espoused in his youth, and adhered through his life, to the cause of its liberty; and who has borne a part in most of the great transactions which will constitute epochs of its destiny.

"The advice nearest to my heart and deepest in my convictions is, THAT THE UNION OF THE STATES BE CHERISHED AND PERPETUATED. LET THE OPEN ENEMY TO IT BE REGARDED AS A PANDORA WITH HER BOX OPENED, AND THE DISGUISED ONE AS THE SERPENT CREEPING WITH HIS DEADLY WILES INTO PARADISE."

THE END.

INDEX